Margaret Fuller

❖❖ STUDIES IN AMERICAN THOUGHT ❖❖
AND CULTURE

Series Editor

Paul S. Boyer

Observing America: The Commentary of British Visitors to the United States, 1890–1950
Robert P. Frankel

*Cosmopolitanism and Solidarity: Studies in Ethnoracial, Religious, and
Professional Affiliation in the United States*
David A. Hollinger

Margaret Fuller: Transatlantic Crossings in a Revolutionary Age
Edited by Charles Capper and Cristina Giorcelli

Margaret Fuller

Transatlantic Crossings in a Revolutionary Age

Edited by

Charles Capper

and

Cristina Giorcelli

Foreword by

Lester K. Little

THE UNIVERSITY OF WISCONSIN PRESS

This book was published with the support of
THE ANONYMOUS FUND
OF THE COLLEGE OF LETTERS AND SCIENCES
at the University of Wisconsin–Madison.

The University of Wisconsin Press
1930 Monroe Street, 3rd Floor
Madison, Wisconsin 53711-2059

www.wisc.edu/wisconsinpress/

3 Henrietta Street
London WC2E 8LU, England

1   3   5   4   2

Printed in the United States of America

Library of Congress Cataloging-in-Publication Data
Margaret Fuller : transatlantic crossings in a revolutionary age /
edited by Charles Capper and Cristina Giorcelli;
foreword by Lester K. Little.
p.   cm.—(Studies in American thought and culture)
Includes index.
ISBN 0-299-22340-X (cloth: alk. paper)
1. Fuller, Margaret, 1810–1850—Criticism and interpretation.
2. Fuller, Margaret, 1810–1850—Homes and haunts—Italy.
I. Capper, Charles.   II. Giorcelli, Cristina.
III. Little, Lester K.   IV. Series.
PS2507.M26   2007
818'.309—dc22   2007011771

Contents

Foreword

This collection of essays evolved out of an international conference, "Margaret Fuller: tra Europa e Stati Uniti d'America," held November 20–22, 2000, at the American Academy in Rome. To mark the occasion as well as commemorate Fuller's contribution to the Italian movement for independence, with the permission of the mayor of Rome, Francesco Rutelli, a tablet was affixed to the wall at number 60 in the Piazza Barberini, where she lived from November 1848 to May 1849. The conference was co-organized by Professor Cristina Giorcelli of the University of Rome Three and Professor Giuliana Limiti, president of the Mazzini Society, Rome, who were kind enough to invite the American Academy in Rome to participate in this project as well. That such a specialist in nineteenth-century American literature as Professor Giorcelli, not to mention her university department or several Italian colleagues who are experts in American cultural history, had an interest in promoting the first-ever conference devoted to the European experience of Margaret Fuller occasions neither surprise nor apology. A few words are called for, though, to explain the willing involvement of the American Academy, beyond the obvious importance of the American-Italian cultural connections involved, and of the Mazzini Society, beyond the plain facts that Fuller met Giuseppe Mazzini in London and then became deeply devoted to and involved in the republican cause in Rome.

The ill-fated battle for the defense of the Roman Republic in the late spring of 1849 was fought at the western-most (and also the highest) section of the city's walls, centered on the San Pancrazio Gate atop the Janiculum Hill. The French army, sent by Louis Napoleon Bonaparte in

response to the urgent request of Pope Pius IX, was concentrated outside the walls, with the advantage of being on slightly higher ground
than the Janiculum itself. Just inside the gate stood the Villa Savorelli, a
seventeenth-century Farnese residence where Garibaldi set up his headquarters for the defense of the Roman Republic. The French began
their bombardment of the walls and republican positions on June 13,
leaving only a partial shell of the Villa Savorelli standing. By the evening of the twenty-first they broke through the walls and on July 3
entered Rome and decreed the end of the republic. Garibaldi's forces
retreated from the city. Margaret Fuller, who was both a war correspondent for the *New-York Daily Tribune* and an organizer of emergency
treatment of wounded combatants, also fled into the countryside with
her officer husband and their child.

All of these things happened nearly a half century before the American Academy in Rome was founded (1894), but in 1909 the Villa Savorelli, long since restored after the damage suffered sixty years earlier and
renamed the Villa Aurelia, was bequeathed to the American Academy,
and the young institution's determined patron, J. P. Morgan, set about
acquiring some ten adjacent acres of land immediately inside the walls
by the gate. Thus it turned out that the privileged grounds now occupied by the American Academy's gardens and buildings were the very
setting for that bloody conflict in which Italian and some foreign soldiers fought for a unified, independent, and republican nation, founded
upon the ideals of the American Revolution. That chapter of Italian history is inextricably a part of American history as well.

As for the Mazzini Society, Anglophone readers should be aware
that Italians refer to this organization in their own language as "la Mazzini Society," and should know the reason behind this momentary in-
trusion of English into their speech. The reason is simple but significant.
This society was founded in New York City in April 1940 by a group of
anti-Fascist Italian exiles. Their purpose was to expose to the American
public, in particular Italian Americans, as well as the American government, their view of the Mussolini regime, and to counter the efforts of
Fascist publicists and spies then working in the United States. In June
they elected Max Ascoli as their first president.

The protofounding, though, goes back to the previous autumn, three
weeks after the outbreak of the war, to a meeting on September 24, 1939,
at the home of Michele and Hélène Cantarella in Northampton, Massachusetts, already for a decade a salon for exiled opponents of the regime.

The key figure in this salon was the noted historian Gaetano Salvemini, then teaching at Harvard. The host, a Sicilian who had served for four years in World War I, was a staunch republican who emigrated in 1922 and who began teaching Italian literature at Smith College in 1929. His wife, Hélène, an American with extraordinary linguistic talent, became Salvemini's English translator. Also present that evening were the art historian Lionello Venturi, specialist on impressionism and teacher of Giulio Carlo Argan; Roberto Bolaffio, an engineer active in organizing fellow anti-Fascist émigrés in New York; and Renato Poggioli, a Slavicist who emigrated in 1938 and after a year at Smith was beginning his first year of teaching at Brown University in Providence.

It was Salvemini who by all accounts proposed the name Mazzini Society. And on that same fall evening in 1939, those present decided to open membership to "Italian and Italian-American intellectuals whose intellectual and political probity and above all loyalty to American ideals are unquestioned."[1] Like the very ground atop the Janiculum, the Mazzini Society is part of the shared heritage of American and Italian history. In the same spirit, Margaret Fuller's claim on our attention extends, as this book amply demonstrates, well beyond the exclusive precincts of American literary history.

LESTER K. LITTLE

Director, American Academy in Rome, 1998–2005

Note

1. Maddalena Tirabassi, "La Mazzini Society (1940–46): un'associazione degli antifascisti italiani negli Stati Uniti," in *Italia e America dalla Grande Guerra a oggi*, ed. Giorgio Spini, Gian Giacomo Migone, Massimo Teodori (Venice, 1976), 141–58. I am grateful to Professor Ernest Benz of Smith College for supplying me with some of the material I have included here.

Preface

If Margaret Fuller's bold traversing of social and cultural boundaries established her celebrity as the most famous American intellectual woman
of her generation, none of her crossings contributed more to that fame
than her simple act of traveling across the Atlantic. In its literal sense,
of course, she was hardly alone. Although only a tiny number of mostly
upper-middle-class Americans in the antebellum era traveled to Europe, they included almost every notable author in America. Most of
them even expected to achieve something of her purposes: cultural vali-
dation, an enhanced professional reputation, and a deepened sense of
national identity through directly encountering its dangerously influential European "Other." There were significant differences, however.
First, she was her country's prepared transatlantic traveler par excellence. A master of most of Europe's literary canon and its most sophisticated interpreter to Americans, she had been mentally crossing the Atlantic long before setting sail on August 1, 1846. At the same time, she
was a preeminently anguished mental traveler. The literature of Germany, Italy, and France all held for her deep personal meanings that
enabled her intellect and defined much of her outlook but also, she
feared, often disabled her from speaking in the idiom of her compatriots. Precisely because of that, though, she reflected on the proper stance
an American should assume toward Europe more complexly than probably any writer before Henry James. Finally, she was her country's ulti-
mate accidental traveler. In serendipitously happening upon her future
husband, the Italian Marquess Giovanni Angelo Ossoli, and arriving on
the eve of Europe's greatest political upheaval before World War II, she

sealed her fate in ways unimaginable to any other nineteenth-century "passionate pilgrim."[1]

Just as much as in her life, Fuller's European experience has loomed large in imaginings of it. Indeed, in one sense, probably too large. Although scholars and critics have attached to it different values, almost all have portrayed it as the central teleology of her life. It was out of a shared commitment to look freshly at the complexities of Fuller's transnational path that roughly a hundred scholars from the United States, Italy, Germany, Russia, Poland, Greece, and elsewhere in Europe gathered in November 2000 at the American Academy in Rome to examine its meaning, intellectual and political context, and unanticipated ramifications. Historic memory was inviting. A little over a hundred and fifty years ago, the Roman Republic of which Fuller was the premiere foreign defender had been established. The contemporary moment was also provoking. Although the Cold War had ended and the terrorist destruction of the Twin Towers in Manhattan was still a year a way, triumphalist claims about the end of nationalism and "history" had faded in the face of genocidal wars of "ethnic cleansing" in Eastern Europe, Asia, and Africa. Occasionally, during the conference, one heard echoes of these concerns. One time a scholar from Russia and one from Poland furiously disputed the relative importance of their respective cultures for understanding the thinking of Romantics like Fuller. Even old myths about "innocent" America and "cynical" Europe occasionally insinuated themselves into sessions. When one American literary scholar applied Antonio Gramsci's theory of "hegemony" to Fuller's conception of the thinking American traveler, an Italian critic leaped to her feet to remind the attendees that behind Gramsci's theories lay tragic failures of his Communist Party to understand Italian republicanism. Then there was the place. The sessions were held at the American Academy in Rome just down the street from the academy's Villa Aurelia, which had served as Garibaldi's headquarters during the French siege of Rome. At the grand dinner at the Capitol financed by the Municipality of Rome, we could see the beautiful surroundings and almost hear the cannon balls fired by the French on the Roman population thereabout. The conference ended fittingly with a ceremony unveiling an official plaque in honor of Fuller in Piazza Barberini at which the "assessore alla cultura" of Rome and Professor Giuliani Limiti, the president of the Mazzini Society, gave the principal addresses.

The conference papers chosen for this volume are grouped under three broad topics: Fuller's European-American transnational crossings, her "Italy" as text and context, and her posthumous image in literature. All in varying ways make two central points. First, Margaret Fuller was one of America's first truly cosmopolitan intellectuals, one fully engaged with the larger currents of Western civilization, not only as manifested in Antiquity, the Renaissance, the Enlightenment, and Romanticism, but also in the messy yet exhilarating reality of mid-nineteenth-century European culture and politics. The second unifying theme, however seemingly antithetical to the first, is in fact deeply complementary: wherever she traveled, imaginatively or physically, Fuller remained firmly rooted in the American soil, concerned with her nation's intellectual life, its culture, and its gathering political crisis. The creative synergy that arose from the interaction of these two powerful impulses, the national and the transnational, emerges with compelling clarity in these essays. Yet within that framework, questions abound as they had during the conference. Was Fuller a European exotic in an alien America who found her completion abroad, or an American idealist in an experienced Europe that defeated her attempts to understand it? Did the national cultures she encountered in Europe fundamentally reshape or confirm her sense of her and her country's national identity? Did her understanding of gender and sexuality radically change? What were the nature and significance of the "radical" politics she imbibed in Europe? How well or not did her European experience prepare her to confront either America's or Europe's social and political future? How did it enter into the American and European imagination? The answers given cover a wide spectrum, but collectively they run against the grain of "either/ or" judgments that have dominated Fuller scholarship for more than a century.

The overarching question, of course, was the exact relation between Fuller's America and her Europe. In my essay on Fuller's "American Transnational Odyssey" that opens the collection, I find the seeds of her transnationalism paradoxically emerging out of her widening national self-consciousness in reaction to a successive series of confrontations with international sites of social and cultural reform. I conclude with reflections on her transnationalism's possible futures in postrevolutionary Europe and the pre–Civil War United States as well as its legacies for twentieth-century American modernism and recent ideological criticism in American Studies. In their essays Joseph C. Schöpp and Robert N. Hudspeth explore how Goethean and Emersonian strands of heroism and self-culture helped Fuller flesh out and clarify her transnational Romanticism before even setting foot in Europe. Offering a specific case study of Fuller's transnationalism in action, Schöpp, in his "Playing the Eclectic: Margaret Fuller's Creative Appropriation of Goethe," shows how her creative readings of Johann Wolfgang von Goethe allowed her not only to critically engage key Goethean ideas but also to reproduce in distinctive ways the Goethean ideal of dialogic hermeneutics. Making a similar point while shifting from a writer to a concept, Hudspeth, in "Margaret Fuller and the Ideal of Heroism," examines how she constructed her notion of the heroic life out of personal and literary ideals she had cultivated in America. He concludes, however, that she was able to make their private and aesthetic side complement their public and the political one only in Europe. In Anna Scacchi's meditation on the transference of Fuller's maternal preoccupations from America to Italy, "Margaret Fuller's Search for the Maternal," she argues—against American feminist critics who have downplayed the question—that ideas, fantasies, and tropes of motherhood were central to Fuller's self-fashioning from childhood on, remaining at the end both emancipatory and problematic. In so doing, she questions Hudspeth's progressivist narrative and Bell Gale Chevigny's later positive interpretation of Fuller's merger of the personal and political in Italy.

In Italy Fuller tested politically her transnational ideas and sensibility. Yet as with Fuller's "maternal," Italy served both as a reality she encountered within certain historical contexts and a text she like other nineteenth-century Anglophone authors and travelers constructed. Probably the biggest difference between their constructions and hers was her overriding commitment to the present and future of an ancient nation they overwhelmingly appreciated solely for its past. If Italy was to experience a new breath of freedom and influence, she knew it needed to destroy the social and political structure on which for over two millennia had rested its magnificent past culture that she too loved as deeply as the most conservative Italophiliac. Chevigny and John Paul Russo present different but complementary versions of that double-consciousness. In "Mutual Interpretation: Margaret Fuller's Journeys in Italy," Chevigny makes this important concept in Fuller's literary criticism into a reflecting mirror of her thought and writings both in America and Europe *and* the key to her fulfillment in Italy as a political critic and activist and as a woman. Russo's essay, "The Unbroken Charm: Margaret Fuller, G. S. Hillard, and the Tradition of Travel Writing on Italy," offers a comparative look at Fuller's travel writings in Italy and George S. Hillard's classic *Six Months in Italy,* published three years after her death. Placing both within the great tradition of nineteenth-century travel literature both in New England and Europe, Russo finds in Fuller's dialectical and historicist method of observation the sources for her rare appreciation of Italy's glorious past, contradictory present, and unknown modern future. By contrast, the meaning and significance of Fuller's transnational liberal politics are contested in the essays by Francesco Guida and Larry Reynolds. In his "Realism, Idealism, and Passion in Margaret Fuller's Response to Italy" Guida offers a partly skeptical reading of Fuller's political reporting on revolutionary Italy and the Roman Republic. While conceding the sophistication of her reportage and the keenness and nuance in many of her judgments, he also notes her lapses, biases, and exaggerations. In "Righteous Violence: The Roman Republic and Margaret Fuller's Revolutionary Example" Reynolds gives us a political Fuller that is at once more radical *and* more available to American appropriation than appears in the narratives of Chevigny and Hudspeth. Indeed, reversing the historical lens of most of the essays in this collection, Reynolds argues that the memory of Fuller's revolutionary words and deeds in Italy were important provocations of her Transcendentalist and antislavery colleagues' later embrace of political violence in the North in the 1850s.

Fuller's memory would have a long afterlife beyond the Civil War in the works of countless writers and activists, from Elizabeth Cady Stanton to Robert Lowell and beyond. If one were to pick, though, two American authors to stand in for them all, one could not do much better than those whose connections with Fuller the last essays illuminate. Henry James's complex portrayals of strong women and self-conscious Romantic characters and their worlds constituted a major theme in several of his most important novels. In "A Humbug, a Bounder, and a Dabbler: Margaret Fuller, Cristina Belgioioso, and Cristina Casamassima," Cristina Giorcelli establishes resonating biographical and literary connections that show Fuller's central place in these masquerades and in James's sometimes malevolently ironical stance toward her and them. While Giorcelli highlights James's preoccupation with theatricality in his constructions of images of Fuller, in "Margaret Fuller on the Stage" Maria Anita Stefanelli analyzes the 1993 play *Alice in Bed* by the late

Susan Sontag, herself arguably our recent time's stand-in for Margaret Fuller, to bring to light Fuller's multiple meanings for Sontag and for us. According to Stefanelli, by juxtaposing Fuller with Emily Dickinson, Sontag reveals the myriad ways in which women as actors, in life and on the stage, destabilize the category "woman" and stage possible ways of freeing female subjectivity from the prison house of male desire. Bringing to a present empirical focal point these backward and forward looks, we include Donato Tamblé's report on newly discovered documents recording conflicts at the Fatebenefratelli field hospital that Fuller directed during the French siege.

All these retrospective essays take on added poignancy as we realize that they largely take up the final three years of Fuller's life — a life that ended in July 1850 in a shipwreck less than three hundred yards off Long Island's Fire Island, New York, as Fuller, just turned forty, returned to America. A further poignant leitmotiv that runs through these essays is also what was arguably most Romantic and, to some extent, modern about Fuller's transnational moves, namely, their riskiness. It was in Europe that she put at risk her dearest American possessions — her idealistic liberalism, her aestheticist passion, her social standing, her professional reputation, her livelihood, and ultimately her life. She died before she had worked out exactly how far she wanted to go in her Europeanization: whether in the mold of a transatlantic American of the later nineteenth century, or of an actual exile of the early twentieth, or, as is likely, something distinctively her own. Certainly, her political radicalism would have pointed her away from the genteel cosmopolitanism of a Charles Eliot Norton just as her critical patriotism would have steered her away from the radical break of a James or a Gertrude Stein. One thing, though, is clear. In both her preparations and her risk-taking, she was, as Ralph Waldo Emerson would insist to Thomas Carlyle, antebellum America's "citizen of the world."[2] As such, she was also its prefiguration of that "trans-national" or "international citizen" that a little over a half century later Randolph Bourne, on the eve of another calamitous international war, would declare to be the only identity possible for a modern cultivated person, whether immigrant, native, or exile. It is no wonder that Fuller's many "transatlantic crossings" continue to provoke, inspire, and even, perhaps, as with James, haunt scholars and nonscholars alike.[3]

The essays that follow underscore that continuing fascination but also something more. In this moment, when calls are coming from almost everywhere in the humanities for an "international American history," "transnational understanding and affiliations," and a new "cosmopolitan" citizenry—often implicitly assumed to have been nonexistent until now—Fuller's transatlantic life and competing transnational ways of understanding take on special relevance. Indeed, when both human rights and national hubris seem to be vying with each other to inherit the mantle of the new globalism, it may turn out to be the very riskiness of her European venture that most speaks to us now.

We wish to thank Giuliana Limiti, president of the Mazzini Society; Lester Little, the former director of the American Academy in Rome; and Francesco Pitocco, director of the Scientific Board of *Dimensioni e problemi della ricerca storica*, which published earlier versions of most of these essays. Generous funding was supplied by the American Academy in Rome, the Department of American Studies of the University of Rome Three, the Department of Modern and Contemporary History of the University of Rome "La Sapienza," and the Department of Philosophy of the University of Rome Three. Instrumental in providing support for the conference out of which this volume evolved were Francesco Rutelli, the mayor of Rome; Gianni Borgna, the commissioner of culture for the city of Rome; the Ministero degli Affari Esteri; the Comune di Roma; and the Associazione Italiana Donne Dirigenti d'Azienda (AIDDA). Thanks go also to Jennifer Brown, who translated earlier drafts of several essays originally written in Italian. Gwen Walker, acquisitions editor at the University of Wisconsin Press, expertly shepherded our volume through the press. Sheila Moermond efficiently oversaw production, Diana Cook provided helpful copyediting, and Blythe Woolston created a useful index. Most important, we received invaluable conceptual advice and editorial help from Paul Boyer, editor of the University of Wisconsin Press series Studies in American Thought and Culture.

CHARLES CAPPER

Notes

Note: All quotations in the text are reproduced as they appear in the original sources cited.

1. For the evidence that Fuller bore her child out of wedlock but eventually married see my *Margaret Fuller: An American Romantic Life*, vol. 2, *The Public Years* (New York: Oxford Univ. Press, 2007).

2. July 31, 1846, quoted in *The Correspondence of Emerson and Carlyle*, ed. Joseph Slater (New York: Columbia Univ. Press, 1964), 407.

3. "Trans-National America," in *The American Intellectual Tradition*, ed. David A. Hollinger and Charles Capper, 5th ed., 2 vols. (New York: Oxford Univ. Press, 2006), 2:178. For the recent scholarship on comparativism, transnationalism, and cosmopolitanism in American history and literary studies, see below, "Getting from Here to There: Margaret Fuller's American Transnational Odyssey," note 32.

I

Transnational Crossings

1

Getting from Here to There

Margaret Fuller's American Transnational Odyssey

CHARLES CAPPER

When I began my own odyssey of writing Margaret Fuller's life, I knew my guiding historical question would necessarily be: how did a woman, who lived three-quarters of her life in the private sphere relegated to antebellum women, manage in a single decade to fashion herself into her generation's most famous cosmopolitan intellectual? By this I mean a self-conscious public "thinker" (to use her preferred term) vitally engaged with national discourses outside her native country. A host of modern scholars has provided one answer: she got out of the United States. Their plot of her needed escape varied according to ideological purpose. For the 1920s progressive Vernon Parrington, America's original sin that Fuller had to elude was its "Puritanism." For the post–World War II existentialist-minded Perry Miller, it was its innocence. For the 1950s "consensus" historian Stanley Elkins, it was the nation's "abstract" and dangerous utopianism. For the 1970s Marx-minded feminist scholars Bell Chevigny and Ann Douglas, it was America's lack of a class-conscious sense of "History." These teleological narratives also varied in historical plausibility. Perry Miller rounded out his modernist fable by speculating that Fuller, facing an alien nineteenth-century

America, may have in fact "elected" to go down with the sinking ship *Elizabeth*![1]

I do not mean to suggest that it is necessarily wrong to play Fuller against American difference from Europe. Since Alexis de Tocqueville's *Democracy in America* (a work Fuller much admired), the idea of America's "exceptional" world status *has* been probably the most relentlessly played theme in American historical writing. And this is true whether this American "exceptionalism" is regarded (as it often was in the nineteenth century) as real and positive or (as it often has been since) mythic and negative. Moreover, the concept rests on a rock bottom historical reality: in the antebellum era, nationality, along with democracy and Protestant Christianity, *did* constitute one of the period's trinity of defining discourses. Finally, the national question clearly shaped Fuller's life. Certainly it drove the politics of the 1848–49 European revolutions that in her last years she embraced. More important still, her struggles with national self-identity give us—to revert to my opening question— a central key to understanding her identity as a cosmopolitan public intellectual.[2]

To find this key, though, we need (to revise Thomas Carlyle's famous sneer) to "accept [*her*] universe." By that I mean accept both its national *and* international halves. If we do this, we can see that American exceptionalism is a profoundly misleading rubric for understanding Fuller's intellectual career in the United States for the simple reason that these spheres were not successive but intimately entangled. So here I want to propose a counter-exceptionalist narrative. First, Fuller *began* her intellectual life in a European-centered mode that opened her to the world but led her into a cultural cul-de-sac. Second, she tried to escape this dead end by adapting her deracinated Romantic cosmopolitanism to a series of "transnational" American reform sites that both included *and* transcended nationality. Third, these moves reached their apogee in New York, where they culminated in a seminal transnational American cultural vision but an uncertain political one. Finally, at the end, I want to briefly indicate how an appreciation of Fuller's American "transnational odyssey" might inject some fresh thinking into recent calls for an "international" or "transnational" American history.

Oscar Wilde says somewhere that Romantics begin at the climax. Fuller's life plot would seem to bear this out. Instead of beginning (as in a good German bildungsroman) with the narrow world of innocence, her life begins with the intellectual equivalent of a very wide world: Latin grammar at six; most of the classical authors by ten; French, Italian, and Spanish works by twelve; and nearly the entire canon of Renaissance and early modern European literature by nineteen. The question, though, remains: how did such a precociously cosmopolitan regimen produce a questing public intellectual, rather than merely, to rephrase Ralph Waldo Emerson's famous disparagement of un-American scholars, a cosmopolite "bookworm"?[3]

To foreshorten the answer radically, we need to notice two psychologically resonant ideologies that infiltrated that precocity. One was the Enlightenment-inspired regimen that her scholarly Jeffersonian Republican father established for her early education. "I love her if she . . . learns to read," Timothy Fuller, writing from the well of the United States House of Representatives, instructed his wife to tell their daughter on the eve of her fourth birthday. "To excel in all things should be your constant aim," he exhorted Margaret six years later; "mediocrity is obscurity." An ambitious rationalist father's stingy parceling out love for learning and dreams of excellence and fame for unremitting work: one does not need to look much further to locate the psychological source for Fuller's "predetermination" (in Carlyle's amazed phrase) "to *eat* this big universe as her oyster or her egg." Her father's classical Enlightenment reading list also kept her hungry and awake to the world: Virgil, Cicero, Horace, and myriad martial and virtue-conscious texts of the later Roman Republic and early empire. By her teens she was devouring histories and memoirs of the great European statesmen of the early modern era, who were men of action and eschewed, she admiringly noted, "Augustan niceties."[4]

This last phrase points to the second cultural ideology infiltrating Fuller's youthful cosmopolitan fantasies beyond that of her Addison-and-Steele-loving father: she was also a daughter of her local milieu's new and yet-to-be battle-tested *Romantic* cosmopolitanism. Contrary to that resentful cosmopolite Henry Adams's picture of the early Republic resolutely turning its back on Europe, she had only to walk up Cambridge's main street to encounter this new transatlantic talk at every turn. Harvard's returning band of German university-trained Ph.D.'s spoke its language. So did Cambridge's influx of liberal exiles returning from failed revolutions in Europe. And so, most earnestly, did a cohort of intellectual-minded Harvard students who invited her to study in their European Romantic extracurriculum, which they thought infinitely more relevant to their dawning individualistic age than the College's

"Common Sense" textbooks. From this virtual college the equally ambitious and alienated Fuller took two theoretically world-transformative
propositions that would guide her all her life: that the subjective life of
the mind contained an infinite ocean of meaning and value — *and* that
heroic individuals might tap into it to re-enchant an otherwise alien and
despiritualized modern world.[5]

Was this vision, though, any less bookishly cosmopolitan than the
Enlightenment regimen of her childhood? To this question, one would
have to respond, how *could* it have been? Barred as a girl from entering Boston-Cambridge's learned professions — even, as with her male
friends, to revolt against them! — she retreated to her prodigious studies
and, after her father's unexpected death, to schoolteaching. Yet, anx-
ious to keep herself free of what she defensively called (quoting Cole-
ridge) that profession's "'strong mental odor,'" she moved on several
fronts to get beyond her suddenly shrunken world. She first turned herself into her young circle's authority on Romanticism's most philosophical (and in America most suspect) literary source, German literature.
She also determined to write for publication. And then she tried to lev-
erage her deracinated Romantic cosmopolitanism into a transnational
project: "teaching" her nation the enormous cultural value of German
Romantic authors. Unfortunately, after publishing one article, "Present
State of German Literature," in the short-lived New York and Boston
American Monthly Magazine, she quickly discovered American periodicals
were uninterested in touting writers most of her country's critics regarded as licentious infidels. She, in turn, stumbled on her own confu-
sion of purpose: if America's English-derived "utilitarian" culture was
(as she argued) totally hostile to her inwardly turned Germans, to whom
was she speaking? Indeed, reading her critically sophisticated but often
awkwardly condescending early essays, one could easily imagine Fuller
becoming not a bookish dreamer but a Germanized version of the
Wordsworthian "monarchist," the elder Richard Henry Dana, who as-
sured *his* oblivion by his precious refusal virtually to publish or speak before his culturally crude compatriots.[6]

Yet she didn't become another Dana. There are many byways
through this tale of why, which I explore in my biography — from the
impact of her father's high-toned Jeffersonianism and her bold German
and French Romantics to her gender self-consciousness and her literary ambition. Here I want to concentrate not on these biographical influences but on the broader historical discourses that she manipulated

in her search to connect her Romantic proclivities with her nation's culture. Specifically, I argue that Fuller's identity as a productive public intellectual emerged from her engagement with four sites of transnational American cultural reform: New England Transcendentalism, women's rights discourse, Western settlement, and New York literary journalism.[7]

The Transcendentalist movement, with which she allied herself the year after her father died, provided her with her first opportunity. Certainly its cosmopolitan synergy struck off sparks. She pressed on the somewhat wary Emerson and his colleagues her "demonic" and Romantically canonized continental writers and artists: Dante, Goethe, Beethoven, George Sand, and the German Romantics. They pressed on *her* their more sublimated English Platonists and Renaissance hermeticists. And this cosmopolitan mix produced one important intellectual result: out of it she formulated her personal cosmology of man's fortunate fall into experience, struggle, and love. Yet the cosmopolitan (not to say cosmic) Transcendentalists also grounded her. Their revolt against their Unitarian church's supernatural rationalist dogmas provoked her first partisan theological talk. Most important, her connections gave her a national project: an invitation to apply their Romantic maneuvers to the reform of American culture through their new magazine, the *Dial*, which they asked her to edit.

Their offer could not have come at a more needed time. Even while organizing the magazine in the winter of 1840, her pessimism about America's crassly commercial burgeoning literary marketplace remained as deep as ever. Perusing all the "hack verbiage from which books and articles without end" were being produced made the present moment seem, she groused in her journal, not her circle's dawn of a new literary age but rather "the late days of a lower Empire." Even in the *Dial*'s inaugural issue, in her sharply critical review of a recent Washington Allston exhibition at Harding's Gallery, she painted a picture of America's artistic conditions and prospects that was starkly bleak. It was doubtful, she said, that the country would anytime soon develop an indigenously imaginative art, since that required not the superficial imitation of European techniques but organic reproductions of the nation's spiritual life, which for the moment was largely barren. Anticipating Henry James's later famous list of American lacks in his *Hawthorne*, she listed her country's deficiencies: "There is no poetical ground-work ready for the artist in our country and time. Good deeds appeal to the understanding. Our religion is that of the understanding. We have no old established faith, no hereditary romance, no such stuff as Catholicism, Chivalry afforded. What is most dignified in the Puritanic modes of thought is not favorable to beauty. The habits of an industrial community are not propitious to delicacy of sentiment." Yet, like a good Puritan Romantic, she also flagellated herself. "I have myself a great deal written," she wrote to her friend the Transcendentalist minister William Henry Channing, "but as I read it over scarce a word seems pertinent to the place or time." Then she put her finger on the cultural tragedy of her American Romantic generation: "How much those of us who have been forced by the European mind have to unlearn and lay aside, if we would act here. I would fain do something worthily that belonged to the country where I was born, but most times I fear it may not be."[8]

Fortunately, she soon got enough Transcendentalist national religion to stop complaining about the woeful state of American culture and start doing something about it. Her first move was to apply a little Romantic historicist analysis. "Since the Revolution," she explained in another throat-clearing letter to Channing, "there has been little . . . to call out the higher sentiments" to counterbalance their new country's inevitable material exploitation and attendant "feverish" petty politics. Then, after pushing aside all her era's falsely touted cultural cures for this malaise—the ossified Unitarians, the superstitious evangelicals, the Anglophile highbrow quarterlies—she brought forward her Transcendentalist circle.

> They see that political freedom does not necessarily produce liberality of mind, nor freedom in church institutions—vital religion; and, seeing that these changes cannot be wrought from without inwards, they are trying to quicken the soul, that they may work from within outwards. Disgusted with the vulgarity of a commercial aristocracy, they become radicals; disgusted with the materialistic working of "rational" religion, they become mystics. They quarrel with all that is, because it is not spiritual enough. They would, perhaps, be patient if they thought this the mere sensuality of childhood in our nation, which it might outgrow; but they think that they see the evil widening, deepening,—not only debasing the life, but corrupting the thought of our people, and they feel that if they know not well what should be done, yet that the duty of every good man is to utter a protest against what is done amiss.[9]

In short, she arrayed her Transcendentalist rebels as the vanguard not (as they appeared to many) of a new church but of a religiously infused national cultural awakening in direct line with the American Revolution.

Finally, in "Short Essay on Critics," which she also published in the first issue of the *Dial,* directly following her coeditor Emerson's opening salvo, "The Editors to the Reader," she added to her historicist vanguard diagnosis and prescription a new *transnational* protodemocratic conception of the "office" of the critic. On one hand, she rested her idea on a classically German Romantic-sculpted base. Against both dominant Anglo American critical methods—the older neoclassical "judicial" and the newer middlebrow "reproductive"—she argued that the critic needed to approach works neither dogmatically nor impressionistically but dialectically. First, she needed to go "inside" the work to "apprehend" the purpose of the writer, then "outside" to determine his formal success in carrying it out, and finally all around to "comprehend" his work's comparative standing in the entire pantheon of world literature determined by a regulative principle underlying the "analogies of the universe." On the other hand, *un*like her German mentors, who made this hermeneutical method the property of a cultural clerisy, she insisted that readers themselves should be encouraged to practice it. Exploiting both Romantic and American republican metaphors, she wrote: "We do not want merely a polite response to what we thought before, but by the freshness of thought in other minds to have new thought awakened in our own. We do not want stores of information only, but to be roused to digest these into knowledge. . . . In books, in reviews, in the senate, in the pulpit, we wish to meet thinking men, not schoolmasters or pleaders." This complexly stringent yet culturally democratic conception of the critic, not as a cheerleader of popular judgments but a provocateur of readers' subjective inquiries in the service of her cosmopolitan Romantic critical ideal, would guide her criticism for the rest of her life.[10]

What, though, were the practical results of Fuller's protodemocratic transnational Romantic maneuvers? On the magazine side, I would say: more than literary historians have noticed. In eschewing academic affiliation, disregarding commercial demands, promoting experimental writing, offending conventional tastes, appropriating avant-garde European writings, and critically engaging the reform ideas of its time, the *Dial* gave birth to a seminal new antiformula for America's modern highbrow "little magazines." Furthermore, they forced this premature birth in an era when American magazines were forever proclaiming the necessity for a new national literature while busily stifling the originality that was needed to produce it.[11]

Yet if one were also to ask how much Fuller's *Dial* writings furthered her transnational project, one would have to say not much. She wrote pioneering essays (in America) on the reviled Goethe, little-known English Renaissance writers, unheard-of female German Romantics, and unperformed European "modern" composers. She also produced a number of German Romantic-influenced dialogues and fables, which had the distinction of being perhaps the most "outlandish" pieces (to use her own ironic word) that the formally experimental *Dial* ever published. But they had little in them that one might call transnational. Indeed, there was little in her articles that was even national. Almost none addressed national issues. She wrote very little criticism of American authors. And she wrote absolutely nothing about the other side of national reform that she and Emerson had promised that their magazine would air: "new demands" on American institutions and social practices. For *that* she needed to discover some reformable social problems. Beginning a year after resigning her editorship, she took up two.[12]

One was the status and culture of women, which Fuller addressed in her 1843 *Dial* article, "The Great Lawsuit: Man versus Men. Woman versus Women," which two years later she would revise and expand into her book *Woman in the Nineteenth Century*. Reading this liberal Romantic essay as a nationalist text might seem wildly off the mark. Its plethora of European myths, texts, tropes, and histories—not to mention its central gender claim that "masculine" and "feminine" are fluid and often-androgynous categories—hardly represented antebellum household artifacts. Yet as both "textualist" and "contextualist" theorists of intellectual history have taught us, meanings in texts often reside in the interspaces between bare arguments. Specifically here, nationality deeply colors both her essay and its context. This is evident in her opening section on the current debate about women's social status, in which she argues that the nation's revolutionary founding (whose Declaration she rewrites Romantically to read, "All men are born *free* and equal"), because of its respect for individual ethical integrity, surpasses the liberating but licentious French Revolution as *the* lynchpin of that modern discourse. Moreover, its principal prescription—that women develop collectively and individually psychic self-reliance through temporary withdrawal—drew directly from "come-outer" ideas afloat among her American Transcendentalist colleagues.[13]

Lastly, in that same section she advances the country's abolitionist movement as a vital buttress of her individualistic nationalist gender argument. This was a momentous departure for her. Six years earlier, in a letter to her famous mentor the pro-Garrisonian abolitionist Harriet Martineau, she had lambasted Martineau for making her *Society in America* an "ultraist" and "abolitionist" book and therefore (she said with some postcolonial umbrage) a "presumptuous" and "hasty" anti-American screed. And only two years before, while paying proper liberal Transcendentalist obeisance to the principle of antislavery but declaring her neutrality over the Garrisonians' specific abolitionist platform and tactics, she had cavalierly dismissed their pro-women's rights abolitionist faction for having *no* program for reforming women's culture beyond antislavery activism. Here, however, she makes precisely the argument that Boston Garrisonians had then made to *her:* that the abolitionists are the political spark lighting all the nation's reform discourses. Indeed, she makes an even broader nationalist argument about the abolitionists' relevance to women's rights talk: they're the *only* group of Americans trying to *act out*, and therefore sincerely express and expand, the living *organic* Declaration, which in a slave-owning nation is otherwise so much hypocritical "cant." In Romantically reformulating the American Declaration as a rights-tract morally revitalized by the Transcendentalists and abolitionists, Fuller offered up to her readers, under the rubric of a gender argument, her first transnational liberal Romantic social critique.[14]

She tried to do something of the same thing with the West in her more literarily Romantic *Summer on the Lakes*, but with more mixed ideological results. In this account of her three-month trip to the Great Lakes and prairie-states region, she lurched into the classic hubris-charged national theme of America as the world's pastoral. Or, rather, four pastorals. One is simplicity: the settlers' escape from eastern fashion and New England jargon. A second is organic nature: the West as a hybrid "garden" both wildly expressive and humanly cultivatable. The other two pastoral "types" are more unconventionally Romantic. One is diversitarian organic culture: the West as an entry point for old-world cultures bringing with them their devotion to nonutilitarian folk arts. The last, and most Fulleresque, is boundlessness: the trope of a vast continent shaping national identity by beckoning ever beyond itself. "The Greeks worship[ped] a god of limits," she writes, contrasting the "all new, boundless, limitless" land of the northern Illinois prairies with the constricted cultural practices of most western women. Invoking the

German Romantics' critique of their worshipped Greek culture, she declares: "I say, that what is limitless is alone divine." Indeed, so enthusiastic does she wax about northern Illinois's "all new, boundless, limitless" land that she reports experiencing a cosmopolitan nationalist epiphany on the morning of July Fourth, which she spent meditating on the top of an enormous bluff, fittingly named Eagle's Nest, overlooking the parklike vistas of Oregon, Illinois. "Certainly I think I had never felt so happy that I was born in America. . . . I do believe Rome and Florence are suburbs compared to this capital of nature's art."[15]

Yet her pastoral tropes perversely refuse to remain stable. Eastern female settlers absurdly try to "domesticate" the West by dragging untunable pianos to their new homes. Western farmers escape from eastern artifice only to exploit the "limitless" new land by destroying its beautiful trees for commercial harvesting. Cultivated immigrants break down in the face of poverty, isolation, and the irrelevance of their arts to the needs of the new bustling West. But the most truly inhuman perversion of her "limitless" pastoral that she exposes is white settlers' expropriation of Indians' *un*virgin land and near extermination of Indian culture, which cause her to blurt out scorching jeremiads that make her antislavery denunciations in "The Great Lawsuit" seem comparatively tame. As for her hope of finding organic folk cultures that she had studied in German Romantic texts just before leaving for her trip, she frankly confesses that she found the "mental experiences" of the Germans, Norwegians, Swedes, and Swiss that she spied disembarking on the pier in Milwaukee (unlike Indians' mythic lore that she extensively analyzes) impenetrable. So she remains at the end, shooting the rapids with her Chippewa guide off Mackinaw Island, alone with western nature, dreaming her national dreams "some time to be realized, but not by me." If she *were* going to find a wide transnational space for her expanding liberal Romantic hopes, it was clear she would need to look beyond her "optative" Transcendentalist cultural vanguard, her nationally despised abolitionist "Jacobins," and her vanishing multicultural West.[16]

Six months after publishing *Summer on the Lakes*, Fuller moved to New York City to accept Horace Greeley's offer to assume the new position of literary editor of his *New-York Daily Tribune*. For her project of finding a cosmopolitan American nation, her move would seem to have been a godsend. Gotham was the country's commercial center. Greeley, who had lavished praise on her book as a paean to the West, was (unlike her

New England Whig friends) an expansive nationalist. And his paper matched his outlook: read by tens of thousands of farmers, mechanics, shopkeepers, and small merchants and their families and neighbors all over the North, it was the closest thing that America had or would ever have (until the current *New York Times*) to a genuine national newspaper. Furthermore, her nationalist associates were not only liberal Whigs like Greeley. Soon after arriving she allied herself with the city's pro-Democratic literati, "Young America," who inveighed against (as Herman Melville, their rising star, put it) "this Bostonian leaven of literary flunkeyism towards England," and logrolled writers whose works they deemed to be indigenously "democratic."[17]

At the same time, New York scarcely undermined her cosmopolitan Romantic propensities. Greeley, who professed to admire the Transcendentalists' "un-American" depth of thought, and who also conceived of his paper as a robust yet uplifting alternative to his sensationalist penny-paper competitors, boasted to his readers that he had hired Fuller precisely to expose them to the great works of continental Europe. Her Young America circle was also not exactly a gang of cultural chauvinists. Their favorite firm Wiley and Putnam reprinted many middle-brow and highbrow European books in its new "Library of Choice Reading," edited by the coterie's refined editor Evert Duyckinck, which Fuller frequently reviewed. In fact, of the approximately 125 literary *Tribune* articles and reviews (which constituted roughly half of her total output), 70, or well over half, were on European books and authors, many in Wiley and Putnam's series.[18]

Finally, as she had not done with her *Dial* criticism, she used her columns to advance her cultural vision of a cosmopolitan nation. Partly she did this by trimming her European sails: either she wrote mostly on *contemporary* European works, or, when reviewing American reprints of her favorite Renaissance and Romantic texts, she often carefully noted that Europeans' cultural glories were behind them. More important, she made her Romantic categories do national cultural work. In particular, she expanded her *Dial* idea of a hermeneutic literary community to include authors of less-than-great works. "I never regarded literature merely as a collection of exquisite products," she told her old Cambridge friend James Freeman Clarke, defending her respectful treatment of crude but "sincere" books, "but as a means of mutual interpretation." Most aptly, she appropriated her Romantic transnationalism not to *inflate* American books but to critically *define* a set of national "ideas" that needed to underlie any American literature. "What suits Great Britain," she wrote in her "American Literature" essay, "with her insular position and consequent need to concentrate and intensify her life, her limited monarchy, and spirit of trade, does not suit a mixed race, continually enriched with new blood from other stocks the most unlike that of our first descent, with ample field and verge enough to range in and leave every impulse free, and abundant opportunity to develop a genius, wide and full as our rivers, flowery, luxuriant and impassioned as our vast prairies, rooted in strength as the rocks on which the Puritan fathers landed."[19]

In short, in viewing American cultural identity in nationally *comparativist* terms, she managed to define the mongrel, expansive, impulsive, and idealistic American "idea" that she had only hesitantly glimpsed in the West. Indeed, she said, Europe *inspired* her national ideal. "What we loved in the literature of continental Europe," she testified, "was the range and force of ideal manifestation in forms of national and individual greatness." Finally, that "individual" was critical as well: just as Shakespeare infused the clarity and boldness of English literature with the "rich colouring, and more affluent life, of the Catholic countries," the American literary "genius," she predicted, will be a *transnational* mongrel, too.[20]

Of course, her new cultural ideal of a Romantically nourished nation hardly lacked difficulties. One was its distant fruition. Repeating all the historical obstacles that she had listed in her Allston review in the *Dial*, to which she now added the difficulty of fusing America's "races," she concluded that a national literature wouldn't emerge for at least another generation. Here her unflinching Romantic historicism misled her. Yet it didn't keep her from appraising week after week the literary works that the United States was *already* producing—and with results that were amazingly prescient. For in counterposing the hackneyed products of America's commercial print revolution *and* the provincially "cosmopolitan" borrowings of popular middlebrow writers like Longfellow to the inwardly deep works of Emerson, Hawthorne, Melville, and Poe, she alone among antebellum critics pointed to that cosmopolitan canon of the American Renaissance that wouldn't be "discovered" until the modernist early twentieth century.[21]

A second problem with her cultural vision of a cosmopolitan nation might seem equally hard for her to have finessed: where would she find the social and political "life" that she argued in her "American

Literature" essay was needed to infuse the *"idea"* of America but which she had failed to find in the West? In fact, New England had already given her two sightings, as shown in her new friendliness to the abolitionist movement (if not its Garrisonian leaders) and an increasing interest in Fourierist socialist theory (if not practice). In New York, though, she turned these nascent political gestures into probes of a thick and variegated national political life. Thanks to her connections with the *Tribune* and to Channing's circle of Fourierist and religious socialists in his Society of Christian Union, she got her first taste of real political battles: over the city's horrific penal and welfare institutions, its pro-capital punishment ideologues, its racist nativist movements, its hectoring evangelical moral reformers, and its censoring publishers. In even more of a departure, Gotham gave her a new language: that of "democracy," a term she had rarely used before except pejoratively, but which she now joined in her *Tribune* editorials to the Romantically resonating—and almost equally nationalistic—social democratic concepts of Christian "benevolence" and "mutual education."[22]

But what most decisively raised Fuller's democratic political talk in New York far beyond its local setting—indeed, what transmuted it into a transnational project to match her cultural one—was New York's pressing and multifaceted international character. On the social side, she resided in a city that was exploding with the foreign born—at the time she was living there approaching 50 percent of the city, about half Irish, another quarter German, and with sizeable numbers of English, French, and some Italians. On the journalistic side, not only did Fuller observe all this, but she also *participated* in public conversations about and—more important—*with* these immigrant groups through their thriving presses. Within a month of her arrival, she was regularly reading, translating, and publishing articles in the *Tribune* from across the entire political spectrum of German, French, and Irish newspapers. Finally, on the political side, starting her first summer, she also began periodically attending, and occasionally covering for her paper, meetings of exile groups agitating for support for liberal democratic revolutionary movements in Europe.[23]

From this international stew she extracted a good deal of transnational meat. To be sure, it had in the beginning a liberal but somewhat noblesse oblige flavor. "Too many have come since for bread alone," she wrote after her first month in New York. "We cannot blame—we must not reject them, but let us teach them. . . . Yes! let us teach them,

not rail at their inevitable ignorance and unenlightened action, but
teach them and their children as our own."[24] In subsequent articles,
however, she dropped the teaching of the ignorant and focused on the
railing of the natives. In the city with the strongest nativist party in
America—and in the face of widespread demonization of the Irish as
hopelessly profligate, superstitious, and virtually subhuman by nativists
and reformers alike (including many of her own reform friends)—she
publicly defended the virtues of their culture and pooh-poohed the danger of their Catholicism. She also used her translations from the liberal
monarchical *Courrier des Etas-Unis* and the radical republican *Franco-
Americain* to expose the charms of French popular culture for her often-
starchly Francophobic readers (including her editor). Indeed, hailing
the appearance of a new weekly edition of the *Deutsche Schnellpost,* she
completely avoided the two main "liberal" options of nineteenth-
century antinativism: immigrants' wholesale assimilation into a uni-
formly republican-Protestant "American" culture or the toleration of
their ethnic diversity as long as their labor power fed capitalist economic development (or, in the case of Democrats, the urban Democratic party). Instead, she urged the birth of a new multiethnic America.

> We do want that each nation needs to hear from those of her compatri-
> ots, able to guide and enlighten them. We do want that each nation
> should preserve what is valuable in its parent stock. We want all the ele-
> ments of the new people of the new world. . . . But we want none of
> their prejudices. We want the healthy seed to develop itself into a differ-
> ent plant, in the new climate. We have reason to hope a new and gener-
> ous race[,] where the Italian meets the Dutch[,] the Swede the Jew. Let
> nothing be obliterated, but all regenerated.[25]

We need to cast aside our present ideological blinders to see how
truly radical her position is here. Fuller was no modern relativist or
static pluralist: certainly she doesn't maintain (as would most famously
the early twentieth-century critic Horace Kallen—and also many current partisans of American "multiculturalism") that America is no more
than a conglomeration of equally valid and largely separate unchanging
ethnic enclaves. Rather, in her own Romantic language, she's arguing
here for a dialectical ideal of American ethnicity: *both* the retention of
immigrants' cultural characteristics *and* their regeneration into a spiritu-
ally broader, deeper, and freer mindset than what they had known in
their respective socially conservative countries. Moreover, she regarded
this required regeneration as truly transnational: both foreign *and* native

"souls" needed to be "re-born here." Finally, as she implies here, the new European immigrants had vital cultural capital to contribute to that regeneration. Reviewing a meeting she attended her second winter celebrating the anniversary of the defeated Polish Revolution of 1830–31, after hearing an Italian nationalist speaker (who clearly had been influenced by the ideas of Giuseppe Mazzini) speak about "Nationality" as humankind's "Individualism" *and* "fellow-feeling writ large," she exclaimed: "May the same fervor of heart be turned to forward the good of the adopted land, for where there is genius, greatness and religion, blooms anew the true Italy, the garden of the world!" Besides the obvious prescience of this exclamation for Fuller's later Italy, what's notable about this mutual metaphorical national transposition is its wonderful ambiguity: it's not clear *which* is the "garden of the world"—the "true" America or the "true" Italy.[26]

These multiethnic articles marked the highpoint of Fuller's transnational American nationalism in the United States. And necessarily so: her assumption that the American liberal "idea" and a cosmopolitan liberal world could be made to coincide, however useful and inspiring as a cultural myth, could hardly sustain itself in an era of increasingly revolutionary and counterrevolutionary political shocks. And two came quickly. The first from the national side of her transnational ledger: the ever-more boiling question of the annexation of the Republic of Texas as a future proslavery state. Indeed, one can trace Fuller's rising political temperature that year in her editorials chronicling the fate of Texas. In her "First of August, 1845" article celebrating the anniversary of the West Indies emancipation, following by weeks the formal acceptance of Texas annexation, she wrote: "The most shameful deed has been done that ever disgraced a nation; because the most contrary to consciousness of right. Other nations have done wickedly, but we have surpassed them all in trampling under foot the principles that had been assumed as the basis of our national existence and our willingness to forfeit our honor in the face of the world." Then, right after Texas was admitted as a new slave state at the end of the year, she virtually declared that national pledge as dead. "What a year it has been with us!" she wrote in her "1st January, 1846" state-of-the-world article. "Texas annexed, and more annexations in store; Slavery perpetuated, as the most striking new feature of these movements. Such are the fruits of American love of liberty! Mormons murdered and driven out, as an expression of American freedom of conscience. Cassius Clay's [antislavery] paper expelled from

Kentucky; that is American freedom of the press. And all these deeds defended on the true Russian grounds: 'We (the stronger) know what you (the weaker) ought to do and be, and it *shall* be so.'" Nor was it just a "lust of power" driving hypocritical Americans. "More money—more land! is all the watchword they know."[27]

So what to do as America politically forsook its own cosmopolitan liberal ideals? Now revising her recently restated Transcendentalist hopes that righteously witnessing "private lives" might be all that was needed, she pulled her second shock card from her transnational political deck: Europe. This was truly a cosmopolitan reshuffling. In her political commentary throughout the year, she had repeatedly declared Europe's class-bound society "bankrupt." Indeed, she had made that very point in January 1846 in taking to task the German Social Reform Association's new journal *Der Volks-Tribun*, edited by Hermann Kriege, then a militant twenty-five-year-old German émigré and an advocate of communism and land reform. Claiming that she, too, placed herself on the "'extreme left' of the army of Progress," she nonetheless strongly objected not just to the newspaper's class-warfare tone as "not the spirit for Young America" but, even more so, to what she saw as its source: the editors' obtuseness about the vast difference between conditions in America and Europe. "We cannot wonder, Germans," she lectured them, "if, having thrown off so heavy and galling a harness, you fume and champ to find the bit still in your mouths; yet let this impatience be transient, and prize more justly and deeply the vast privileges you have already attained. Seek to extend them, to complete and elevate their scope."[28]

Yet even as she lambasted the *Volks-Tribun*'s editors for its insufficient appreciation of their "vast privileges" in America, she was already starting to look with new political eyes across the Atlantic. Earlier in the winter she had begun moving from commenting mostly on appealing European manners to remarking about German radical political writers who implicitly challenged her own uneasy faith in America's "exceptional" promise. She even translated a dispatch from *Deutsche Schnell-post*'s Paris correspondent Heinrich Börnstein, who edited the German-language Parisian *Vorwärts! ("Advance!")*, the most radical journal in Europe, then dominated by Karl Marx and Arnold Ruge, who would soon found the Communist League. Following Börnstein's insider's appraisal of the erupting radical socialist movements in Germany, in which he argued that the coming age of humanistic socialism would extend the

French Revolutionary ideal of "abstract" political equality into full economic and social equality, he inserted an account of a recent strike of five thousand carpenters in Paris. Fuller added: "The new era is not far off. The new era, when the laborer shall be thought worthy of his hire, and every man entitled to express the wants that consume him, and ask relief from the cares that now harass so many from the cradle to the grave."[29]

Even more revealing of her anticipatory radical mood than her friendly liberal gloss on Börnstein's article (which the antistrike Fourierist Greeley the next day sharply critiqued) was her lengthy editorial on New Year's Day 1846. There she barely mentioned *any* American movements, even abolitionism, but found instead, as "signs" of the future, filled with "providential meaning," social and political barrier-breaching stirrings in virtually every country in Europe. Indeed, of the new "Associative and Communist principles," which she again liberally interpreted, here as a reawakening of the Romantic socialist ferment of the 1830s, she wrote: "Let the worldling deem as he will about their practicability, he cannot deny [them] to be animated by faith in God and a desire for the good of Man." And the American nation in this coming democratic era, she asked?

> Altogether, it looks as if a great time was coming, and that time one of Democracy. Our country will play a ruling part. Her Eagle will lead the van, but whether to soar upward to the sun or to stoop for helpless prey, who now dares promise? At present she has scarce achieved a Roman nobleness, a Roman liberty, and whether her Eagle is less like the Vulture and more like the Phenix than was the fierce Roman bird, we dare not say. May the New Year give hopes of the latter, even if the bird need first to be purified by fire.

With this soberly ambiguous look at Janus-faced American "Democracy" as future liberator or imperialist, she implied a curious corollary: if America *were* to "lead the van" it would seem to need a good deal of helpful "fire" from elsewhere.[30]

My main purpose has been to show three things: that Fuller's transnationalist outlook had its roots in America; that it evolved dialectically out of a series of American transnational challenges to her Romantic-inspired European cosmopolitanism and her uneasily acquired American nationality; and that it deeply colored her liberal Romantic thinking. Her transnationalism was also prospective. On the cultural side, it defined a new critical cosmopolitanism as far removed from the cosmopolite borrowings and empty "universal" claims for European texts and tropes of Oliver Wendell Holmes and James Russell Lowell—whom she severely critiqued in the *Tribune*—as from the self-congratulatory cultural nationalism that she likewise criticized as stringently in New York as in Boston. Indeed, it wouldn't be until the delayed rise of literary modernism in America over a half-century later that critics would deconstruct with such literary sophistication and buoyant panache the nation's popular binaries of indigenous nationality and European borrowings for the purpose of creating a new cosmopolitan American literature. And if for modernists like Ezra Pound and T. S. Eliot this move required the jettisoning of national democracy and humanistic religion of Fuller and her generation's social Romantics and Transcendentalists, the jury is still out on the question of whether that was a gain or a loss for American literary practice. On the social side, only Whitman's "nation of nations" trope and Melville's fictive mongrel ship *Pequod* bear metaphorical comparison with Fuller's conception of America as a site of *mutual* transethnic appropriation, where individuals neither fixed nor effaced but exchanged—and thereby reconstituted—their ethnic *and* American identities in the public sphere. And, after them, a roughly equivalent conception would not be articulated again until the pre–World War I "Young America" critic Randolph Bourne, reacting to a second wave of European immigration, announced a new version in his famous essay "Trans-national America."[31]

As I indicated at the beginning, I also believe that Fuller's American transnationalism might provoke *us* to think a little more deeply about how to overcome isolationist and exceptionalist American historical narratives. One approach repeatedly advanced by American Studies scholars since the 1960s has been what I would call the strategy of ideological critique: claiming that all appropriations of the American nation have solely served the hegemonic purpose of what Sacvan Bercovitch has punningly called a conservative "rite of assent." An almost mirror-opposite approach has recently been proposed by American historians calling for a new "international" or "transnational" history that would virtually drop or radically reduce the category of "American nation" altogether. Yet if Fuller's moves and movements indicate anything, they suggest that that trope may have had in the nineteenth century more immanent transnational potential than twentieth-century scholars have yet seen. And, contra Bercovitch, liminal ideological potential as well, since for Fuller, American nationality actually *expanded* rather than contracted her sense of democratic possibilities. And that expansion would continue in Europe. Specifically, by transferring in Italy her hopes for liberal idealism and social justice from the world's newest republic to the radical Democratic resurgence aiming to restore its oldest, she captured, as no other nineteenth-century American intellectual, precisely the argument that undergirded that century's European liberal nationalist movements—that nations existed to advance the world's freedom.[32]

Of course, there is a great irony in this last appropriation: not only did the Italian republican revolution fail, but so also did all the European revolutions of 1848. This hard fact would leave Fuller with some hard questions. Was her dream of a cosmopolitan Romantic democratic revolution all a chimera? Did it require abandoning the central faith in democratic progress that most nineteenth-century American *and* European liberals always clung to? Or was that updated liberal dream something, as American radical intellectuals came to be convinced following the revolutionary defeats on the Continent, that could *only* be realized in America? Or, to put this last question more positively, would she have become, like most of *them* in the wake of the northern emancipation of American slaves, once again a cosmopolitan voice for the revitalization not of the world but of America? We will never know, because she died while pondering European revolutionary defeat and before having to face the promises and snares of her country's "Second American Revolution." But there is one thing we do know: her *American* transnationalism transformed her Romantic cosmopolitanism into (in Emerson's phrase) a "new magazine of power" in her struggle to establish herself as a public intellectual. And a private one as well: certainly they grounded her Romantic dreams of heroic individuals reenchanting a mechanical modern world in experiences that even she could not have imagined ensconced thirty years earlier in what her early Victorian biographer Thomas Wentworth Higginson innocently called her Cambridge "nest."[33]

Notes

1. Charles Capper, *Margaret Fuller: An American Romantic Life*, vol. 1, *The Private Years* (New York: Oxford Univ. Press, 1992); Vernon Louis Parrington,

Main Currents in American Thought: An Interpretation of American Literature from the Beginnings to 1920, 3 vols. (New York: Harcourt, Brace, 1927–30), vol. 2, *The Romantic Revolution in America, 1800–1860*, 414–34; Perry Miller, ed., *Margaret Fuller: American Romantic* (Ithaca, N.Y.: Cornell Univ. Press, 1970), ix–xxviii; Stanley M. Elkins, *Slavery: A Problem in American Institutional and Intellectual Life* (Chicago: Univ. of Chicago Press, 1976), 155; Bell Chevigny, *The Woman and the Myth: Margaret Fuller's Life and Writings*, rev. ed. (Boston: Northeastern Univ. Press, 1994); Ann Douglas, *The Feminization of American Culture* (New York: Alfred A. Knopf, 1977), 259–88; Miller, *Margaret Fuller*, xxvii. I have adapted parts of this essay from my preface in *Margaret Fuller: An American Romantic Life*, vol. 2, *The Public Years* (New York: Oxford Univ. Press, 2007).

2. For thoughtful appraisals of Tocqueville's tension-filled "exceptionalist" critique of American democracy, see Cushing Strout, "Tocqueville's Duality: Describing America and Thinking of Europe," *American Quarterly* 21 (Spring 1969): 87–99; James T. Kloppenburg, "Life Everlasting: Tocqueville in America," in his *The Virtues of Liberalism* (New York: Oxford Univ. Press, 1998), 71–81, 201–4. For recent discussions of the pervasive theme of American "exceptionalism" in historical writing, see the works cited in note 32.

3. Ralph Waldo Emerson, "The American Scholar," in *The Collected Works of Ralph Waldo Emerson*, ed. Alfred E. Ferguson et al., 5 vols. to date (Cambridge, Mass.: Belknap Press, 1971–), 1:56.

4. Fuller Manuscripts and Works, Houghton Library, Harvard University, 3:7; ibid., 5:6; *The Correspondence of Emerson and Carlyle*, ed. Joseph Slater (New York: Columbia Univ. Press, 1964), 478; *The Letters of Margaret Fuller*, ed. Robert N. Hudspeth, 6 vols. (Ithaca, N.Y.: Cornell Univ. Press, 1983–94), 1:155.

5. Capper, *Margaret Fuller*, 1:84–87, 91–92, 103–7.

6. *Letters of Fuller*, 1:318; ibid., 6:274; *American Monthly Magazine* 8 (July 1836): 1–13. In addition to her dozen articles published in the *Western Messenger, American Monthly Magazine*, and *Boston Quarterly Review*, Fuller planned or wrote many others that were never printed.

7. I discuss in detail Fuller's engagements with these four transnational sites in my *Public Years*, volume 2 of *Margaret Fuller: An American Romantic Life*.

8. Journal "1840," Fuller Manuscripts and Works, box 1; "A Record of Impressions Produced by the Exhibition of Mr. Allston's Pictures in the Summer of 1839," *Dial* 1 (July 1840): 75; *Letters of Fuller*, 2:125.

9. *Letters of Fuller*, 2:108.

10. *Dial* 1 (July 1840): 6, 7, 10.

11. The still indispensable guide to the twentieth-century's "little magazines" is Frederick J. Hoffman, Charles Allen, and Carolyn F. Ulrich, *The Little Magazine: A History and a Bibliography* (Princeton, N.J.: Princeton Univ. Press, 1946). The best study of their international intellectual contexts remains Henry

F. May, *The End of American Innocence: A Study of the First Years of Our Time* (New York: Alfred A. Knopf, 1959).

12. The only other *Dial* piece to vie with Fuller's sketches for the title of most outlandish was Charles King Newcomb's eerie tale of ritual murder, "The Two Dolons," *Dial* 3 (July 1842): 112–23.

13. *Dial* 4 (July 1843): 8, 43; *Woman in the Nineteenth Century* (New York: Greeley & McElrath, 1845). The methodological question of linking textual analysis and contextual interrogation in intellectual history has received enormous attention over the last thirty years, but for a recent especially cogent appraisal, see Martin Jay, "The Textual Approach to Intellectual History," in his *Force Fields: Between Intellectual History and Cultural Critique* (New York: Routledge, 1993), 158–66. For a now classic "contextualist" approach as applied to American intellectual history, see David A. Hollinger, "Historians and the Discourse of Intellectuals," in his *In the American Province: Studies in the History and Historiography of Ideas* (Bloomington: Indiana Univ. Press, 1985), 130–51.

14. To Harriet Martineau, [ca. November 1837], *Letters of Fuller*, 1:307, 309; to Maria Weston Chapman, December 26, 1840, ibid., 2:197–98; Anne Weston to Margaret Fuller, January 1841, "Weston Papers," Anti-Slavery Collection, Boston Public Library; *Dial* 4 (July 1843): 9. For Unitarianism and antislavery, see Daniel Walker Howe, *The Unitarian Conscience: Harvard Moral Philosophy, 1805–1861* (Cambridge, Mass.: Harvard Univ. Press, 1970), 270–305, and Douglas C. Stange, *Patterns of Antislavery among American Unitarians, 1831–1860* (Rutherford, N.J.: Fairleigh Dickinson Univ. Press, 1977). There exists no adequate study of the Transcendentalists and antislavery. For a classic but tendentious discussion, see Elkins, *Slavery*, chap. 4. More positive recent appraisals of individual Transcendentalists include Len Gougeon, *Virtue's Hero: Emerson, Antislavery, and Reform* (Athens: Univ. of Georgia Press, 1990); Richard F. Teichgraeber III, *Sublime Thoughts/Penny Wisdom: Situating Emerson and Thoreau in the American Market* (Baltimore: Johns Hopkins Univ. Press, 1995), chaps. 3–6; Albert J. von Frank, "Mrs. Brackett's Verdict: Magic and Means in Transcendental Antislavery Work," in *Transient and Permanent: The Transcendentalist Movement and Its Contexts*, ed. Charles Capper and Conrad Edick Wright (Boston: Massachusetts Historical Society, 1999), 385–407; and Dean Grodzins, *American Heretic: Theodore Parker and Transcendentalism* (Chapel Hill: Univ. of North Carolina Press, 2002), chap. 7. In her *Woman in the Nineteenth Century* (1845), Fuller would extend her analysis into more popular and political topics, such as prostitution and Texas annexation, but without altering the transnational liberal Romantic perspective of "The Great Lawsuit," most of whose sections she reproduced verbatim in her book.

15. *Summer on the Lakes, in 1843* (Boston: Charles C. Little and James Brown, 1844), 53, 65.

16. *Summer on the Lakes*, 166; *Dial* 4 (July 1843): 10.

17. "Hawthorne and His Mosses," in *The Writings of Herman Melville*, ed. Harrison Hayford, Hershel Parker, and G. Thomas Tanselle, Northwestern-Newberry Edition, vol. 9, *The Piazza Tales and Other Prose Pieces, 1839–1860*, ed. Harrison Hayford et al. (Evanston, Ill., and Chicago: Northwestern Univ. Press / Newberry Library, 1987), 239–53.

18. Horace Greeley, in *Memoirs of Margaret Fuller Ossoli*, ed. R. W. Emerson, W. H. Channing, and J. F. Clarke, 2 vols. (Boston: Brown, Taggard and Chase, 1852), 2:152; Horace Greeley, "Prospectus for the Year 1845," *New-York Daily Tribune*, November 16, 1844.

19. [Aug. 14, 1845,] *Letters of Fuller*, 6:359 ("mutual education"); S. Margaret Fuller, *Papers on Literature and Art*, 2 vols. (New York: Wiley and Putnam, 1846), 2:124.

20. *Papers on Literature and Art*, 2:123.

21. For the classic modernist "discoveries" of the "American Renaissance," see Lewis Mumford, *The Golden Day* (New York: Boni and Liveright, 1926), and F. O. Matthiessen, *American Renaissance: Art and Expression in the Age of Emerson and Whitman* (New York: Oxford Univ. Press, 1941).

22. These developments are traced in the second volume of my biography of Fuller.

23. The best recent discussions of German and Irish social and political life in antebellum New York City may be found in Stanley Nadel, *Little Germany: Ethnicity, Religion, and Class in New York City, 1845–80* (Urbana: Univ. of Illinois Press, 1990); Richard B. Stott, *Workers in the Metropolis: Class, Ethnicity, and Youth in Antebellum New York City* (Ithaca, NY: Cornell Univ. Press, 1990); and Ronald H. Bayor and Timothy J. Meagher, eds., *The New York Irish* (Baltimore: Johns Hopkins Univ. Press, 1996), 1–209. For an example of the deep hostility harbored by many antebellum radical reformers toward the Irish, in this case by one of Fuller's ideologically closest friends in New York, see Lydia Maria Child to Maria Weston Chapman, Apr. 26, [1842,] in *Lydia Maria Child: Selected Letters, 1817–1880*, ed. Milton Meltzer and Patricia G. Holland (Amherst: Univ. of Massachusetts Press, 1982) 169–70.

24. "New Year's Day," *New-York Daily Tribune*, December 28, 1844, 1.

25. "Deutsche Schnellpost," *New-York Daily Tribune*, January 25, 1845, 1.

26. Ibid.; "Anniversary of the Polish Revolution," *New-York Daily Tribune*, December 1, 1845, 2. For Kallen's theories of ethnic "pluralism" and their later legacies in discussions of "multiculturalism," see David A. Hollinger, *Postethnic America: Beyond Multiculturalism*, 2nd ed. (New York: Basic Books, 2000), chap. 4. See also Werner Sollors, "A Critique of Pure Pluralism," in *Reconstructing American Literary History*, ed. Sacvan Bercovitch (Cambridge, Mass.: Harvard Univ. Press, 1986), 250–79.

27. "First of August, 1845," *New-York Daily Tribune*, August 1, 1845, 1; "1st January, 1846," *New-York Daily Tribune*, January 1, 1846, 1.

28. "New Year's Day," *New-York Daily Tribune*, January 1, 1845, 1; "First of August, 1845," *New-York Daily Tribune*, August 1, 1845, 1; "Der Volks-Tribun," *New-York Daily Tribune*, January 17, 1846, 1.

29. "The Social Movement in Europe," *New-York Daily Tribune*, August 5, 1845, 1 ("communism").

30. "1st January, 1846," *New-York Daily Tribune*, 1.

31. Bourne, "Trans-National America," *Atlantic Monthly* 118 (July 1916): 86–97.

32. Sacvan Bercovitch's influential discussion of American rituals of consent may be found in his *American Jeremiad* (Madison: Univ. of Wisconsin Press, 1978), but for a partly revised recent restatement, see his *The Rites of Assent: Transformations in the Symbolic Construction of America* (New York: Routledge, 1993). For calls for a new "transnational" or "international" history that would variously drop, reduce, or make highly permeable the concept of the nation in American historical scholarship and American Studies, see Ian Tyrrell, "American Exceptionalism in an Age of International History," *American Historical Review* 96 (October 1991): 1031–55; and most of the articles in "The Nation and Beyond: Transnational Perspectives on United States Identity," Special Issue of *Journal of American History* 86 (December 1999). For perspectives that retain more of the concept of the American nation within a comparativist framework, see Carl N. Degler, "In Pursuit of an American History," *American Historical Review* 92 (February 1987): 1–12; Michael McGerr, "The Price of the 'New Transnational History,'" and "Ian Tyrrell Responds," *American Historical Review* 96 (October 1991), 1056–72; and David A. Hollinger, "The Historian's Use of the United States and Vice Versa," in *Rethinking American History in a Global Age*, ed. Thomas Bender (Berkeley: Univ. of California Press, 2002). Transnational and comparativist antebellum intellectual histories are still comparatively rare. The two most ambitious recent works in the genre—James T. Kloppenberg, *Uncertain Victory: Social Democracy and Progressivism in European and American Thought, 1870–1920* (New York: Oxford Univ. Press, 1986), and Daniel T. Rodgers, *Atlantic Crossings: Social Politics in a Progressive Age* (Cambridge, Mass.: Harvard Univ. Press, 1998)—both begin their stories in the 1870s. The only comparable study to extend its search backward, Dorothy Ross's *The Origins of American Social Science* (Cambridge, UK: Cambridge Univ. Press, 1991), argues that American "exceptionalist" ideology permeated American social science from its inception. Carl J. Guarneri, "Brook Farm, Fourierism, and the Nationalist Dilemma in American Utopianism," in Capper and Wright, *Transient and Permanent*, 447–70, likewise highlights the conservative impact of nationalist ideology on Transcendentalist Fourierism. Yet some American intellectual and

literary historians have recently begun returning to an older interest in ante-
bellum American-European cross-"influences," albeit in new ideological and
transnational ways. See Lawrence Buell, "American Literary Emergence as a
Postcolonial Phenomenon," *American Literary History* 4 (Fall 1992): 411–42; and
Thomas Bender, *A Nation among Nations: America's Place in World History* (New
York: Hill & Wang, 2006). For two much-noted reclamations of the idea of
American nationhood for versions of contemporary left-liberal political criti-
cism, see Richard Rorty, *Achieving Our Country: Leftist Thought in Twentieth-Century
America* (Cambridge, Mass.: Harvard Univ. Press, 1998); and Hollinger, *Post-
ethnic America*, chap. 6. Hollinger further develops his ideas in his *Cosmopolitanism
and Solidarity: Studies in Ethnoracial, Religious, and Professional Affiliation in the United
States* (Madison: Univ. of Wisconsin Press, 2006).

    33. Higginson, *Cheerful Yesterdays* (Boston: Houghton, Mifflin, 1899), 3.

2

Playing the Eclectic

Margaret Fuller's Creative Appropriation of Goethe

JOSEPH C. SCHÖPP

> To me, our destinies seem flower and fruit
> Born of an ever-generating root.
> Margaret Fuller, "The One in All"

"No author," remarks Octavius Brooks Frothingham in the first significant study of American Transcendentalism, "occupied the cultivated New England mind as much as [Goethe] did."[1] Although of all German authors Goethe undoubtedly ranked first in number of magazine articles and books in translation, New England was deeply divided over the literary standing of the scandalous "Old Heathen," as he was frequently called. If there was one German author, argues Charles Capper, "who was almost universally excoriated in all the American journals, it was Goethe. Political liberals disliked him because of his political conservatism; religious conservatives, both Unitarian and orthodox, abhorred him because of his supposed pantheism; and virtually all denounced him for the supposed libertinism of his personal life and the unashamed sensuality of some of his writing." While for George Bancroft he held "perhaps the lowest place" in everything that related "to firmness of principle, to love for truth itself, to humanity, to holiness, to love of freedom," the verdict of the three major New England Transcendentalists was somewhat more balanced and qualified.[2]

Thoreau, though "not much acquainted with the works of Goethe," as he freely admitted, deemed him important enough to include in his poetic portrait gallery of *A Week on the Concord and Merrimack Rivers*. The picture that he draws, however, is far from flawless. Lacking the vatic power of a poet, Goethe, "the city boy, whose toys are pictures and works of art, whose wonders are the theatre and kingly processions and crownings," is seen as one who is diametrically opposed to Thoreau himself, the country boy whose wonders are those of *The Maine Woods, Walden*, and *Cape Cod*. Far from being the poetic genius, "an originator, an inspired or demonic man, who produces a perfect work in obedience to laws yet unexplored," he appears as a latter-day artist who merely "detects and applies the law from observation of the works of genius." He is, as it were, a mimetic rather than a poetic artist, twice removed from the divine source of inspiration, who merely arranges into an "artistic completeness" what the genius long before him had originally explored.[3]

In Emerson's œuvre Goethe, the scholar and writer, appears in a more favorable light as both the true representative of his age and as Emerson's own alter ego. "No more instructive name occurs," he argues, "than that of Goethe, to represent the powers and duties of the scholar or writer."[4] Though born "into an overcivilized time and country, when original talent was oppressed under the load of books and mechanical auxiliaries and the distracting variety of claims" (*EL* 760), he was able to make the most of these limitations. Aware of the encyclopedic nature of the age, he "found himself the master of histories, mythologies, philosophies, sciences and national literatures" (*EL* 751). This mastery made Goethe, in Emerson's eyes, a *Meister*-like poet after all, a "poet of a prouder laurel than any contemporary" (*EL* 752).

Margaret Fuller was, as Amanda Ritchie argues, among the very few Americans who had "read *all* of Goethe that was available to her" and had thus achieved "a degree of expertise on Goethe's collected writings that would rival almost any published study of the poet and his life." She was aware of the contents of the first fifty-five volumes of the *Vollständige Ausgabe letzter Hand*, as the notes in one of her unpublished manuscripts on Goethe indicate. Fuller regarded Goethe as "one of the master-spirits of this world" who would lead New England—"this naked, unatmospheric land of ours," as Emerson would later characterize it in a letter to Fuller—out of its provincial narrowness and moral illiberalism so that it would one day perhaps play a more significant part in the concert of *Weltliteratur*, a concept developed by Goethe in the later years of his life.[5]

Especially in the post-Napoleonic era Goethe's awareness of a world of intercultural relations and literary transactions had grown; he now intensified his efforts as a translator and saw his role, typical of a mercantilistic age, increasingly as that of a literary agent and entrepreneur "in a marketplace in which all nations offered their commodities." Despite its limitations, translation, in his eyes, could advance to "one of the most important and dignified businesses in world-trade."[6] Such a world-literary project that transcended narrow national boundaries and helped intertwine the diverse strands of cultures appealed to Fuller and her fellow-Transcendentalists who feared nothing more than cultural stagnation in "the *morgue* of conventions" (*EL* 761).

When Fuller, still in her teens, makes her first acquaintance with Goethe's writings, he appears to her as a sublime, superhuman Olympian figure. His "perfect wisdom and merciless nature" at first overwhelm her (*M* 1:117). In a letter to James Freeman Clarke dated ca. August 1, 1832, in which Goethe's name is mentioned for the first time in her correspondence, she remarks:

> It seems to me as if the mind of Goethe had embraced the universe. I have felt this lately, in reading his lyric poems. I am enchanted while I read. He comprehends every feeling I have ever had so perfectly, expresses it so beautifully; but when I shut the book, it seems as if I had lost my personal identity; all my feelings linked with such an immense variety that belong to beings I had thought so different. What can I bring? There is no answer in my mind, except "It is so," or "It will be so," or "No doubt such and such feel so."[7]

Fuller read other major German writers: Lessing, "strong, but not deep" (*L* 6:202); Jean Paul Richter with his "exuberant sentiment"; the Schlegels, who could "find plausible meaning for the deepest enigma"; and, above all, Novalis, "an uncommon person" in a "common-place" world, whose "pure mystic sweetness" appealed to her own mysticism. But none "could fill Goethe's place."[8] His "interior truth," as Emerson had characterized it (*EL* 756), his "largeness and depth"[9] of thought provided the challenge that she sought. Therefore she would "persevere in reading the great sage, some part of every day, hoping the time will come when [she] shall not feel so overwhelmed" (*L* 1:177), when she will not just give in and dutifully respond Amen, "It is so" or "It will be so." "What can *I* bring?" was the challenging question that required an answer.

Submissiveness, an essential element in an antebellum "true woman,"[10] was never in Fuller's vocabulary nor was it an adequate attitude for someone determined to write the life of Goethe. Initially "contented to learn a little every day, as becomes a pupil" (*L* 1:177), she increasingly abandoned the role of the obedient disciple and developed a more independent and critical stance well becoming a biographer. "All the scandal about Goethe—about his marriage and so forth," she wrote to Frederic Hedge while collecting her biographical material, "only puzzles and disturbs me" (*L* 1:293). That "his son was illegitimate, that he lived out of wedlock with the mother for twenty years and only married her on acct of the son," at first greatly pained and troubled her, as she remarked in a letter to James F. Clarke in 1836. She had no idea, she continued, "that the mighty 'Indifferentist' went so far with his experimentalizing in *real life*" that he made practically no distinction between *l'homme et l'œuvre*. "[She] had not supposed he '*was*' all he had '*writ*'" (*L* 6:287).

Fuller eventually abandoned her plan of writing *The Life of Goethe*, although "she had collected a large mass of notes and observations" by 1838.[11] Her decision can only in part be explained by a deep feeling of inadequacy and a lack of important biographical information.[12] What is at least of paramount importance is that her decision to translate Johann Peter Eckermann's *Gespräche mit Goethe in den letzten Jahren seines Lebens* coincided with the abandonment of the biographical project.[13] Through Eckermann, it seems, Fuller learned to know her *real* Goethe, the mature artist, critic, and thinker who should largely determine the future course of her own literary career. In a letter to Emerson dated July 3, 1837, she had already confessed that she primarily saw Goethe "as a great thinker, who makes me think, a wonderful artist who gratifies my tastes" (*L* 1:288). Goethe, "the scholar or writer," as Emerson had characterized him, the "artist," as Thoreau saw him, and, above all, the "thinker" whose ideas made her—in the words of Bettina Brentano—think "on and on [*fort und fort*] till we live in them,"[14] characterizes Fuller's newly gained attitude toward "the great sage" of Weimar. "Let us not in surveying his works and life abide with him too much in the suburbs and outskirts of himself," she wrote. "Let us enter into his higher tendency" (*DG* 41).

It is equal partnership, "walk[ing] by his side,"[15] rather than submissive discipleship that marks Fuller's later, more mature position vis-à-vis Goethe. Appropriation, the term I use in my title, implies nothing less than her creative agency of absorbing and unfolding those Goethean ideas that she found most conducive to her own work as a writer. The

translatio, i.e., the transfer of new texts into her native context, Fuller believed, would eventually lead to a renewal of her New England culture
that, in the eyes of her Transcendentalist friends, was in need of a regeneration. Therefore, the motto for George Ripley's *Specimens of Foreign
Standard Literature*, a series of translations in which Eckermann's *Conversations with Goethe* appeared, seemed aptly chosen since it testified to this
intercultural regenerative endeavor: "As wine and oil are imported to us
from abroad, so must ripe understanding, and many civil virtues, be imported into our minds from foreign writings;—we shall else miscarry
still, and come short in the attempts of any great enterprise."[16]

Creative agency also meant a critical sifting of those ideas with
which she would not agree. Far from being merely "a blind admirer of
Goethe,"[17] she assumed an increasingly "sceptical attitude" toward him.
His greatest weakness, she thought, was his cold intellect, which became
a key word in her *Dial* essay of 1841. His intellectual faculty was "too
much developed in proportion to the moral nature," which resulted in
"a deep mind and a shallow heart" (*DG* 2). As a minister and courtier,
he too easily "lost sight of the highest aim" (*DG* 21). Too much a "man of
the world and man of affairs" (*DG* 4), he undervalued the restless aspirations of more "flame-like natures" like Novalis (*DG* 2). Lacking the vatic
powers of a true Romanticist, the world, as it were, was too much with
him and "was to him an arena or a studio, but not a temple" (*DG* 20).
His works, in short, "are not instinct and glowing with the central fire"
of nature transfigured (*DG* 27), a critique that she shared with both
Emerson and Thoreau.

Fuller, it seems, learned more and more to choose and "play the Eclectic" (*L* 1:198) somewhat like Goethe himself who regarded the eclectic as one who, among the things surrounding him, would appropriate
what he deemed appropriate to and in accordance with his nature.[18]
Following Fuller's example I will also act as an eclectic and concentrate
on those Goethean ideas that I consider of crucial importance to her literary œuvre. I want to show that she did not pick these ideas haphaz-
ardly but with great deliberation and that they form a stringent inner
coherence. I also want to demonstrate that through the creative appropriation of these ideas she helped transcend the cultural limitations of
her time and place so that, on the shores of New England, "fresh currents of life [could] call into life fresh thoughts," as she would later
phrase it in her essay "American Literature" (1846), whose subtitle
programmatically stated that a mere affirmation of the "Position in the

Present Time" was insufficient and that "Prospects for the Future" had
to be envisioned, a future less narrow and provincial than the present.[19]
The Goethean ideas adopted and unfolded by Fuller that I will discuss
next revolve around the notions of translation, self-culture, the Daimonic, the role of woman, and the status of art.

Heeding her own advice to abandon "the suburbs and outskirts" of
Goethe's life and "enter into his higher tendency" of art, Fuller therefore appropriates Goethe through his writings rather than through his
biography. *Torquato Tasso*, the dramatic representation of "a personage
more living than the other great poets," was the first major work to
be translated by Fuller, a play about an artist and his art, which after
Goethe's first Italian journey had marked his artistic reorientation, if
not his rebirth as an artist after the period of Sturm und Drang. With
her translation of *Tasso* Fuller not only gained access to the Emerson
circle (*M* 1:201), but *Tasso* also helped define her own role as a writer and
served "as a vehicle for her own entry into literary history," as Christina
Zwarg has convincingly shown.[20]

Inspired by Goethe's notion of the translator as cultural interpreter
(Dolmetscher), Fuller regarded translation as more than just "an act of
simple importation—bringing yet another treasure or text from the Old
World" to be exhibited in the New World. Translations in the Goethean sense were meant to initiate a dialogue between cultures. Despite
Fuller's emphasis of transcriptive accuracy and clarity, a translation
from one language into another is more than that; it is essentially a creative act. "Translation is writing," argues Jacques Derrida, "that is, it is
not translation only in the sense of transcription. It is a productive writing called forth by the original text." Goethe, with his writings, provoked new texts in Fuller, his thinking made her think *fort und fort*, and,
as she said in her *Dial* review of a new book on Tasso, "we are always
more and more interested to see what gloss a new mind will put on the
old text."[21] By glossing over the text of Goethe's *Torquato Tasso* her *Tasso*
becomes a sort of palimpsest, that is, a text that can claim a status all its
own, as the changed title clearly indicates. As editor of *Dial* and as a
translator she acted as an agent and interpreter in a complex process of
cultural transactions that helped advance the status of American literature in a world-literary context.

Despite her objections to some of Goethe's personal traits, Fuller
sympathized deeply with him as an artist who kindled in her "an earnest

desire . . . always to have some engrossing object of pursuit" (*M* 1:121).
The "Seeker" who is "nobler than the Meister" (*DG* 3), the "effort"
rather than the "success" were the goals that she found worth pursuing.[22]
With Goethe, Clarke maintained, she "from first to last" sought "*self-
culture*"; from early on she "*knew that the only object in life was to 'grow.'*" What
the notion of growth implied was "again made much more clear to her
mind by the study of Goethe, the great master of this school, in whose
unequalled eloquence this doctrine acquire[d] an almost irresistible
beauty and charm" (*M* 1:132–33). Distancing herself from an evangelical
notion of self-culture conceived as a conscious commitment to Christ
undertaken at a single dramatic moment, Fuller and her Transcendentalist friends followed a more liberal concept of self-culture as a continuous process of individual growth. While Emerson and Thoreau defined
this quest for selfhood in spiritual terms as a "Platonic quest" invoked
"through oratory, poetry and prose," Fuller recognized the imbalances
of such a one-sided spirituality that, in her eyes, "lacked appreciation for
carnality," as Daniel Walker Howe has shown. The corporeal, carnal
self that Fuller promoted both as a person and a writer stressing alternative "art forms unfamiliar to New Englanders, such as sculpture and
drama," she would find represented in the writings of Goethe.[23]

Growth also evoked associations with Goethe's organicist thinking
with his lifelong interest in plants, especially the *Urpflanze* in which he
saw the "secret" *(geheime)* and "eternal laws" *(ew'gen Gesetze)* of Nature at
work according to which the various and manifold forms and figures of
life would "silently unfold" *(still entfaltend)*, as he had phrased it in his
poem "Die Metamorphose der Pflanzen."[24] Toward the end of his life,
in *Conversations with Eckermann,* he would declare that in his search "to
find out what all plants without exception had in common," he had discovered metamorphosis as the fundamental law governing the processes
of life.[25] Growth then had to be understood as an ongoing transformation in which ever-new forms came into being.[26] It closely resembled
the Emersonian notion of nature in flux, that is, in a ceaseless process
of transition and of becoming.[27] Since everything was in motion, nothing was permanent, everything provisional. The self, therefore, had to
be seen as becoming, incessantly unfolding and advancing into shape
after shape as Goethe in his writings had shaped "forms new and more
admirable than life has yet produced"[28] and as Fuller would take on
shape after shape and transform herself into figure after figure from
Mariana in *Summer on the Lakes* to Miranda in *Woman in the Nineteenth*

Century, from Minerva passing into the Muse and Mary, the Madonna, without ever exhausting the meaning of herself or reaching a final stage of perfection.

For Goethe and Fuller alike, the journey was an ideal representation of this ongoing process of self-becoming. The traveling self was the one that passed through various transformative stages; it was, as it were, a self that was constantly in transit. Traveling through Italy, they both experienced a metamorphosis; their selves began to grow, to expand and to develop. Goethe remarked that between Weimar and Palermo he had undergone many a change, that in Rome he had been born again and could here therefore celebrate a second birthday. On her grand tour from Scotland and England to France and Italy, Fuller experienced a similar rebirth and, at her arrival in Rome, could exclaim in a Goethe-like exuberance: "Ah! how joyful to see once more *this* Rome, instead of the pitiful, peddling, Anglicized Rome" as so frequently described in the Anglocentric travelogues of the time with their stock responses that she found neither inspiring nor joyful to read. For both Fuller and Goethe the ruins of Rome were more than merely stony antique sites; they became alive and began to speak.[29] While Goethe gained an ever-increasing self-assurance in Italy as both naturalist in search of the *Urpflanze* and artist, Fuller, who had almost gotten lost on Ben Lomond, during the revolution of 1848–49 found her new private and political self in the streets of Rome.

In the course of such a metamorphic process, when older forms pass into newer ones, nothing is essentially lost; the former self is, as it were, transformed and re-formed. Metamorphosis, for Goethe as for Fuller, always implied that the previous, more primitive forms were never wholly repudiated by the later, more advanced ones, that the earlier state was always *aufgehoben* in the later one, that is, "transcended" and at the same time "preserved" in the Hegelian double sense of the word. The self passing through various forms thus never lost sight of the secret and eternal laws that governed and silently unfolded it. Unlike Goethe who, in her eyes, had "lost sight of the highest aim" (*DG* 21) and overemphasized the concept of "natural growth," Fuller favored a view that would redress the imbalance between the natural and the spiritual. If Goethe ever "went astray," she penned in one of her journals, "it was, *à moi,* that he so loved gradation and natural growth that he hated miracles." Despite such reservations, Goethe's "Gesetz der Metamorphose" can be seen as an essential element in Fuller's as well as her friends'

Transcendentalist thinking.[30] As reformers in search of more advanced personal as well as cultural formations, the Transcendentalists recognized the inherent dynamic, if not the explosive potential of the metamorphic law. The cultural stagnation of their native New England, they hoped, could thus be overcome and subjected to a ceaseless process of change and advancement.

The intrinsic force that propelled and energized this transformative process Goethe, who "in his love of form . . . was a Greek," had identified with the ancient Greek power of the Daimon.[31] In his poem "Urworte. Orphisch" Goethe has the Daimon speak and characterize him/her/itself somewhat paradoxically as a transgeneric "minted form" *(geprägte Form)*, yet vital and continuously developing *(lebend sich entwickelt)*, a power, as it were, that governs and determines individual forms of life.[32] The Daimon then would be synonymous with one's character, one's fate to which (s)he was subject. *Dichtung und Wahrheit* contains the most detailed discussion of the Daimonic: "[It was something] which manifested itself only through contradiction, and therefore could not be comprehended by any conception, much less defined by a word. It was not divine, for it seemed without reason, not human, because without understanding, not devilish, because it worked to good, not angelic, because it often betrayed a petulant love of mischief. It was like chance, in that it proved no sequence; it suggested the thought of Providence, because it indicated connexion" *(DG* 18–19). The Transcendentalist attitude toward the Daimon as an ungraspable, not fully explicable force was somewhat ambiguous. Emerson, a lover of "daylight," in his lecture "Demonology" rejected "these twilights of thought" and found it "somewhat wilful, some play at blindman's-buff, when men as wise as Goethe talk mysteriously of the demonological,"[33] while he at the same time readily admitted that there was a "last closet" that never opened, "a residuum unknown, unanalyzable" *(EL* 406).

Fuller, more mystery-conscious than Emerson, showed a greater affinity to Goethe's idea of the Daimonic. Like Goethe for whom the Daimon symbolized contradiction par excellence, Fuller regarded it "not necessarily either malignant or the reverse . . . not devilish, only daemonic." It represented a pre-Christian, prerational power, an elemental and pervasive force, *"instinctive,"* spontaneous, incalculable, uncontainable; "it refuses to be analyzed by the understanding, and is most of all inaccessible to the person who possesses it" *(L* 6:141). Since the Daimonic was more effective in the artist, since he differed "from other men only in this, that the voice of the demon within the breast speaks louder," it can also be seen as synonymous with the creative genius.[34] Wilhelm Meister, the archetypal artist figure, for Goethe and Fuller alike embodied the Daimon par excellence. Wilhelm belonged, as Goethe had remarked to Eckermann, to the most incalculable creations to which even he as Wilhelm's creator lacked the key. Wilhelm had no center; he was, as it were, conceived as a fluid self somewhere between, if not beyond, good and evil, conforming to his own code of conduct, acting according to an inner necessity rather than external rules.[35] As a fluid and decentered self, Wilhelm is also a metamorphic figure passing into ever-new forms, a nonconformist who refuses to conform to the commonly accepted mores of society.

The mysterious force of the Daimonic had a greater impact on Fuller than it had on Emerson; she was, as it were, more responsive to the Daimon's "twilights of thought." "A 'youthful prodigy' by day, by night a victim of spectral illusions, nightmare and somnambulism," as she characterized herself in her "Autobiographical Romance" (*EMF* 26), she from early on suffered under long spells of severe headaches that interrupted her writing process; she often felt that "for weeks and months, the daemon work[ed] his will" until, in the midst of "the bad time," quite unexpectedly an uncontrollable power, now more beneficent and creative, would take possession of her (*M* 1:225). James F. Clarke saw in her a Daimonic figure par excellence, not easily comprehensible, because her "complex & various nature [drew] her in many directions." "What a Sphynx is that girl!" he remarked. "Who shall solve her?"[36] And Fuller's own "Credo," as laid down in her journal of 1842, was thoroughly Daimonic and abounded with heterodox allusions transforming the Judeo-Christian Godhead, as it were, into a Goethean Daimon within which "all manifestation is contained, whether of good (accomplishment) or of evil (obstruction). To itself its depths are unknown."[37]

Apart from the more personal affinity that she felt for the Daimonic, it was, above all, the inherent cultural potential that fascinated Fuller. As an incalculable and uncontrollable force, it was capable of unexpected cultural interventions and transgressions. It could transcend the limitations of a routinized, commonplace existence, and new uncommon, charismatic possibilities, not to be culturally contained, would open up. All that limits us, Goethe had argued, the Daimon seemed to penetrate; "it seemed to play at will with all the elements of our being; it compressed time and dilated space" (*DG* 19). It would also change the cultural fabric of New England since it was, in Goethe's words, a power that "if it be not opposed to the moral order of the world, nevertheless does often so cross it that one may be regarded as the warp, and the other as the woof."[38] As a scandalous force that constantly violated the dominant moral order it, of course, met with severe opposition in a thoroughly moralistic culture.

The Daimonic also shows a certain affinity to the metamorphic, as Fuller's "Credo" discloses, in which the heterodox divinity of the Daimon is identified as a force "evolving plants, animals, men, suns, stars, angels, and, it is to be presumed, an infinity of forms not yet visible in the horizon of this being who now writes."[39] Metamorphosis for Fuller is characterized by an inherent incalculability rather than a linearly progressive development toward a given *telos*. "Nature," she argues with Goethe, "seems to delight in varying the arrangements, as if to show that she will be fettered by no rule" and "human nature goes not straight forward, but by excessive action and then reaction in an undulated course" (*EMF* 288, 343). Nature's course, in short, is far from unilinearly progressive; it meanders, digresses, and, in its digressions, discloses unexpected views and vistas that the linear-minded progressivist is unable to detect. Thus Fuller delights "in the varying arrangements" of her M-figures Mariana, Miranda, Minerva, the Muse, and the Madonna, who do not develop in a linear sequence but advance in a rather undulated course in various directions. As plants exfoliate into leaves and flowers are governed by a secret and eternal energy *(energeia)* rather than the goal-oriented notion of what the Greeks called *entelecheia,* Fuller's self, propelled by an intrinsic Daimonic force, passes incessantly through ever-new forms. The metamorphic permutations never solidify, they know of no end. Finality would imply stasis that, in turn, entails death.

Metamorphosis was also a notion greatly conducive to Fuller's conceptualization of woman in *Woman in the Nineteenth Century*. Inhabiting the private sphere, "a place so narrow" (*EMF* 284), her desire to grow and expand into wider, more open spaces increased. Though she loved "best to be a woman," she confessed, "womanhood [was] at present too straitly-bounded to give [her] scope" (*L* 6:143–44.).

Writing provided an ideal scope for Fuller to transcend the narrow bounds of true womanhood; "when I write, it is into another world," she once remarked in a letter to William H. Channing, "not a better one perhaps, but one with very dissimilar habits of thought to this where I am domesticated" (*L* 2:125). This other world was one in which the strict

gender rules that privileged man and domesticated woman were sus-
pended. The "two sides of the great radical dualism" she envisioned
as "perpetually passing into one another. Fluid hardens to solid, solid
rushes to fluid. There is no wholly masculine man, no purely feminine
woman" (*EMF* 310). Goethe's image in mind, "that the noble woman is
she who if her husband dies can be a father to the children," she con-
structs and imagines a whole series of such androgynous figures with
very uncommon habits of thought. She sees women as sea captains, the
muse equipped with Minerva's intellect and javelin, the Madonna "with
child on one arm and the gun on the other" (*L* 6:131), "the soft arms of
affection" armed with "the steel bracelets of strength" (*EMF* 263). The
rigid barriers between the two genders are thus broken down, and new
forms bespeaking "the nature of the coming era" (*L* 6:131) originate in
her writing.

Metamorphosis is finally to be seen in close relation to both Goethe's
and Fuller's notion of woman as a creative force. In his *Conversations with
Eckermann,* Goethe explained the enigmatic scene of Faust's descent into
the innermost caverns of the earth as a *descensus ad inferas,* that is, a return
to the realm of the mothers, who for Goethe represented the force en-
ergizing the ever-generating process of creation and growth, destruction and reconstruction. The mothers were, in Eckermann's words, the
central powers from which the various earthly phenomena emanated,
evolved, and received their unmistakable form.[40]

For Fuller, Goethe was a poet who always represented "the highest
principle in the feminine form" (*DG* 26). In her *Dial* essay "Goethe," her
prose gains a rhapsodic quality when she is able to talk about Ottilia,
"that being of exquisite purity, with intellect and character so harmo-
nized in feminine beauty, as they never before were found in any portrait of woman painted by the hand of man" (*DG* 32), or Iphigenia, "the
full beauty of virgin womanhood, solitary but tender, wise and innocent, sensitive and self-collected, sweet as spring, dignified as becomes
the chosen servant of God" (*DG* 41).

In *Woman in the Nineteenth Century* Fuller's discussion of the "feminine
form" takes its most extensive shape. From Goethe's "poetic soul," she
argues, "grew up forms new and more admirable than life has yet produced, for whom his clear eye marked out paths in the future." Wilhelm
Meister's various female encounters are described as an ascent from
such "common forms of feminine character" as Mariana and Philina to
Mignon, "the electrical, inspired, lyrical nature," then advancing "into
the region of thought" where he would encounter Natalia before he will

finally reach "the house of Macaria, the soul of a star, *i.e.* a pure and perfected intelligence embodied in feminine form, and the center of a world whose members revolve harmoniously round her." What Goethe had identified as the eternally feminine *(das ewig Weibliche)* may be seen as the magnetic force attracting Wilhelm and leading him on his "upward path" from "the hours passed by the side of Mariana to these with Macaria," indeed "a wide distance for human feet to traverse" *(EMF* 316–19).

This distance traversed may, on the one hand, be interpreted as a soul's progress "through the various forms of existence" *(DG* 21) on its way to personal selfhood, while, on the other hand, it marks the stages of Wilhelm's development as an artist. Whereas Mariana, in this context, symbolizes the world of quotidian existence in which a work of art should always be rooted, Mignon, "electrical, inspired, lyrical," takes on the part of the Muse, whose "eye is over-full of expression, dilated and lustrous," and Macaria with her "pure and perfected intelligence" assumes the role of Minerva who had once sprung from Jupiter's head and functions as "regulator" checking and channeling the ecstatic visions of overinspired females, such as Justinus Kerner's Seeress of Prevorst in *Summer on the Lakes* (*EMF* 318, 303, 150–70). Though often critical of Goethe as artist and aware of a "want felt in his works" *(DG* 3), Fuller here agrees with his artistic ideal of a perfect balance between the subjective and objective, the ideal and the real that defied excessive subjectivity and wanted "thought or feeling made universal."[41]

Art, in Goethe's view, was experience *dargestellt*, that is, formed, transformed, and thus elevated to a higher level of representation. Goethe's *Darstellungsgabe* (*L* 2:49), a term that Fuller regarded as so essentially Goethean that she did not even bother to translate it, may be seen as the site where Mariana, Mignon, and Macaria could finally meet and, as it were, cooperate, an act of cooperation that implied that Wilhelm's previous feminine encounters were not rejected but again *aufgehoben* in the Hegelian sense that they are transcended and at the same time preserved in a higher state of art. Fuller once again sees the artistic process as a metamorphic one raising the common, quotidian world of Mariana, by virtue of Mignon's inspiring faculties and Macaria's intelligence to the level of a true work of art. Only minor poets, Fuller argued, would write "verses merely as vents for the overflowing of a personal experience" while poets of Goethe's magnitude had a gift to objectify their subjective experiences and thus make their feelings universally accessible. Of her own verses, Fuller confessed in a letter to Caroline Sturgis, she felt ashamed when she thought that there was "scarce a line of *poetry* in them," that they were all "'rhetorical and impassioned' as Goethe said of Me de Staël" (*L* 2:49). Though she may not always have achieved her artistic goals she—in a Goethean manner "always striving" *(immer strebend)*—believed in a state of lifelong apprenticeship *(Lehrjahre)* rather than mastery.

Goethe, Emerson maintained, had been Fuller's teacher. To her he represented "the most powerful of all mental reagents,—the pivotal mind in modern literature,—for all before him [were] ancients and all who ha[d] read him [were] moderns." Nowhere, Emerson continued, "did Goethe find a braver, more intelligent, or more sympathetic reader" than in Fuller (*M* 1:242–43), which, however, did not mean that her readings were not critical. Their differences, temperamental as well as cultural, were too striking to make her a merely blind admirer. There was Goethe, the serene Olympian, "Jove-like and calm," a "self-collected" (*DG* 20), cold man of the mind, and there was Fuller, a much more impassioned person. There was Goethe with his Old World love of aristocratic "gradation," and there was Fuller with her New World belief in republican equality and "the great onward movement now obvious throughout the civilized world."[42] There was Goethe, both the Greek classicist with his love of form and the post-Romantic modernist, as Emerson saw him, and there was Fuller, the Romanticist with her deep sympathies for more "flame-like natures" like Novalis. Despite such differences there were numerous points of agreement where "she found her moods met, her topics treated, the liberty of thought she loved, the same climate of mind" (*M* 1:243). Goethe, the man thinking, made her think onward and onward, *fort und fort,* and Goethe the artist inspired her to pursue her very own artistic goals. Absorbing his ideas she, together with her Transcendentalist friends, helped enrich the literature of her country, still unilaterally oriented toward England, so that its voice would from now on be distinctly heard in the chorus of what Goethe had called *Weltliteratur.*

Notes

1. Frothingham, *Transcendentalism in New England* (New York: Putnam, 1876), 57.

2. Capper, *Margaret Fuller: An American Romantic Life*, vol. 1, *The Private Years* (New York: Oxford Univ. Press, 1992), 129; Bancroft quoted in Henry A. Pochmann, *German Culture in America: Philosophical and Literary Influences, 1600–1900* (Madison: Univ. of Wisconsin Press, 1957), 679, 329–32.

3. Henry D. Thoreau, *A Week on the Concord and Merrimack Rivers* (Princeton, N.J.: Princeton Univ. Press, 1983), 325–30.

4. Ralph Waldo Emerson, "Goethe; or, the Writer," in *Essays and Lectures* (New York: Library of America, 1983), 746–61, 750 (hereafter cited in text and notes as *EL*).

5. Ritchie, "Margaret Fuller's First Conversation Series: A Discovery in the Archives," *Legacy* 18 (2001): 223, 230; *Memoirs of Margaret Fuller Ossoli*, ed. R.W. Emerson, W. H. Channing, and J. F. Clarke, 2 vols. (Boston: Roberts Brothers, 1881) (hereafter cited in text and notes as *M*); *The Letters of Ralph Waldo Emerson*, ed. Ralph L. Rusk and Eleanor Tilton, 8 vols. (New York: Columbia Univ. Press, 1960–82), 3:447.

6. See Goethe's review of Thomas Carlyle's *German Romance* (Edinburgh, 1827); *Gedenkausgabe der Werke, Briefe und Gespräche*, ed. Ernst Beutler, 27 vols. (Zurich: Artemis, 1948–71), 14:932–33. See also Victor Lange, "Nationalliteratur und Weltliteratur," *Goethe-Jahrbuch* 33 (1971): 15–30.

7. *The Letters of Margaret Fuller*, ed. Robert N. Hudspeth, 6 vols. (Ithaca, N.Y.: Cornell Univ. Press, 1983–94), 1:177 (hereafter cited in text and notes as *L*).

8. *L* 1:177; "Menzel's View of Goethe," *Dial* 1 (January 1841): 342.

9. Fuller, "Goethe," *Dial* 2 (July 1841): 19 (hereafter, this essay in *Dial* will be cited in text as *DG*).

10. See Barbara Welter, "The Cult of True Womanhood, 1820–1860," in her *Dimity Convictions: The American Woman in the Nineteenth Century* (Athens: Ohio State Univ. Press, 1976), 21–41.

11. Arthur R. Schultz, "Margaret Fuller—Transcendentalist Interpreter of German Literature," in *Critical Essays on Margaret Fuller*, ed. Joel Myerson (Boston: G. K. Hall, 1980), 199.

12. "But shall I be fit for anything till I have absolutely re-educated myself? Am I, can I make myself, fit to write an account of half a century of the existence of one of the master-spirits of this world? It seems as if I had been very arrogant to dare to think it; yet will I not shrink back from what I have undertaken—even by failure I shall learn much." *M* 1:128.

13. Translated as *Conversations with Goethe in the Last Years of his Life*, Eckermann's book appeared as volume 4 in George Ripley's series *Specimens of Foreign Standard Literature* (Boston: Hilliard, Gray, 1839) in which Fuller's *Life of Goethe* was supposed to appear had it ever been completed.

14. Fuller, "Menzel's View of Goethe," 341.

15. Ibid., 340.

16. The motto, taken from Milton's *History of Britain, Book 3*, faces the unpaginated front page of *Conversations with Goethe*.

17. *Conversations with Goethe*, xx.

18. "Ein Eklektiker aber ist ein jeder, der aus dem, was ihn umgibt, aus dem, was sich um ihn ereignet, sich dasjenige aneignet, was seiner Natur gemäß ist." *Gedenkausgabe*, 9:585. On Fuller's "eclectic method of work" see also Renate Delphendahl, "Margaret Fuller: Interpreter and Translator of German Literature," in *Margaret Fuller: Visionary of the New Age*, ed. Marie Urbanski and M. Olesen (Orono, Maine: Northern Lights, 1994), 64ff.

19. *Margaret Fuller: Essays on American Life and Letters*, ed. Joel Myerson (New Haven, Conn.: College and Univ. Press, 1978), 381.

20. Fuller, review of R. H. Wilde, *Conjectures and Researches Concerning the Love, Madness, and Imprisonment of Torquato Tasso, Dial* 2 (January 1842): 399; in a letter to Grand Duke Karl August dated Rome, March 17, 1788, Goethe reports that he has found himself as an artist: "Ich habe mich in dieser anderthalbjährigen Einsamkeit wiedergefunden; aber als was? —Als Künstler!" *Gedenkausgabe*, 19:105; Christina Zwarg, "Feminism in Translation: Fuller's *Tasso* and *Günderode*," in her *Feminist Conversations: Fuller, Emerson, and the Play of Reading* (Ithaca, N.Y.: Cornell Univ. Press, 1995), 80.

21. Zwarg, *Feminist Conversations*, 61; Jacques Derrida, *The Ear of the Other*, quoted in *Feminist Conversations*, 59; Fuller's review appeared together with "Act Second, Scene First" of her *Tasso* translation in *Dial* 2 (January 1842): 399.

22. See Fuller's preface to *Conversations with Goethe*, xviii.

23. Howe, *Making the American Self: Jonathan Edwards to Abraham Lincoln* (Cambridge, Mass.: Harvard Univ. Press, 1997), 211, 226.

24. "Denke, wie mannigfach bald diese, bald jene Gestalten, / Still entfaltend, Natur unsern Gefühlen geliehn." *Gedenkausgabe*, 1:516–18.

25. Eckermann, *Gespräche mit Goethe in den letzten Jahren seines Lebens, Gedenkausgabe*, 24:237.

26. Goethe referred to the *Urpflanze* as the quaintest creature in the world and saw in it a model for new plants that would exfoliate practically ad infinitum: "Die Urpflanze wird das wunderlichste Geschöpf von der Welt, um welches mich die Natur selbst beneiden soll. Mit diesem Modell und dem Schlüssel dazu kann man alsdann noch Pflanzen ins Unendliche erfinden . . . Dasselbe Gesetz wird sich auf alles übrige Lebendige anwenden lassen." *Gedenkausgabe*, 11:353.

27. In his essay "Self-Reliance" Emerson had characterized "the moment of transition from a past to a new state" as that "one fact the world hates, that the soul *becomes*." *EL* 271. See also Jonathan Levin, *The Poetics of Transition: Emerson, Pragmatism and American Literary Modernism* (Durham, N.C.: Duke Univ. Press, 1999).

28. *The Essential Margaret Fuller*, ed. Jeffrey Steele (New Brunswick, N.J.: Rutgers Univ. Press, 1992), 316 (hereafter cited in text and notes as *EMF*).

29. "An diesen Ort [Rom] knüpft sich die ganze Geschichte der Welt an, und ich zähle einen zweiten Geburtstag, eine wahre Wiedergeburt, von dem Tage, da ich Rom betrat." *Italienische Reise, Gedenkausgabe*, 11:160; Fuller, "*These Sad But Glorious Days": Dispatches from Europe, 1846–1850*, ed. Larry J. Reynolds and Susan Belasco Smith (New Haven, Conn.: Yale Univ. Press, 1991), 168. The dispatches abound with passages in which Fuller severely castigates the conventional descriptive modes of her contemporary Anglo-American travel writers. See also my article "Transitions: Margaret Fuller's European Journey from Romanticism to Republicanism," in *Cultural Encounters in the New World*, ed. Harald Zapf and Klaus Lösch (Tübingen: Gunter Narr, 2003), 19–31; see Fuller's enthusiastic remark in a letter to her brother: "I passed the Villa where Goethe lived when in Rome; afterwards the houses of Claude and Poussin. Ah, what human companionship here, how everything speaks! . . . Read also Goethe's Year in Rome and Romish Elegies." *L* 5:181. Goethe in his "Römische Elegien" addresses the stones, palaces, and streets to speak ("Saget, Steine, mir an, o sprecht, ihr hohen Paläste! / Strassen, redet ein Wort!"); they would later respond. See *Gedenkausgabe*, 1:163ff.

30. Fuller quoted in Ritchie, "Fuller's First Conversation Series," 217; *Gedenkausgabe*, 24:237. The term "metamorphosis," though infrequently used by Fuller, abounds in Emerson's essays and journals.

31. See Fuller's preface to *Conversations with Goethe*, xiii.

32. The words of the Daimon in the original read as follows: "Nach dem Gesetz, wonach du angetreten. / So mußt du sein, dir kannst du nicht entfliehen, / So sagten schon Sybillen, so Propheten; / Und keine Zeit und keine Macht zerstückelt / Geprägte Form die lebend sich entwickelt." *Gedenkausgabe*, 1:523–24.

33. *The Complete Works of Ralph Waldo Emerson*, 12 vols. (Boston: Houghton Mifflin, 1903–4), 10:24.

34. Fuller, "Lives of Great Composers, Haydn, Mozart, Handel, Bach, Beethoven," *Dial* 2 (October 1841): 149.

35. "Es gehört dieses Werk [Wilhelm Meister] übrigens zu den inkalkulabelsten Produktionen, wozu mir fast selbst der Schlüssel fehlt. Man sucht einen Mittelpunkt, und das ist schwer und nicht einmal gut." *Gedenkausgabe*, 24:141.

36. Quoted in Capper, *Margaret Fuller*, 314.

37. Fuller, "A Credo," quoted in Frederick Augustus Braun, *Margaret Fuller and Goethe* (New York: Henry Holt, 1910), 247–57.

38. Goethe, *Truth and Poetry: From My Own Life*, tr. John Oxenford, 2 vols. (London: Bell and Daldy, 1871), 2:157–59.

39. Fuller, "A Credo," quoted in Braun, *Fuller and Goethe*, 247–57. See also Howe, *Making the American Self*, 219–20.

40. The term "creative" *(schaffend)* is one of Eckermann's key terms in his discussion of the Mothers. They are "schaffende Wesen," "schaffende Gottheiten," "das schaffende und erhaltende Prinzip, von dem alles ausgeht, was auf der Oberfläche der Erde Gestalt und Leben hat." *Gedenkausgabe*, 24:384–86. The paradoxical formulation "schaffend und erhaltend" is strongly reminiscent of Goethe's "Urworte. Orphisch," where the "minted form" *(erhaltend)* is seen in a continuous process of vital development *(schaffend)*.

41. *L* 2:33. In *Summer on the Lakes, in 1843* Fuller's ideal artist figure is envisioned as follows: "no thin Idealist, no coarse Realist, but a man whose eye reads the heavens while his feet step firmly on the ground. . . . A man religious, virtuous and—sagacious; a man of universal sympathies, but self-possessed." *EMF* 132.

42. Fuller, preface to *Conversations with Goethe*, xv.

3

Margaret Fuller and the Ideal of Heroism

ROBERT N. HUDSPETH

To write an essay on heroism is probably rash, for there is perhaps only one other nineteenth-century cliché so grand and so amorphous, and that is "genius," which uncomfortably tends to merge into "hero." Yet the topic was on the minds of Margaret Fuller and her contemporaries, and to understand it better is to understand how they thought and to what they were responding. If "heroism" is an idea that Fuller followed, it is a path that is remarkably circular, for it began early in her reading about Rome, and it came to an end there with the revolution of 1849 in shambles. It was where Fuller at last found her ideal fulfilled: heroism had a "local habitation," and the hero a name, Giuseppe Mazzini. But it is a long journey from Cambridge, Massachusetts, to Rome, though it took Fuller only fourteen years to make it (and one needs remember that this woman of large accomplishment had a public life of only fifteen years, a bare decade and a half from 1835 to 1850). Fuller had an abiding concern for heroism—though one that fluctuated in its importance to her—that informed her literary criticism and shaped her political writing in Italy, that moved from books to revolution.

Born in 1810 to a politically engaged father, Fuller grew to adult-hood in the first decades of the nation's existence. "The United States" was still a fairly new idea that had been badly undercut by near-rebellion in New England and by the continued sectional schism caused by slavery. Growing up in Cambridge, Fuller was immersed in an edu-cation made intense by her father's rigorous tutelage. She later recalled her ambivalence about that education when she defined it as "heroic common sense," and described its embodiment in "those great Romans, whose thoughts and lives were my daily food during those plastic years." Her earliest notion of heroism derived from the power of men who "take up things with their naked hands," in whom there is "no divinity, no demon, no unfulfilled aim, but just the man and Rome, and what he did for Rome." She could not resist the pull of this life of action and accom-plishment, though she knew—at least by 1840—that such an ideal meant that "my own world sank deep within, away from the surface of my life" and thus became repression.[1] Apparently from the start, she was both beguiled and frustrated by the very possibility of "heroism." Nor was this unusual, for when, in later years, Emerson came to write his book of heroes, he titled it *Representative Men*, unlike Thomas Carlyle who unabashedly made his *On Heroes, Hero-Worship and the Heroic in His-tory*. Something there is in American culture that does not love a hero.

The very nature of heroism was for Fuller a question of the past. Heroism is what men *did,* not what they do; our conception of the hero derives from mythology, for he is a demigod, a mediator between the purely human and the purely divine. Thoreau caught this quality ex-actly when he noted in his journal that "the past is only so heroic as we see it—it is the canvass on which our idea of heroism is painted—the dim prospectus of our future field." We dream of heroism as possibility, but most often as just that: possibility. That makes a contemporary hero all the more powerful, as Fuller found in 1825, when the Marquis de La-fayette visited Boston. Here was a genuinely great man who had heroi-cally served the cause of freedom. Not only that, he was close enough for her to write directly to him! "Sir the contemplation of a character such as yours fills the soul with a noble ambition." To an American teenager, the idea of the heroic existed, and she could even think it pos-sible that it lay within her grasp, though she understood the problem she faced: "Should we both live, and it is possible to a female, to whom the avenues of glory are seldom accessible, I will recal my name to your rec-ollection."[2] If "it is possible to a female": therein lay the challenge for

Fuller. That Roman duty so much a part of her character ran afoul of her gender. If heroism were ever to be made present and to live outside the literature of the past, if it were to mean anything specific to her, she was going to have to address the male prerogative.

In May 1830, still short of her twentieth birthday, in a letter to James Clarke, a minister friend, Fuller took on the challenge of the heroic more directly and personally: "I have greatly wished to see among us such a person of Genius as the nineteenth century can afford—ie. one who has tasted in the morning of existence the extremes of good and ill both imaginative and real—I had imagined a person endowed by nature with that acute sense to Beauty (ie Harmony or Truth) and that vast capacity of desire which give soul to love and ambition." She has to keep the male pronoun, but she clearly projects herself into the idealized vision, a romantic one of the lone, suffering advocate of the soul's deep promptings:

> I had wished this person might grow up to manhood *alone* (but not *alone in crowds*). . . . I wished this being might be launched into the world of realities his heart glowing with the ardor of an immortal towards perfection; his eyes searching every-where to behold it; I wished he might collect into one burning point those withering palsying convictions which in the ordinary routine of things so gradually pervade the soul; That he might suffer in brief space agonies of disappointment commensurate with his unpreparedness and confidence. . . . Such a man would suddenly dilate into a thing of Pride, Power, and Glory—A centre round which asking, aimless hearts might rally—A man fitted to act as interpreter to the one tale of many-languaged ages! (*L* 6:167–68)

"Such a man"—she can hardly phrase it any other way, but it most certainly is her idealized version of her own aspirations, for she saw that perhaps she might be the "interpreter to the one tale of many-languaged ages." However, not only was there the gender question, but there was the latent problem that her vision is a bookish one constructed out of her extensive, cosmopolitan reading. So far, this notion of the heroic was unconnected with political activity, either theoretically or practically. For example, in 1842, when Thomas Dorr led a "rebellion" in Rhode Island—where Fuller had just been teaching—she apparently ignored the whole episode, even though one might have found his cause of constitutional government to be heroic.

Throughout her early writings, Fuller explores ideas that will abide in her work: the hero/genius will be a reconciler of extremes, a symbol of growth, and an interpreter. It was this last term, the "interpreter," that gave her an immediate opening (and implicitly tempered the gender question), for in the 1830s, Fuller became a literary critic, and so everything she wrote or implied about heroism became a function of the critic's mind and responsibility and, at least for a time, was shaped by literary examples, and not only literary but modern ones. In her "Modern British Poets," for example, an essay from 1836, Fuller wrote that some poets are "pilot-minds of the age," who "win from the raging billows large territories, whose sands they can convert into Eden bowers, tenanted by lovely and majestic shapes." This impassioned but vague language points toward conceptions but cannot make them concrete. Finally, she finds her focus: "thought itself is [as] immortal as the soul from which it radiates." Thinking becomes the center of human activity. "Wherever we perceive a profound thought," she goes on to say, "we offer a higher homage than we can to common-place thoughts." This is the same idea that had led her to write only a few months earlier that the most important "benefactors" of mankind were those who "suggest thoughts and plans," who comprise "intellects of the higher order."[3] At this point, in the mid-1830s, Fuller had committed herself to the workings of the intellect. It was in intellectual power that heroism originates. Her own role as critic was to interpret those minds to a reader. In doing so, Fuller appropriated at least a part of what she thought "heroic."

However, something still was lacking, Fuller thought, for "thought," as important as it was to her, stopped short of fulfilling an ideal. We can see that problem best in her essay on Goethe published in the *Dial* in 1841. First, she explains Goethe's conception of the *Dämonische*. It is, in many ways, the obverse of the intellect, for, as Fuller describes it, it is "an individuality . . . gifted with an instinctive, spontaneous force, which at once, without calculation or foresight, chooses the right means to an end." She makes it clear that what she finds in Goethe's idea is a force of being, a presence, not a set of activities. Those individuals who are *Dämonische* are not necessarily people of accomplishment; they may be quite obscure. What they have is a magnetic self: "by his eye and voice he rules all around him."[4] Without using the term, Fuller has described the heroic personality. Moreover, as it was earlier in her first essays, the idea here is apolitical. The heroic is presence, not activity; it is private, not public; it does not of necessity *do* anything.

It is not until later in the essay that she develops a concern for activity that joins to the *Dämonische,* to become a heroic ideal. After quoting Goethe on the one "'who would do great things'" and who would "'give us freedom,'" Fuller says that "there is a higher spiritual law always ready to supersede the temporal laws at the call of the human soul." This clearly represents her faith in human agency rooted in a spiritual reality. Fuller has, however, a demanding standard for the "soul" because a being who "is too content with usual limitations will never call forth this unusual manifestation."[5] Embedded in her interpretation of Goethe's heroism is a rebellion against much of what society has taken for granted.

When she wrote the essay on Goethe, Fuller had become close friends with Ralph Waldo Emerson, a man who attracted and frustrated her, a man whose undoubted genius she readily acknowledged but whose limitations were equally clear to her. In some ways, her essay on Goethe and its protoheroic idealism emerges from the same current as did Emerson's essay "Heroism," published in his 1841 *Essays.* There, Emerson begins with Plutarch (an author Fuller knew well) to champion a martial "arming of the man" in order to resist both the predations of nature and the limitations of society. It is "a military attitude of the soul." Yet, as he makes this claim, Emerson goes on to say that "heroism feels and never reasons, and therefore is always right,"[6] which speaks directly to the limitation she had found in Roman heroism, for, she thought, that it did *not* feel, that it denies emotion. The Emersonian version of heroism would have appealed to Fuller on precisely the grounds she most needed.

Not only is this new form of heroism emotionally complex, but Emerson also specifically claims that it is open to women. After scoffing at the notion that heroism is foreign to women simply because we cannot imagine it, he says: "Let the maiden, with erect soul, walk serenely on her way, accept the hint of each new experience, search in turn all the objects that solicit her eye, that she may learn the power and the charm of her new-born being, which is the kindling of a new dawn in the recesses of space." Such a one, Emerson continues, "inspires every beholder with somewhat of her own nobleness. The silent heart encourages her; O friend, never strike sail to a fear."[7] Both Emerson and Fuller grounded heroism in resistance, for to them, contentment seemed a great failure. Like Emerson, Fuller in the 1840s assumed that what must be resisted is the sum of all the forces in the culture that work against self-development. The resistance implied by heroism is deeply personal and individual. There is as yet no notion of social commitment; heroism begins and ends in self-culture.

So, by the time Fuller wrote *Woman in the Nineteenth Century* in 1844, she was committed to an ideal of heroism that was both intellectually ambitious and personally electrifying, still inward looking. As usual, she turned to history and found in the Countess Emily Plater, who was born in Lithuania and later became a hero in the Polish struggle for independence, a woman "capable of all sweet affections, capable of stern virtue." This praise lets Fuller confront the lingering problem created by the gendering of the word "hero," for again she felt compelled to explore the ill effects of the masculine associations. Using her alter-ego figure of Miranda, Fuller brings into the open the fact that "the use of ['manly'] where a heroic quality is to be described" inevitably frustrates any attempt to think about heroism and women. Miranda goes on to claim that "persistence and courage are the most womanly no less than the most manly qualities" and that she would ungender the word so as to mean "'a heavenward and instructed soul'" rather than either "manly" or "womanly." Almost as a corollary to this, Fuller praises Abby Kelly, a radical woman's rights advocate: "'She acted like a gentle hero,'" says Fuller under the guise of a correspondent who wrote to her, "'all heroism is mild and quiet and gentle.'" Here Fuller consciously and pointedly demilitarizes heroism, as she had done with the figure of Panthea, wife of Abradatus, whose story she found in Xenophon. The husband had fulfilled his warrior role by dying a noble death in combat. Xenophon, however, accords to the wife's suicide a dignity that is equal to the husband's heroism. Fuller holds Panthea up as an exemplar of nobility whose heroism is in her self-command, her peace, and her faithfulness, all qualities matched evenly against a masculine warrior code.[8]

Fuller's method in *Woman in the Nineteenth Century* allows her to experiment, to offer contrasting ideas as possibilities of how we understand women's lives. Here she uses her fictional yet autobiographical Miranda; she creates a fictional letter; she uses a Greek historian. All of this allows her to move the notion of heroism into new forms, to challenge the reader to surrender stereotypes, to uncouple "manly" from "heroic." All of these figures are less extreme than the Goethean ideal of *Dämonische;* each is less intellectually intense. *Woman* among other things grounded the possibilities of heroism in daily life and located possible living exemplars, for Fuller's interest in George Sand, Harriet Martineau, and Abby Kelly gave substance to the claim that what a woman needs is "not as a woman to act or rule, but as a nature to grow, as an intellect to discern, as a soul to live freely and unimpeded, to unfold such powers as were given her."[9] It is, in short, an opening to heroism redefined and localized, and to a heroism that begins to have a social context.

But, having repositioned the idea of heroism, Fuller regresses in her essays written in the *New-York Daily Tribune* to an ideal of hero worship. In a piece on Beethoven, Fuller says that "there is as high a joy in worshiping the hero as in emulating him," and in a review of Milton's prose works, she says "we love hero-worship, where the hero is, indeed, worthy the honors of a demi-god." She simply could not do without the idea that the hero has "a character governed by a principle of its own, and not by rules taken from other men's experience," a line that comes from a little-known essay on the relationship between beauty and time that she wrote in April 1846. In order to discuss individuals who become more attractive as they age, Fuller says that heroes are individuals with an "originality of character," a "spontaneity of action" who grow with time, whose experiences "expand the soul, deepen and vary the experience, refine the perceptions and immortalize the hopes and dreams of youth." Amid the several themes that converge in this figure, Fuller again addresses the gender issue. She takes as her title Shakespeare's description of Cleopatra, "Age could not wither her nor custom stale / Her infinite variety," but toward the end of the essay rewrites the line to make it gender-neutral "Age cannot wither them nor custom stale / Their infinite variety."[10] Souls—the center of her conception of heroism—do not have genders. No matter whether she starts from the masculine or the feminine, Fuller habitually converges on a neutral center.

In this brief essay based on Shakespeare, Fuller seems to fall back on an earlier view of heroism, for again her notions of heroism are drawn from books. Though in *Woman* she had acknowledged the possibility of real women being heroic, she still was ambivalent. The power of the imagined hero proved irresistible to a woman so committed to literary study. As long as she lived in the United States, Fuller was an intellectual who was more concerned with a hypothetical state of being rather than with the accomplishment of living souls.

By the time Fuller left New England for New York City, the idea of heroism had become liminal. It never went away, but it never came wholly to the fore, for to her self-culture and self-expression were more immediately interesting and problematic in a culture that, she thought, worked against both. In many ways, her intellectual life did not "change" in content so much as in focus when she moved to New York City in late 1844; her energies moved among several possibilities, one of which increasingly became overt social reform. She was powerfully interested in the reform of prostitutes and the rehabilitation of former female convicts; the work on the *New-York Tribune* gave her the opportunity to see reforming institutions at close hand.[11] In the mid-1840s, the ideal of heroism was probably too grand, too hypothetical to make it worth pursuing as a topic in itself, and almost all of Fuller's writing in New York City was in response to immediate stimuli, both literary and social.

By chance, the opportunity for new topics came to Fuller in 1846, when she was able to make a long-delayed visit to the Europe that had so fascinated her through its literature. In Manchester, in Edinburgh, in London, and in Paris, she met a procession of European intellectuals, politicians, and reformers. These were not heroes, but they were committed men and women who had a larger sense of the public responsibility and several of whom had the rebellious "contempt of some external good" that Emerson had named as a heroic quality in his essay.[12]

As Fuller passed from capital to capital, she was the model of the woman of letters abroad: she was curious, thoughtful, perceptive, and, though sometimes exhausted by the pace, stimulated by the people she met. Especially in France, she was astute in reading the political situation: "While Louis Philippe lives, the gases, compressed by his strong grasp, may not burst up to light; but the need of some radical measures of reform is not less strongly felt in France than elsewhere, and the time will come before long when such will be imperatively demanded." Looking squarely at the need for reform, Fuller thought immediately of Charles Fourier, whose thought had had a specific impact on her friends at Brook Farm and among some of her acquaintances in New York City. "The doctrines of Fourier are making considerable progress," she wrote. While "the mind of Fourier is, in many respects, uncongenial to [hers]" his views are "large and noble" but she finally had little faith that the public would embrace his socialism: "the unthinking mob has found stones on the highway to throw at the prophets" (*SG* 119–20).

Her specific reservation about Fourier was that "he commits the error of making soul the result of health of body, instead of body the clothing of soul." This passage succinctly marks a profound problem for her: how was one to think of genuine social and political change and yet work from something other than a basis of "gross materialism" that constituted Fourier's education? (*SG* 120). Though she did not yet wholly understand it, an answer was at hand in one of the many European intellectuals she had already met—Giuseppe Mazzini. Fuller's understanding and involvement with European revolution, indeed, her final, deepest understanding of "heroism" came all by chance. She just happened to be in Europe in 1848 when revolution broke out; her private involvement with Giovanni Ossoli kept her in Rome for the proclamation of the republic in 1849. A series of unplanned events put her on the spot; a lifetime of reading and thinking made her adequate to the crisis. Nothing Fuller could have planned, nothing she could have sought, nothing she could even have imagined, could match her friendship with Giuseppe Mazzini, for that friendship involved her experience with revolution, war, defeat, and triumph of principle. A passing friendship begun in London evolved into an occasion to observe real heroism in action, and an old ideal vividly lived from day to day in the harrowing months that led up to the Roman Republic and through to its bloody demise in 1849.

Fuller was taken by Mazzini when they first met in London: "By far the most beauteous person I have seen is Joseph Mazzini," she wrote to a friend. "He is one in whom holiness has purified, but nowhere dwarfed the man." Mazzini was indeed physically striking, and he attracted many intellectual women, including Harriet Martineau and Jane Welsh Carlyle.[13] Fuller elaborated this brief, private estimation in a *Tribune* account of him: "[He] is not only one of the heroic, the courageous, and the faithful—Italy boasts many such—but he is also one of the wise. One of those who, disappointed in the outward results of their undertakings, can yet 'bate no jot of heart and hope,' but *must* 'steer right onward,' for it was no superficial enthusiasm, no impatient energies, that impelled him, but an understanding of what *must* be the designs of Heaven with regard to Man, since God is Love, is Justice." For Fuller, "he is one of those same beings who, measuring all things by the ideal standard, have yet no time to mourn over failure or imperfection." Fuller quotes Milton's Sonnet 22, where the poet refuses to despair over his blindness. Milton goes on to say that he lost his eyesight

> In liberty's defense, my noble task,
> Of which all Europe talks from side to side.
> This thought might lead me through the world's vain masque,
> Content though blind, had I no better guide.

Fuller connects Milton's heroic confrontation with loss to define Mazzini's character. Finally, Milton's claim echoes the one Fuller made in her Cleopatra essay, discussed above, that such men (and she would include Mazzini) had impulses that "proceeded from a fullness and certainty of character, that made it impossible they should doubt or repent, whatever the results of their actions might be."[14]

Superficially Fuller and Mazzini shared a number of interests: like her, he had begun his career as a literary critic; they both admired Schiller's poetry; both had befriended the impecunious, erratic Danish writer Harro Harring, and each deeply admired the work of George Sand.[15] So, there was a community of thought that lay behind Fuller's public praise. She immediately perceived his value, for he combined a will to action with a fullness of mind, but, equally important, Mazzini had a deep religious faith in divine guidance. When Fuller says he measures "all things by the ideal standard," she praises him in her highest terms. From the very first she found him to be the charismatic, intellectual, spiritual leader she had been trying to define throughout her career. She apparently did not overtly contrast him with Fourier, but Mazzini offered her the religious grounding that the Frenchman lacked.

In the ordinary course of things, Mazzini would have remained a deeply attractive, morally compelling man, one of several whom Fuller met. He gave her letters of introduction to friends in Paris; she visited his mother in Genoa when she arrived in Italy; he sent more letters of recommendation and she defended him in print.[16] But then the world changed: as Fuller foresaw, the French monarchy fell to a revolution; then uprisings spread—to Austria, to the several Italian states—and Fuller found that her travelogues became war dispatches. As she watched the events of 1848 unfold, she always had Mazzini in mind, and her assessment of the swirl of political and military events was ideologically close to his republican and "Italian" point of view.

Fuller early saw that the Italians had problems about who was to lead. At first Fuller and many others thought that the new pope might be that leader, for, when Giovanni Maria Mastai-Ferretti became Pius IX in 1846, he proclaimed a political amnesty that looked to be the start of a reforming program. Fuller's estimate of him in October 1847 was cautious but hopeful: "I saw with pleasure the Pope, who has not in his expression the signs of intellectual greatness so much as of nobleness and tenderness of heart, of large and liberal sympathies." She sounded a similar note privately to Emerson: "He is a real great heart, a generous

man. The love for him is genuine, and I like to be within its influence."
By the end of 1847, however, Fuller was having serious doubts about
Pius's leadership: he was, she wrote, "terribly afraid to be or seem to be
less the Pope of Rome, in becoming a Reform Prince, and father to the
fatherless." Then, in April 1848, Pius disavowed revolution and condemned the idea of republican reform, thus, to Fuller, confirming the
limitations of his mind that she had already begun to see. From the start
she doubted his intellect: "It was necessary to be a great thinker, a great
genius, to compete with the difficulties of his position. I never supposed
he was that; I am only disappointed that his good heart has not carried
him on a little farther." The protohero of 1847 became an object of contempt: "Poor Pope! how has his mind been torn to pieces in these later
days." The advice Pius received from his counselors came to "cloud his
mind."[17] As we have seen, from her earliest writing Fuller believed that
heroes had unusual mental talents; that they thought more clearly,
more deeply.

Fuller's residence in Rome and her friendship with Mazzini brought
her to frame the developing crisis in terms of his heroic leadership.
Throughout her *Tribune* essays she consistently contrasted Mazzini with
his rivals to show how he alone could lead the Italians to freedom. The
first and most important of these contrasts was with Pius, who failed his
opportunity to be the liberating hero. Mazzini was a man of thought
and spirituality, both qualities Pius lacked. Where Pius's mind had been
"torn to pieces," Mazzini's was clear and powerful. "Mazzini is a man
of genius," wrote Fuller, "an elevated thinker, but the most powerful
and first impression from his presence must always be of the religion of
his soul" (*SG* 264). Throughout the increasingly tense days of 1848 and
1849, Pius and Mazzini were linked in Fuller's imagination as the failed
and the true heroes.

The second of her contrasts was that of Mazzini and Abbé Vincenzo
Gioberti, who was taken seriously as a leader in the revolution and who,
Fuller thought, could challenge Mazzini. In a dispatch of February 20,
1849, Fuller said that she "always looked upon [Gioberti] as entirely a
charlatan, who covered his want of all real force by the thickest embroi-
dered mantle of words." Though she gave Gioberti credit for opposing
the Jesuits, she finally found him too bound up with Charles Albert, the
king of Piedmont-Sardinia, who was both weak and not interested in social reform. In direct contrast to Gioberti she goes on to say that "mean-
time the thought of Mazzini had echoed through Tuscany" (*SG* 254–55).

Typically, it is Mazzini's ideas that mattered. Though he himself was absent, his ideas about republican government, about social reform, and about unification had taken root and were flourishing despite the appeal of Gioberti to those Italians for whom open revolution was not thinkable because it would also mean social revolution.

The third contrast Fuller made at this time was between Mazzini and Count Pellegrino Rossi, the exile who had returned to Rome and become prime minister of the Papal States, but who was assassinated as he arrived to take up the office. Fuller explicitly discussed the two together in March 1849 by pointing out that both were outsiders, former exiles who, when they came to Rome, were named "Citizen of Rome." Rossi, however, was an extension of the pope's failed policies and was murdered because he was despised; Mazzini was elected a citizen by the people of Rome. The one outsider died an outsider; the other was embraced by the people and became one of them. Fuller even risks approving of assassination in her contrast, for the symbolism is so intensely meaningful to her.[18]

When it came to symbols, Fuller and Mazzini had together made productive use of "Rome." Fuller's 1840 memoir made the city a symbol for her ambivalent reactions to classic heroism; Mazzini's symbol when he addressed the Roman Constituent Assembly (a speech Fuller translated and used in her *Tribune* dispatch of March 20) was a city being reborn into its third life: as the Roman empire had been succeeded by the Rome of the popes, that now-degraded Rome was giving way to republican Rome. In his words, "After the Rome of the Emperors—after the Rome of the Popes, will come the Rome of the People." Like Fuller, Mazzini was an outsider (a Genoese by birth, he had never been to Rome before 1849) but Rome had lived in his imagination as a place of possibility. To Fuller, he had now come to be the living embodiment of the virtue and heroism Rome had symbolized. That which in literature she had found repressive now had a new and vibrant life: "the genius of Rome [that] displayed itself in Character" was no longer an abstraction, for Mazzini now stood in the assembly as a man in whom "thought passed into action."[19] That heroism she had found in her early reading was no longer a figment of the imagination of the past; it stood before her; the "single thought and indomitable will" that had repelled her as much as it attracted in early life now served freedom.

Fuller was never blind to what she considered Mazzini's limitations, for she rightly understood that he had no faith in the socialism that drew her to Fourier's writings, and she clearly said so: "And yet Mazzini sees not all: he aims at political emancipation; but he sees not, perhaps would deny, the bearing of some events, which even now begin to work their way. . . . I allude to that of which the cry of Communism, the systems of Fourier, &c. are but forerunners." Still, throughout her analysis of the events of 1848–49, she consistently defended Mazzini against the charges made by both the "moderates" in Lombardy and the conservatives who would restore the pope. (For instance, to her liberal Milanese friend Costanza Arconati Visconti, who had been offended by an open letter Mazzini sent Pius, Fuller wrote: "I do not wonder that you were annoyed at his manner of addressing the Pope; but to me it seems that he speaks as he should,—near God and beyond the tomb; not from power to power, but from soul to soul, without regard to temporal dignities.") As the crisis grew, Fuller had come to see Mazzini as "the inspiring soul of his people." First he became a triumvir, then the political leader of the new republic and began to institute reforms.[20]

Margaret Fuller had few illusions about the success of the republic in the face of the united hostility of the European powers, but she saw that Mazzini had brought new life to the Romans. "He is become the inspiring soul of his people. He saw Rome, to which all his hopes through life tended, for the first time as a Roman citizen, and to become in a few days its ruler. He has animated, he sustains her to a glorious effort, which, if it fails, this time will not in the age. His country will be free" (*L* 5:240). She knew by then that even though a hero might fail politically, there was a success in the future that he had created. The cost was horrific—as she saw repeatedly in her role as director of a hospital to which the wounded Roman soldiers were brought: "After [June] 22d, the slaughter of the Romans became every day more fearful. . . . Those who were brought into the Hospitals were generally grievously wounded, very commonly subjects for amputation" (*SG* 303).

As early as 1847, Fuller had paid tribute to "constancy," a trait necessary for progress: "who could be constant to those moments in which he has been truly human—not brutal, not mechanical—is on the sure path to his perfection and to effectual service of the Universe." Rome tested that idea in the harshest way, for Mazzini refused to capitulate to save his men's lives. Fuller deeply felt the force of her ideal being put into practice: "After the attempt at revolution in France failed," she wrote to William Henry Channing, "could I have influenced Mazzini, I should have prayed him to capitulate, and yet I feel that no honorable terms can be made with such a foe, and that the only way is *never* to yield." This was heroism directly and painfully observed, but it pained her deeply: "but the sound of the musketry, the sense that men were perishing in a hopeless contest, had become too terrible for my nerves."[21] Mazzini had a larger vision of republican virtue that meant it was better to die than to surrender. Even knowing the cost of that vision, Fuller still found in him that personal growth and public responsibility that marked the hero.

After the republic fell to French firepower, Fuller again returned to Rossi and Mazzini, but this time she added a third name to her contrast, the French general Oudinot, who led the conquering force. This "triumvirate," unlike the one that led the republic, has but one hero. Fuller emphasizes the cruel irony that Rossi, Mazzini, and Oudinot all had been named Citizen of Rome, yet Rossi had his honor from the disgraced pope and Oudinot had his by force of conquest. Mazzini alone was made a citizen by his fellow citizens. He alone became the possible democratic hero who, though an outsider, originally had been elected and empowered by those whom he led. Significantly, Fuller returns to the term she applied to Abby Kelly in *Woman in the Nineteenth Century* when she praised "the unyielding mildness of Mazzini" (*SG* 313). The supposedly "feminine" quality made Mazzini unique among his contemporaries for Fuller.

To trace Fuller's ideas about heroism is to discover that it is a topic that informs much of what interested her. She was a literary critic first and then a journalist and, finally, a historian. Throughout her career she had an ideal of resistance, for she understood that her own culture left much to be desired, that it was materialistic and greedy, that it seldom rewarded serious thought or imaginative literature. There was an emptiness and drift to American culture that angered her, so she turned to European models or to the far past of antiquity. Mazzini's slogan, "Dio e Popolo" (God and the people), rang true for Fuller, for she could fantasize about a worldwide democratization: "It seems as if Fate was at work to bewilder and cast down the dignities of the world and democratize Society at a blow." But even as she says this she acknowledges the failures in her native land: "My country," she writes, "is at present spoiled by prosperity, stupid with the lust of gain, soiled by crime in its willing perpetuation of Slavery, shamed by an unjust war." A failed President Polk had pursued an unjust war; a flawed general, Zachary Taylor, had just been elected to succeed him. "It is not the making a

President out of the Mexican War," Fuller wrote, "that would make me wish to come back" (*SG* 229, 230). No matter whether it was Xenophon, Goethe, or Mazzini, Fuller's hero was a symbol of even better things to come. The hero was always an imagined version of our potential "best self," a figure that could embody vision and accomplishment, who was endowed with power and wisdom, who had a spiritual depth and a magnetism of personal presence.

To return for a moment to the "genius" letter she wrote James Clarke in 1830, we can recognize the youthful enthusiasm that allowed her to imagine herself as the hero of the nineteenth century, for surely all imaginative, ambitious young people have some notion of a heroic possibility for themselves. By July 1849, Fuller had seen a genuine hero; she had measured what it cost him personally to be the great man, and she could acknowledge that she "owned myself not of that mould" (*L* 5:247). And yet, if she was not to be the hero, she had a significant role to play. From literary critic acting as the interpreter who mediates between the creative genius of the author and the inquiring reader, Fuller had become the mediator between the heroic Mazzini, whose actions she did not always accept nor understand, and an American public who had no conception of what heroism could mean. Fuller had come far in a few years: from the youthful need to find heroism in personal growth of the sort championed in Goethe, she had come to a fully political understanding. After the fall of the Roman Republic, Fuller had no illusions about organic growth. A corrupt political world needed heroes who could combine the power of mind and the demanding constancy she found in Mazzini. Fuller clearly knew that there was to be a day of reckoning in her slave-holding native land; she knew full well that as she wrote about Mazzini and the dying young men of Rome that most Americans were oblivious to the need for a hero and to the cause which would inevitably create one.

In her penultimate letter to the *Tribune*, written after she and Ossoli had fled to Florence, Fuller sends "love to my country," and then makes an audacious prayer: "O Lucifer, son of the morning, fall not this time from thy chariot, but herald in at last the long looked for, wept for, bled and starved for day of Peace and Good Will to men" (*SG* 320). Here she envisions Lucifer's redemption; Satan becomes redeemed into a figure of peace; he returns to being the "bright morning star" as Fuller reverses the tradition that reached from Isaiah to Milton. She dares to rewrite one of the most potent myths of English literature. Where Fuller might have been expected to call for Christ's return to earth to fulfill his original promise, she turns instead to the self-ruined angel, not to the incarnated God/man. Jesus, because he is divine, cannot be a hero to Fuller; Lucifer, the fallen angel, more closely symbolizes human experience. It is to the fallen that Fuller looks for her next hero.

The Roman Republic had ended; Mazzini was in exile; lives had been given for no immediate benefit, but an exhausted Fuller refused to despair. The ideal of heroism that had been a backdrop now lived; no longer was it the past on which heroism was inscribed, now it was the present, and more importantly, it had a future. Margaret Fuller's last published lines, written on Epiphany day 1850, begin, "Joy to those born in this day," and close, "Joy to them; and joy to those their heralds, who, if their path was desert, their work unfinished, and their heads in the power of a prostituted civilization, to throw as toys at the feet of flushed, triumphant wickedness, yet holy-hearted in unasking love, great and entire in their devotion, fall or fade, happy in the thought that there come after them greater than themselves, who may at last string the harp of the world to full concord, in glory to God in the highest, for peace and love from man to man is become the bond of life" (*SG* 322–24). Heroism had not made a republic, but it had made something even more important: the power of individuals to make the world better.

In his *Representative Men,* which appeared in January 1850 just as Fuller came to terms with the failed Roman revolution, Emerson says, "Great men are thus a collyrium to clear our eyes from egotism, and enable us to see other people and their works." It was just that sort of eye-cleaning that Mazzini worked upon Fuller and, that, in turn, allows us to estimate exactly what "heroism" had become for her. First, Mazzini as the active hero led Fuller to accept the bloodshed and horror of the war, even against her natural instincts. "Since the 30th April," she wrote Emerson, "I go almost daily to the hospitals, and, though I have suffered,—for I had no idea before, how terrible gunshot-wounds and wound-fever are,—yet have I taken pleasure, and great pleasure, in being with the men." She tried to maintain her faith in a pacific socialism "that may lead to the redress of the frightful social ills of Europe, by a peaceful though radical revolution instead of bloody conflict" but it did not negate her understanding of how entrenched the powers of repression were. Writing to Marcus Spring, a month after her public praise of socialism, she said: "You, Marcus, could you let a Croat insult

Rebecca, carry off Eddie to be an Austrian serf; and leave little Marcus bleeding in the dust? . . . You have the truth, you have the right, but could you act it, Marcus in all circumstances?"[22] This is a significant change for Fuller: her experiences with the revolution and her understanding of Mazzini's leadership made the "heroic" encompass the bloody reality of genuine social reform. In observing the Romans, Fuller saw that freedom was not an abstract proposition but a concrete reality that could only be attained by sacrifice through an unflinching, horrifying willingness to die so that others might live in freedom.

Second, Fuller had passed from literary observations of the idea of heroism and of that ideal being expressed imaginatively (and biographically) by literary productions. Read in the light of her experience and acceptance of the revolution, her 1836 praise of the great man quoted above is necessarily callow, for it thinks of heroism as a quality in and of itself; the hero matters because he is heroic. The tautology in that position becomes clear, for what Fuller could praise in the 1830s and 1840s as the fulfillment of human potential and the sum of self-culture was, by 1849, not only inadequate but also irrelevant. When she was immersed in literature, she was looking to the past for examples; Mazzini stood— literally—before her eyes. Because the revolution had failed, it now was the future to which Fuller looked. At the very moment the French entered Rome, she wrote in a *Tribune* letter that Mazzini was "a man to whom only the next age can do justice, as it reaps the harvest of the seed he has sown in this" (*SG* 311).

Heroism might not lead to a united, republican Italy in 1849, but it made it possible—even inevitable—that the future would be affected by it. Fuller had this insight even before the republic came into being. In December 1848 she wrote: "amid the blood and tears of Italy, 'tis joy to see some glorious new births.—the Italians are getting cured of mean adulation and hasty boasts; they are learning to prize and seek realities." That is, they were learning how to be heroic in themselves, how to become citizens of a world of which they as yet had no direct experience. A scant year later, in her last *Tribune* dispatch, Fuller made a prophecy: "The seeds for a vast harvest of hatreds and contempts are sown over every inch of Roman ground, nor can that malignant growth be extirpated, till the wishes of Heaven shall waft a fire that will burn down all, root and branch, and prepare the earth for an entirely new culture. The next revolution, here and elsewhere, will be radical." The failure of the revolution of 1849 was not to be the last fact, for, Fuller continues, "the power of positive, determinate effort is begun. A faith is offered — men are everywhere embracing it; the film is hourly falling from their eyes and they see, not only near but far, duties worthy to be done" (*SG* 237, 321–22). New sight: the necessary effect of heroic leadership — as both Emerson and Fuller were claiming — was the result of a heroism made new, immediate, and potential all at once.

The social critic Fuller had become by the end of the revolution had seen "heroism" come to life in political action. Mazzini's leadership was not important because it made him "great"; it was important because it came as he led people. He was very directly a "citizen-hero," a man whose strength derived from his connection with the people, not only of Rome, but of all Italy. When Fuller praised the Romans for calling him to citizenship she made it clear that his was a heroism that connected him with, not one that put him above, his fellow citizens. To Fuller, Mazzini acted as the instrument of the Romans, not the other way around. They called him; he was adequate to the task, and it was never a question of his ego or of his personal satisfaction. One of her final descriptions of him focuses on his personal suffering: "in two short months, he had grown old; all the vital juices seemed exhausted; his eyes were all blood-shot; his skin orange; flesh he had none; his hair was mixed with white; his hand was painful to the touch." It is at the close of this description that she says, "in him I revered the hero, and owned myself not of that mould" (*L* 5:247).

She was, however, too hard on herself. The original question she posed to Lafayette and James Clarke had become moot: she had been painfully privileged to witness a new form of heroism, one that she thought was not her lot to share as a public figure. Nevertheless, Fuller was adequate to the call: she did what she was trained to do — she wrote. Margaret Fuller turned her accomplished pen to describing a world wholly foreign to her American audience and correspondents; she faithfully represented Mazzini's vision to her own people, pled for their support, and worked again and again to educate them to a higher vision. One cannot but see this labor — conducted often in the midst of the actual cannonade of the siege, always with a fear that her husband, a member of the republican guard, might at any time be killed, separated from her child, whom she left in the Abruzzi mountains — as itself a genuine form of heroism. And so it was.

Notes

1. *Memoirs of Margaret Fuller Ossoli*, ed. R. W. Emerson, W. H. Channing, and J. F. Clarke, 2 vols. (Boston: Phillips, Sampson, 1852), 1:18.

2. Henry D. Thoreau, *Journal*, ed. Elizabeth Hall Witherell et al., 7 vols. to date (Princeton, N.J.: Princeton Univ. Press, 1981–), 1:148; *The Letters of Margaret Fuller*, ed. Robert N. Hudspeth, 6 vols. (Ithaca, N.Y.: Cornell Univ. Press, 1983–94), 1:150 (hereafter cited in text and notes as *L*).

3. Fuller, "Modern British Poets," *American Monthly Magazine*, n.s., 2 (October 1836): 321, 327; Fuller, "The Life of Sir James Mackintosh," *American Monthly Magazine*, n.s., 1 (June 1836): 574

4. Fuller, "Goethe," *Dial* 2 (July 1841): 18.

5. Ibid., 29.

6. *The Collected Works of Ralph Waldo Emerson*, ed. Alfred E. Ferguson et al., 6 vols. to date (Cambridge, Mass.: Belknap Press, 1971–), 2:178.

7. Ibid., 2:153.

8. Fuller, *Woman in the Nineteenth Century*, ed. Larry J. Reynolds (New York: W. W. Norton, 1998), 25, 23, 66, 54–55. Julie Ellison reads Fuller's interest in heroism in useful ways: "Central to the dynamics of heroism is the problem of aggression, which Fuller very early understood as a problem of gender." Her reading, however, leads her to find this section of *Woman in the Nineteenth Century* to be less conclusive than do I: "Avoiding conflict in the name of self-sufficiency or literary tradition, Miranda implies, accomplishes nothing in either the social or the textual domain. Such an ethic makes a difference to the individual woman who lives it, but not to others." *Delicate Subjects: Romanticism, Gender, and the Ethics of Understanding* (Ithaca, N.Y.: Cornell Univ. Press, 1990), 217, 282. Ellison cogently explores the use of Miranda as a figure who is less skeptical than Fuller herself.

9. Fuller, *Woman in the Nineteenth Century*, 20.

10. Fuller, "The Beethoven Movement," *New-York Daily Tribune*, September 3, 1845, 1; Judith Mattson Bean and Joel Myerson, eds., *Margaret Fuller, Critic* (New York: Columbia Univ. Press, 2000), 246; Fuller, "'Age could not wither her . . . ,'" *New-York Daily Tribune*, April 10, 1846, 1.

11. See, for example, three from 1845: "St. Valentine's Day—Bloomingdale Asylum for the Insane" in the *Tribune* for February 22; "Our City Charities . . . ," March 19; and "Asylum for Discharged Female Convicts," June 19.

12. Emerson, *Collected Works*, 2:149. Among the many she met, Fuller described Wordsworth and Harriet Martineau, Joanna Baillie, the Howitts, Lamennais, and Béranger, Pauline Roland, and George Sand. It is worth noting that she described Baillie and Roland "as the best specimens which have been

hitherto offered of women of a Spartan, Roman strength and singleness of mind, adorned by the various culture and capable of the various action opened to them by the progress of the Christian Idea." Fuller, *"These Sad But Glorious Days": Dispatches from Europe, 1846–1850,* ed. Larry J. Reynolds and Susan Belasco Smith (New Haven, Conn.: Yale Univ. Press, 1991), 89 (hereafter cited in text and notes as *SG*).

13. *L* 4:240. Denis Mack Smith says that "Mazzini shone best in female society," and quotes him: "'Despite my lack of social graces, I get on well with almost every woman who knows me because I much prefer them to men.'" *Mazzini* (New Haven, Conn.: Yale Univ. Press, 1994), 45.

14. *SG* 99; John Milton, "Sonnet XXII," in *The Complete Poetical Works of John Milton,* ed. Douglas Bush (Boston: Houghton Mifflin, 1965), 197; Fuller, "'Age could not wither her,'" 1.

15. Mack Smith, *Mazzini,* 3, 25, 45, 54. Roland Sarti describes Mazzini's commitment to literary criticism in terms not far from those one would ascribe to Fuller: "It was literary criticism that intellectuals of Mazzini's generation chose as their battleground. They were brought up on classics that paraded before them ideals of civic virtue, but while they adopted the ideals of citizenship that classic literature inspired, they rejected its literary forms. Mazzini saw it as the task of his generation to propagate those ideals in a style that appealed to the emotions." *Mazzini: A Life for the Religion of Politics* (Westport, Conn.: Praeger, 1997), 32.

16. Joseph Rossi, *The Image of America in Mazzini's Writings* (Madison: Univ. of Wisconsin Press, 1954), 52–56.

17. *SG* 155; *L* 4:315; *SG* 189, 199, 244.

18. *SG* 262–63; Julie Ellison may be right in her observation about Fuller's reaction to such scenes: "Revolutionary violence seems to strike her as a foregone and wholly justifiable conclusion. There is perhaps an element of relief for Fuller in seeing violence externalized rather than felt as a savage personal impulse, as there was in seeing passion and suffering played out visibly before her. Fuller's own passional life was so powerfully shaped by fantasies of heroism, including military heroism, that a degree of vicarious wish fulfillment may also be at work." *Delicate Subjects,* 295. Ellison's discussion of Fuller in Rome is part of a larger argument that aims to explore feminism and romantic thought in Fuller's work. Much of what Ellison says is thoughtful and provocative, but she overplays Fuller's role as a romantic critic: "Political action is aestheticized not only because it is staged by the picturesque Italians, but because the historian is an artist, seeking out the vantage points from which to be moved and stirred" (292). This is true for some of Fuller's writing from Rome, but it diminishes the keen political understanding Fuller had and her deep commitment to the idealism she found embodied in Mazzini.

19. *SG* 263; *Memoirs of Fuller,* 18.

20. *SG* 225; *L* 5:49, 5:240. Though his reforms had no chance to take full effect, Mazzini encouraged popular education and ended the "monopoly in university teaching"; he ended clerical censorship of the press and abolished the death penalty and protective tariffs; he appointed a lay judiciary to replace the secret ecclesiastical courts, and supported religious toleration. Mack Smith, *Mazzini*, 68–69.

21. *SG* 166; *L*, 5:247. Larry J. Reynolds argues that Fuller was more prone in her letters than in her *Tribune* dispatches to admit her emotional distress: "the private Fuller, the woman concerned with human beings as opposed to abstract ideas, is more heroic, because of her vulnerability, than the persona of the *Tribune* letters, and perhaps Fuller knew this." *European Revolutions and the American Literary Renaissance* (New Haven, Conn.: Yale Univ. Press, 1988), 77. His argument that Fuller has a different persona for public and private writings is right, but I do not think that the private writing was less "heroic." In fact, my argument is that each form of expression was necessary for her evolving idea of heroism, that finally there is no contradiction between her emotional testing and her public analyses of revolutionary heroism but rather that the two complement each other.

22. Emerson, *Collected Works*, 4:15; *L* 5:239; *SG* 320; *L* 5:295–96.

4

Margaret Fuller's Search for the Maternal

ANNA SCACCHI

> The other day, I met a decrepit old man of seventy, on a journey, who challenged the stage-company to guess where he was going. They guessed aright, "To see your mother."
>
> Margaret Fuller, *Woman in the Nineteenth Century*

The Life of a Woman

In recent years various scholars have lamented the fact that the life of Margaret Fuller continues to attract more attention than her works. Because of this undue focus, they remark, we still lack critical editions of fundamental texts, which circulate in the censored versions edited by her brother Arthur after her death.[1] Although this state of affairs is now changing, the number of biographical studies dedicated to Fuller by American scholars is indeed quite large. Christina Zwarg, in her *Feminist Conversations* (1995), convincingly argues that this emphasis on the woman rather than the writer has produced damaging misinterpretations of her work. But, in linking the pathos of Fuller's life to the neglect of her writing, she seems to place the blame not only on the critics, who are guilty of a biographical approach, but also on Fuller herself, *guilty*, in turn, for having lived such a romantic life. Zwarg writes, "The dramatic text of Fuller's life has always generated reader interest; new biographies have appeared with rhythmic regularity since her death in a shipwreck in 1850. But because her *provocative personal narrative*, with its

66

cosmopolitan scale and power, has remained the central focus of scholarly attention, the bulk of her writing continues to remain veiled in mystery or misreading."[2]

Not only have Fuller scholars put together a narrative that assigns primacy to life over texts—a major essentialist sin in times that tend to attack the idea that subjects exist outside language—they have also plotted it as an initiation story, in which the heroine becomes a freer, more self-conscious person thanks to her dislocating experience in the Old World. And initiation stories, with their naive reliance on the notion that an integral self *can* be achieved, do not fare well today. Fuller's European experience is read by a majority of scholars as representing a strong break with her original formation. In their eyes it constitutes the beginning of a process of evolution and self-awareness at both the ideological and literary levels. The problem with this hypothesis, Zwarg maintains, is that it encourages us to neglect all of Fuller's works prior to her travels in Europe. If they are read at all, it is in order to confirm her former ideological dependence on the Transcendentalists.[3]

The critical paradox of an approach founded on biography and structured around the idea of a progress toward self-awareness, according to Zwarg, is that it results in a sort of interpretive negativity. That is, all of Fuller's writings prior to her Roman experience are either given short shrift or judged more or less negatively, if not hurriedly dismissed. At the same time, a work that does not exist—that mysterious *History of the Roman Republic* swallowed up by the sea and perhaps, according to the judgment of nay-sayers like Nathaniel Hawthorne, never written—is exalted as the apex of her literary production.[4] Her real writing, that which is actually accessible, is often neutralized in order to emphasize "the work that we literally cannot read."[5]

Zwarg's is an interesting version of a new postfeminist tendency in the critical literature dedicated to Fuller that privileges the texts and their rhetorical structures over the events of her life.[6] Despite the recent revival of attention on her, Fuller continues to be placed at the margins of the nation's nineteenth-century literary panorama, and is still considered of interest mainly to feminists, as a champion of women's rights, or to historians, for her connections with the Transcendentalist network. New emphasis on Fuller's writing rather than on her biography will produce significant changes in the breadth and depth of studies dedicated to her and this will surely be welcomed. I have the impression, however, that the opposition *fact-fiction* that Zwarg's approach more or less explicitly intends to deconstruct ends up unchanged, despite the shift of emphasis from the *real* events of Fuller's life to the rhetorical strategies of her self-fashioning. Although she argues against the essentialism of earlier feminist scholars, Zwarg seems to assume a *real* Margaret Fuller that was less than her writing and more embarrassingly contradictory as well. As a consequence, in order to best appreciate Fuller's valuable work—which for Zwarg does not include her most autobiographical texts—she deems it safer to place her life backstage.

The aim of this essay, on the contrary, is to defend women's interest in the lives of other women as a reading strategy, in part because I myself approached Fuller as a writer through the mediation of her biography. I must confess that I initially found *Woman in the Nineteenth Century* abstract and ineffective, albeit feeling uncomfortable about it, because in this I seemed to share the opinion of so many of her contemporaries about her literary value, while I rejected outright their representation of women with intellectual aspirations as *unnatural*. But while I felt no intellectual attraction to the brilliant rhetorician that was being uncovered by postfeminist readings, I developed an intense interest in her life. Looking for the woman in her work, I also found the writer, and she was more than Emerson's theoretical interlocutor in my eyes. Because Fuller's stirring life responds to my own interest in women's lives, I discovered a more interesting author than I had anticipated. Her "life"—a multifaceted text deriving from her words, the contrasting narratives of her biographers, and my own search for a narrative itinerary in the events of her biography—helped me to overcome my discomfort with her writing. A better knowledge of her work, in its turn, enabled me to gain a different perspective on her apparent rejection of nineteenth-century women's culture, to which I tended to impute her digressive and highly contrived style.

To explain the value I give to Fuller's life as a path leading to her works, I will resort to the words of the Italian feminist philosopher Adriana Cavarero, who has sternly criticized postmodern tendencies to emphasize language at the expense of history in her *Relating Narratives: Storytelling and Selfhood*. Cavarero distances herself from the tendency of contemporary criticism, feminist criticism included, to focus exclusively on the rhetorical dimension of autobiographical narration: for "by swallowing life, the text also risks swallowing the unrepeatable uniqueness of the existent."[7] She reminds the reader of women's interest in other women's lives, borrowing a scene evoked by Liz Stanley in a well-known essay on autobiographical writing. In the scene, a female reader enters a bookstore, picks up a volume on Hegel and feminism, puts it back immediately; picks up the latest mystery by a feminist, considers it for a moment, and then puts it back; glimpses the new biography of X, takes it, reads the cover attentively, flips through it, and then goes to the pages of photographs in the middle and stops to scrutinize them carefully.

Cavarero asks why "women—feminists included—are happy to read biographies of women, written by women," and also, why "there are many women who write life-stories of other women, in order to appeal to the reading public of women." The answer, for her, lies in a pact between the writer and the reader based on the common desire for a life-with-meaning. Anglo American feminists' critique of the notion of a unique self—an ideological, patriarchal construction—is thus invalidated:

> It is more than likely that our reader shows an interest not so much in a deconstruction of the text, but rather for a life-story that is capable of narrating the *uniqueness* of its protagonist. Indeed, what else is she looking for in the photographs if not this uniqueness in the form of a body and facial expression? . . . It is indeed quite probable that the desire to read auto/biographies of others is a sort of spontaneous reflex of the narratable self's desire for narration. And it is symptomatic that, in the perspective of reading others' stories, the distinction between biography and autobiography no longer counts. Unlike what happens in narrative friendships, there is here neither relation nor exchange. In this case the narratable self decontextualizes her desire and transfers it to the ready-made work.[8]

Women's interest in other women's lives, then, cannot be treated merely as an act of vicarious living or escapism or a naive belief in patriarchal versions of subjectivity. We read the lives of other women and look into the unrepeatable singularity of their existence in the hope of discovering a witness who might also speak for our own uniqueness.

Margaret Fuller's life, considerably larger than most of us could dream of living and at the same time so much more limited by fate and historical context, lends itself particularly well to the female reader's desire for such a narration. It offers any number of inchoate events and circumstances capable of being shaped in a variety of narrative itineraries. The female reader's interest, then, is not merely the result of the cosmopolitan dimension of Fuller's seductive biography, where the tragic force of her death—resembling that of a heroine of mass culture who, caught up in a Hollywood tearjerker, is seized by destiny just as she is on the brink of a new life—diverts our attention from what is really important about her. It is also the result of the extraordinary capacity of Fuller's story to respond to our desire for a significant life, a life-with-meaning. In other words, her life-story's intrinsic power of seduction does not depend on a deplorable excessiveness that strikes our melodramatic imagination, distracting us from the texts and reabsorbing their capacity for cultural criticism, as Christina Zwarg insinuates. Rather, its power depends on her life's ability to stimulate a narrative relationship in which all the parts—she who narrates herself to us, the biographer, the reader—satisfy their desire for narrating the self.[9]

The auto/biographical mode, however, can be an empowering hermeneutic strategy and a trap at the same time. The danger, of course, is turning Fuller into a pretext for fashioning one's own autobiography. For many feminist readers "Margaret Fuller," an intermingling of life and text, has been and continues to be a palimpsest through which to interpret their own individual and collective story. In this perspective Bell Gale Chevigny's work seems to me paradigmatic of the ways a literary foremother can help today's feminists to articulate their own narrative and write a revisionist genealogy placing a woman "at the beginning"—and, in the process, become a hybrid text inscribing both the artist's and the interpreter's story. Chevigny's pioneering volume, *The Woman and the Myth*, published in 1976 and reprinted in an augmented edition in 1994, is a perfect example of the archaeological activity that in the seventies English and American feminists began with the intent to recover forgotten women writers of the past. In appearance Chevigny repeats the rhetorical gesture of Ralph Waldo Emerson, William H. Channing, and James Freeman Clarke, editors of the controversial *Memoirs*. She chooses, as they did, to put together a composite picture of Fuller based on a continual dialogue, in which Margaret's voice is woven together with those of her friends and contemporaries. But in reality Chevigny's editorial repetition, motivated by rage, is both a re-vision and a vindication, where the feminist biographer aims to replace the postmortem analysis carried out on Fuller's corpus by her male friends with a truer life. That first anatomy, it is worth recalling, not only domesticated but also mutilated the writing. Because they wanted to protect the reputation of the woman, whose scandalous Italian union continued to be a source of gossip and wild conjecture, the editors used scissors to suppress passages where Fuller probably appeared too unconventional for contemporary standards of feminine propriety.

Or they added phrases that conveniently dispelled doubts about her marriage.

Chevigny's, then, is a *counter*-portrait, specifically aimed at unmasking the bias of the *Memoirs* volume and governed by the desire to bring to light Fuller's nonconformity. She writes in order to transform the patriarchal narrative—telling the story of a gender anomaly that produced suffering and unease—into a feminist narrative that celebrates an ideal mother. In Chevigny's counter-portrait the editor's voice adopts the feminist perspective of the search for those foremothers reduced to silence and censured in the name of patriarchal notions of respectability and female decorum. Furthermore, it sets out not only to separate the woman from the myth, the truth from ideology, and Margaret from the skewed portraits of her, but also to guide the ideal female reader in the search for Fuller's authentic voice. In the new introduction to the revised edition of *The Woman and the Myth*, the search for Margaret is suggestively interspersed with Chevigny's own search for self, so that "Margaret" also becomes an instrument of self-knowledge for the biographer.[10] This new introduction and Chevigny's "Daughters Writing" essay, which appeared in *Feminist Studies* in 1983, seem to me equally exemplary of the ability of "Margaret Fuller" to transform herself into an interpretive palimpsest. I find it revealing and in many respects moving that Chevigny's discovery of Margaret as a foremother is occasioned by Fuller's life rather than by her writing, and that it is openly presented as a vindication and not as a detached reconstruction. Coming after her early, unquestioning acceptance of conventional portraits of Fuller as an eccentric old maid, the biography is a symbolic act signifying Chevigny's own growing self-awareness.

The auto/biographical mode, then, seems to impose itself on the reader from inside the writings of Margaret Fuller. "Margaret Fuller," understood as the intermingling of life and writing, continues to present itself to the attention of scholars as an enigma, a knot to be untangled. Both Fuller's life *and* work seem to require a strategy of subtraction: they refuse facile interpretations, they reveal themselves to be consistently furrowed by contradictory tendencies, and they refer to each other in a continuous dialogue, in a strenuous effort of reciprocal definition. Reading her works and the literature dedicated to her (starting with the wave of testimony of friends and acquaintances that invaded the American press for a few decades after her death), one cannot but note how much both are characterized by the same, almost obsessive desire to

explain, analyze, and draw from the irreconcilable contradictions a unified portrait in which all the details will finally reveal the pattern and
add up to a meaningful story. On the other hand, as Chevigny comments on Poe's well-known cameo of Fuller ("Her acts are bookish, and
her books are less thoughts than acts") citing Thoreau, in this overlap-
ping of life and writing she signaled that she belonged to her age: "To
live deliberately, to invent one's biography—these were, of course,
Transcendentalist aspirations, but no one else carried them, literally
and figuratively, so far as she."[11]

A veritable incarnation of the romantic artist, Fuller wrote in order
to validate her own biography and lived her life as a source of inspiration for writing. Referring to her conscious acts of self-construction,
Hawthorne commented, "She took credit to herself for having been her
own Redeemer, if not her own Creator; and, indeed, she was far more a
work of art than any of Mr. Mozier's statues." If we were able to forget
the malevolent vein of Hawthorne's portrait, the true-false opposition
that sustains it, we could even appreciate his insight into Fuller's understanding of identity as performance. But he then went on to pronounce
the failure of her romantic attempt to create herself, a failure in his
opinion determined by a "rude old potency" (her woman's body), which
she was unable to shape into more refined and spiritual matter. He
seemed to rejoice in her fall from the pedestal of intellectual aspirations
like "the weakest of her sisters" and even to consider her unsuccessful attempt to free herself from her body, which trapped her in biology, a due
punishment for her unfeminine hubris.[12] Hawthorne's bias against
Fuller's bold attempt to step outside the nineteenth-century "woman's
sphere"—a bias shared by many of her contemporaries—can explain,
to some extent, the opposite view taken by Chevigny and other feminist
readers. In the effort to distance themselves from Hawthorne's and
other derogatory portraits of the past, some feminist narratives turn
Fuller's "fall from the realm of the intellect" into the achievement of
control over her body and desires, that is, the apex of her liberation
from an oppressive patriarchal culture.

This essay considers facts from her biography—in particular, her
becoming a mother at a late age, away from home, possibly out of wedlock, and with a partner who she knew would shock all of her American
friends—and weaves them together with the recurring narrative themes
in her writing, which I will refer to as her search for the maternal. Life
and texts are analyzed against the backdrop of nineteenth- and

twentieth-century interpretations of Margaret Fuller, which have invariably singled out biological motherhood as the most meaningful and change-producing event in her life. My hypothesis is that Fuller's search for the maternal found in both the maternal body and maternal ideology an obstacle larger than she had probably anticipated, and this threatened the political agency she had just begun to fashion for herself. By way of a cautionary note, I do not want to offer what follows as a better portrait of Margaret Fuller, one nearer to the truth than others. Like other scholars, I got caught in the tangle of her life and responded to it with my own reading of her writings. Although I believe that the "real" Margaret Fuller is for us inaccessible if not through the mediation, the filter, of "Margaret Fuller," nevertheless, this textual dimension does not alter the fact that, just like Cavarero's female reader of biographies, I am attracted to her by the desire to capture the uniqueness of her existence.

Who Am I? Where Do I Come From?

Margaret Fuller's writing is always profoundly autobiographical, even when it superficially seems projected completely outward. It returns constantly to the questions that she remembers having asked herself as a child: "I remembered how, a little child, I had stopped myself one day on the stairs and asked, how came I here? How is it that I seem to be this Margaret Fuller? What does it mean? What shall I do about it? I remembered all the times and ways in which the same thought had returned."[13] These questions signal an anxiety to arrive at a sense of self, at an objectification and distancing by which she could find an identity. They also signal a search for origins ("how came I here?") and an urgency to reunify the internal and external, private and public, and individual and social realms ("I" and "this Margaret Fuller"). As a child and then an adolescent, she perceived her anxiety of identity on an individual plane, but later she turned it into a collective issue. She transformed those questions into a broader cultural critique: first through the Boston Conversations, in which she posed the same questions to her students in the first person plural, and with an emphasis on the issue of their identity as women; and then through *Woman in the Nineteenth Century*, in which she confronted the separation between the definition of self and social identity as a problem of power and asymmetrical gender relations.

Fuller's anxiety of identity forced her to translate herself continually through a series of self-portraits: Mariana, Miranda, the various autobiographical personae narrating her life as one marked by diversity and solitude. Taken individually, they emphasize not so much the simultaneous presence of different selves as the temporary isolation of a single trait that then becomes the interpretive key, if not the glue, that unifies the contradictory fragments into a coherent pattern. Or perhaps it would be better to speak of impersonations displaying an infinite series of Margarets, a testimony to her prominent theatricality (widely recognized by friends and acquaintances) that, in the puritan fabric of New England, would have appeared as an exotic and artificial trait. William Henry Channing, in fact, confessed that after meeting her he was negatively struck by an attitude that seemed false to him: "I then suspected her of affecting the part of a Yankee Corinna."[14] Any attempt to read Fuller's masks as literally autobiographical, then, is doomed to failure, even though they do refer, more or less obliquely, to actual events in her life. Rather, her fictional selves seem to be the outcome of an interpretive strategy, relying on writing as a technique to understand and invent her own self. This might explain why Fuller often resorted to using a filter in her self-portraits, that is, a voice *en travesti*, or a narrating "I" who does not coincide with the narrated self.

First, there is her adolescent self-portrait in *Summer on the Lakes*. Mariana, the exuberant and passionate individualist, is so extraneous to the reserved character and rigor of New England that Fuller feels the need to give her an exotic origin: "She was, on the father's side, of Spanish Creole blood." Interestingly, Emerson and Channing did the same with her, in their attempt to get to the bottom of the Fuller enigma.[15] Mariana, pure uncontrolled energy and a true reversal of the submissive femininity that Fuller was sent to the school of Susan Prescott to learn, is censured by her companions for her rebellious behavior.[16] She is forced to accept the idea that women exist in networks, the only mode of existence that the society in which she lives seems to offer her, and cannot presume they are free, independent selves. Such a relational identity, one must note, is achieved not through the version of romantic love spun by the sentimental narrative voice, determined to be "the wise and delicate being who could understand her," but through the autobiographical story told to her by her teacher.[17] And it is an identity that allows her to be welcomed back as a sister by her companions, but condemns her to silence and obscurity: "A wild fire was tamed in that hour of penitence at the boarding school."[18]

Then, in *Woman in the Nineteenth Century*, there is Miranda, the serene and distant daughter born out of her father's head, who from the height of her own exceptionality looks benignly down on her as a yet unemancipated sister.[19] We also have the narrative voice of the "Autobiographical Romance," written in 1840, which is modulated in mournful tones: mourning for her own natural, spontaneous, irretrievably lost self and for her childhood, dominated by a strict father who demanded discipline, hard work, the suppression of emotions, and the total control of her own social identity.[20] Finally, we have the masculine masks adopted in other autobiographical fragments, like the six undated pages in her manuscripts where the death of her mother, a recurrent dream that haunts Fuller as a child and adolescent, becomes a "real" episode.[21] Then there are the masks adopted in her letters. These display an infinite array of possible subjectivities: the obedient child aware of her own intellectual superiority, the adolescent overwhelmed by strongly sensual passions for peers of both sexes and for feminine maternal figures, the caring yet lucidly critical teacher, the seductress, the prophet, the accomplice, the vestal virgin, the Baccante, Minerva, the Muse, and so on. Ann Douglas has written that "Fuller always operated through an intricate blend of rigorous self-scrutiny, conducted in her journals, her correspondence, and in her ever-vigilant consciousness, with imaginative but not always well-controlled role-playing."[22] I am not sure that I share Douglas's confidence in a self that exists before role-playing, or, better, that can control it. Yet I agree with her that self-scrutiny and role-playing were Fuller's ways of being in the world. Indeed, she collapsed them into one activity.

Fuller, however, was not satisfied with this fragmented and multifocal subjectivity. She seemed rather to use the variety of masks and autobiographical voices to search, like Oedipus, for the story of her self and of her own origin: who am I, where do I come from? In her search for identity she oscillated between pride in a state of singularity that distinguished her from other women and a painful sense of isolation. Her difference, as she was well aware, did not result in an authentic freedom from the constraints of gender but only made her relations with men and women more difficult. The writing through which she invented possible responses to her quest is pervaded, until adulthood, by two themes that play off each other: the absence of her mother and the desire to substitute for this absence—which generates fear and nostalgia— a symbolic fullness, through an inventory of female figures capable of returning to her the original maternal figure that she lacked.

"Man is of woman born," writes Fuller in *Woman in the Nineteenth Century*, "and her face bends over him in infancy with an expression he can never quite forget." The distant memory of a maternal face bent over her own in childhood seems to obsess her as well. In all the autobiographical personae she employed in looking for the original that might explain to her who she was and help her in her effort at self-parturition—thereby finally bringing together the I and the social mask in an organic whole—Fuller depicted herself as motherless. This absence adds up to loss and mourning in her "Autobiographical Romance," where the secret space of the maternal, the garden, is accessible to the narrator only as flight, as the moment stolen from paternal control and enjoyed in total solitude. An excerpt from her diary, dated November 1831, recounts her flight into the woods, where she had a mystical experience during which she asked herself those gnawing questions about her origins. The episode is significantly framed by an act of rebellion against paternal and religious authority—"I was obliged to go to church or exceedingly displease my father"—that is also an act of rebellion against her country—"It was Thanksgiving day." Significantly, this scene takes place in a natural landscape evoking the maternal from which the wandering orphan feels repelled: "I paused beside a little stream, which I had envied in the merry fullness of its spring life. It was shrunken, voiceless, choked with withered leaves. I marveled that it did not quite lose itself in the earth. There was no stay for me, and I went on and on, till I came to where the trees were thick about a little pool, dark and silent. I sat down there. I did not think; all was dark, and cold, and still."[23]

In Miranda's public voice the absence of the mother is only an emptiness that does not generate mourning or nostalgia on the conscious level, but simply singularity and isolation. Like many other women before her, Miranda fears the ambiguous power of the body to ground her and at the same time imprison her in biology. The lack of a maternal origin neutralizes the body and assigns to women an interiority devoid of the coloration of gender: "What woman needs is not as a woman to act or rule, but as a nature to grow, as an intellect to discern, as a soul to live freely and unimpeded." The bodiless Miranda—who is all soul—gains in universality, but that leaves her a disembodied icon of the intellectual possibilities of women:

> She was fortunate in a total absence of those charms which might have drawn to her bewildering flatteries, and in a strong electric nature,

which repelled those who did not belong to her; and attracted those who did. With men and women her relations were noble, affectionate without passion, intellectual without coldness. The world was free to her, and she lived freely in it. Outward adversity came, and inward conflict, but that faith and self-respect had early been awakened which must always lead at last, to an outward serenity and an inward peace. . . . She had taken a course of her own, and no man stood in her way . . . the many men, who knew her mind and her life, showed her confidence, as to a brother, gentleness as to a sister.[24]

In the eyes of the narrating "I" that speaks with her and embodies an intermediary position between the uniqueness of the father's chosen one and the feminine masses left in ignorance by less enlightened parents, Miranda is an example of the infinite possibility of female expansion. The problematic nature of this vision is that the absence of the mother generates an emptiness and a lack of connection. In her social intercourse Miranda is guilty of the same intellectual rarefaction that Fuller fiercely attacked in Emerson, because she could not be satisfied with the detached friendship he bestowed on her. Mariana's story is similarly marked by the absence of the mother, and in her too the problem of the missing origin generates an imbalance of identity, a disharmony. But Mariana's lack or excess is the opposite of Miranda's. While the latter is pure mind, Mariana is fire, passion, erotic energy, body. Just as Miranda, who is gifted with a self-reliance that makes her relations with others sterile, is turned inward, so Mariana is extroverted, mimetic, and invaded by a desire for the gaze of others that, paradoxically, isolates her.

If the process of identification starts with the image of self that the child sees reflected in her mother's eyes, it is comprehensible that the questions concerning her own origin (who am I? where do I come from?) would repeat themselves obsessively throughout Fuller's life. Until recently, Fuller's reconstruction of a solitary childhood spent in the study of the classics, far from a mother in fragile health and always involved in the care of younger siblings, was accepted by biographers without reservation. Actually, if we interpret her autobiographical writings in a literal sense, Fuller surely exaggerated both the separation from her mother as well as her own extraneousness to the domestic sphere. In the first place, as Charles Capper and Joan von Mehren have amply demonstrated, as unusual as was the curriculum of studies to which she was subjected, it went along with what was considered normal for boys—and it was not exceptional among girls belonging to the elite families of New England, especially those active in the political arena.[25]

Clearly the adult Fuller's criticisms of her father's principles of child rearing were amply influenced by her teaching experience as well as by her Romantic vision of the child as "the father of the Man." As a teacher at Temple, Bronson Alcott's coeducational institute in Boston, she had become familiar with his innovative pedagogy, which stressed the need to adapt the learning process to the individual rhythms of young minds. She probably speculated on the terrible effects that her father's pedagogy, based on early and continuated stuffing of "empty vessels" with indigestible notions, had had on her spiritual well-being. The retroactive self-pity, that is, probably derives less from the memories of her experience as her father's chosen one than from her intellectual rejection of his educational principles. In addition, as Capper points out, Timothy was not the only person in the family responsible for his child's moral and intellectual upbringing, because Margarett Crane never completely delegated to her husband the decisions regarding her daughter's education. Timothy was absent for most of the day and his political engagements often kept him away from home. Initially he was directly involved in his child's instruction during the evening hours, but he was eventually forced to leave this duty to his wife and to the proper institutions.

He did reserve for himself the role of supervisor, which he exercised at a distance through letters. But obviously his absence reduced the effectiveness of his authority and gave the young Fuller the opportunity to occupy her time in frivolous activities. She read novels and went to dances, though she knew that her father would not approve. We should also consider that the relationship between Timothy and his wife, however asymmetric, was modeled on the ideal of the companionate marriage that had spread among the American intellectual elite at the beginning of the century. Margarett Crane was sufficiently able to take advantage of the power of influence that it gave her, and this emerges clearly in her letters to her husband. Astutely, she expressed fears, suggestions, and advice and reported the opinion of influential friends with the intention to guide her husband in the direction that seemed to her most opportune.[26] When Margaret's behavior started to strike relatives and friends as improper for a young lady, her parents steered their educational course away from the menacing rock of an unmarriageable daughter.

In addition, while the Fuller family enjoyed prestige, it certainly was not rich. Their economic conditions became more difficult when the parents decided to move to Groton. The domestic help, already minimal in Cambridge, was reduced to only one person. Margaret might have been spared part of the domestic duties that all women in the nineteenth-century family were expected to do, but she was certainly forced to participate in daily activities. As we learn from her letters, she often regretted that the care of children, house cleaning, food preparation, and sewing took so much time away from her reading. The black-and-white picture we are familiar with depicts a woman who is clearly different from other women—even painfully so—because she was raised "as a man" and was spared the feminine sphere of the home. But, looked at in this light, the picture takes on a series of intermediate tones. Therefore we must reconsider the idea, still common today, that Fuller's exceptionality depended on the "masculine" upbringing she was privileged to enjoy and on the fact that her father, to use the words of Ann Douglas, "forcibly cut her off from the feminine subculture, a world governed by etiquette books and sentimental novels."[27] And we are forced to note that this way of explaining Fuller's anomalous status is paradoxically similar to the rationale that dominated nineteenth-century biographies of her. The main difference is that while within the domestic ideology her lack of domesticity was interpreted as a condemnation to unhappiness, for many contemporary feminists hers was a fortunate escape from the world of women's trivia.

Nevertheless, this explanation is confirmed by Fuller herself in her autobiographical writings. She tended to represent herself as split into two halves—masculine and feminine, intellect and heart, soul and body—and incapable of forging the androgynous self to which she aspired. However, the condition of the orphan through which she represented herself should not be read merely as a symptom of her precocious removal from the jurisdiction of Margarett Crane. It is, I would say, the metaphor for an absence that has little to do with her biological mother. What she was missing was a maternal symbology, an absence of which she was painfully aware. Raised by her father to dominate the language of reason and excel at it, she was seduced by its power but was eventually forced to realize that it did not belong to her. She needed a symbolic "maternal" that would instantiate her origin and have the power to ground her, so that she could flee from both the bodiless destiny of Miranda and the hysterical fate of Mariana. Contemporary feminists have learned the political importance of rewriting the past in order to change the future; they have also learned that undue emphasis on the vanguard's novelty leads only to isolation. By anticipating their theoretical moves, Fuller provides us with what we might appropriately call an archaeology of the feminine. Sacking the myths of all cultures and all historical periods, from the most remote times to the very present, she engaged in a hunt that might transform the missing origin into a fortifying presence.

In her "Autobiographical Romance," written when she was thirty, Fuller seems to interpret the privilege of her classical education through the lenses of a patriarchal ideology that considered women constitutionally too weak to be involved in intensive intellectual activity. This could only have been a paradox for someone like Margaret who, a few years later, would declare, "Let them be sea captains, if they will!" The exaggerated curriculum of study imposed on her by her father, she says, generated nightmares, sleepwalking, and nervous excitement. Ultimately, it destroyed her health forever, leaving her unable to apply herself in work and study for more than a few hours at a time. But perhaps the rancor with which she viewed her destiny as her father's chosen daughter is still more profound and subterranean. Perhaps it has to do with the skepticism with which she began to look at her future and at the possibility of using her education for a purpose not merely ornamental. Perhaps it has to do with the knowledge of having been misled, by her mother as well as by her father, into believing that her "masculine" upbringing would guarantee her a different destiny as an adult. The ideal of the "Republican Mother" was at bottom the reason for Timothy Fuller's choice of a classical curriculum for his daughter. He thought that it would make her the ideal intellectual companion for an American citizen, but he probably never envisioned for her a role different from the traditional ones of wife and mother. This could not have been enough for Margaret Fuller. Moreover, it was that very upbringing that became an obstacle for her in her relationships with men, who often resented her competitive attitude or were unwilling to engage in the kind of "conversation" she yearned for, a total act of communication where both participants came naked, without reserve.

Intellectual independence, then, did not allow Fuller access to the masculine public realm, and at the same time it precluded the feminine realm of private affection. But she perceived in teaching, and later in her social journalism, with its utopian drive, an intermediate space that allowed her to achieve a voice where the contrasting discourses of public and private could mingle.[28] Her father's Lockean educational precepts were based on the idea that the child was an empty container, and their aim was to teach intellectual and moral rigor and precision of expression through constant application and the memorizing of the classics. Fuller now substitutes this *paideia* with a Socratic model based on the involvement of the teacher in a conversation that she guides but cannot, nor wishes to, totally control. Her use of questions in the classroom is designed to bring to light what the student already possesses within herself. The objectives of rigor and precision remain her father's, but the relationship between master and student recovers the "mother" figure absent from Fuller's childhood. In effect, the educational process is now modeled explicitly on the mother-daughter relationship, which promises the delivery of that which was already there.[29]

The Mother Rediscovered

On December 20, 1847, nine months after arriving in Italy, Fuller wrote a letter to Emerson in which she seemed to distance herself definitively from him and from the United States as well: "I find how true was the lure that always drew me towards Europe. It was no false instinct that said I might here find an atmosphere to develop me in ways I need. Had I only come ten years earlier! Now my life must be a failure, so much strength had been wasted on abstractions, which only came because I grew not in the right soil." This image of an exile who has finally returned home recurs several times in her correspondence: "Italy receives me as a long-lost child, and I feel myself at home here" (*M* 2:224–25, 220). Rome, "the Mother of Nations," as she defined it in a letter to the *Tribune* on May 6, 1849, is always present in Fuller's reports from Italy, not as a mere backdrop or stage in which the events she relates take place, but as a maternal figure that cries, hopes, and watches over the destiny of her children. Rome is also "my Rome," the absent mother, denied, who finally allows herself to be embraced. But Fuller soon abandons the tone of the returning daughter for another, quite different one: that of the Mater Dolorosa, through which she identifies herself with Rome as a mother.

It is easy to make this role reversal coincide with her motherhood, which required her to abandon the city at the beginning of the summer of 1848 and interrupt her reports on the Roman Republic for six months. In the stories that have accumulated over the years, Italy, and especially Rome, always represents the place in which Margaret Fuller's search is completed or begins to be completed. Rome, the city of the soul, comes to symbolize in a certain sense a place of initiation. It is in Rome that her potentialities unfold and take on meaning, and the coveted union between "I" and "this Margaret" is realized. Fuller herself says so when she repeatedly describes her residence in Rome as a homecoming, and all those who study her—not only the biographers of the nineteenth century but also contemporary scholars—repeat it to varying degrees. Even those who, like Zwarg, want to deconstruct Fuller's story "from . . . to" tend to underscore the passage from a position of observation and distanced speculation to that of first-person participation.

But in this narrative of self-revelation and realization that culminates in Rome, what Rome means for Fuller depends on what we believe Fuller *really* was from the beginning. It reveals, in other words, what objective we assign to her torturous search for self. In the stories narrated by her friends and her nineteenth-century biographers, Rome is fatally linked to her encounter with Ossoli and to her pregnancy. Reciprocated love, sexual fulfillment, and motherhood are read as the satisfaction of a secret desire always held in check by her meager ability to attract a husband, which was the source of all her eccentricities. Emerson, Channing, and Clarke explicitly constructed their biography of Fuller as a path that goes from a profound existential awkwardness to the final recognition of her own natural destiny, tragically interrupted by fate. The anomaly of Fuller, for them, lay in her failure to realize a natural feminine vocation, suffocated and perverted by the exaggerated development of the intellectual, masculine talents that were artificially imposed on her. According to this patented reading, she is "cured" by Rome and by the Marquis Ossoli. The shipwreck comes as a fatal interruption of the process of her domestication. Everyone seems sure of it now that she is dead, but when she was still alive and spoke of her intention to return to the United States, the reaction instead was one of worry and fear. Besides the question of her marriage, regarding which Fuller did not seem willing to dispel doubts, there was the problem of her political ideas, apparently even more radical than when she had left. A gathering of her dearest friends—Emerson, Channing, Marcus and Rebecca Spring—came to the conclusion that it was better for her to remain abroad, and they hurried to communicate this to her. "If you return you will lose the power to write," Rebecca warned her, using words that seem to suggest that in the United States her reputation as a socialist might possibly lead to her being banned from the literary market. "It's because we love you we say 'stay!'"[30]

Despite his admiration and esteem for Fuller's intellect, William Henry Channing was among the first to credit the portrait of Fuller as a woman who had invested an energy in her studies that she was not able to expend more appropriately:

> But the tragedy of Margaret's history was deeper yet. Behind the poet was the woman,—the fond and relying, the heroic and disinterested woman. The very glow of her poetic enthusiasm was but an outflush of trustful affection; the very restlessness of her intellect was the confession that her heart had found no home. A "bookworm," "a dilettante," "a pedant," I had heard her sneeringly called; but now it was evident that her seeming insensibility was virgin pride, and her absorption in study the natural vent of emotions which had met no object worthy of life-long attachment. At once, many of her peculiarities became intelligible. Fitfulness, unlooked-for changes of mood, misconceptions of words and actions, substitution of fancy for fact,—which had annoyed me during the previous season, as inconsistent in a person of such capacious judgment and sustained self-government,—were now referred to the morbid influence of affections pent up to prey upon themselves. (*M* 2:37)

In *Recollections of a Busy Life*, Horace Greeley quoted Channing's interpretation of Fuller's peculiarities to explain what he found wrong with her, but then translated the latter's Transcendentalist jargon in the direct and concrete idiom of a New York businessman: "If I had attempted to say this, I should have somehow blundered out that, noble and great as she was, a good husband and two or three bouncing babies would have emancipated her from a deal of cant and nonsense." His gross reduction of Fuller's desire to a false goal only reveals what lies hidden in the homage written by her three devoted friends to celebrate the "woman behind the poet": the idea that a happier woman would have killed the poet or, in other words, the idea that Fuller never was a "true" poet. Hawthorne, in a less crude but perhaps meaner way than Greeley's, writes:

> Thus there appears to have been a total collapse in poor Margaret, morally and intellectually. . . . She took credit to herself for having been her own Redeemer, if not her own creator; and, indeed, she was far more a work of art than any of Mr. Mozier's statues. But she was not

working on an inanimate substance, like marble or clay; there was
something within her that she could not possibly come at, to re-create
and refine it; and, by and by, this rude old potency bestirred itself, and
undid all her labor in the twinkling of an eye. On the whole, I do not
know but I like her the better for it,—the better because she proved
herself a very woman, after all, and fell as the weakest of her sisters
might.

In the clash between nature and culture, body and spirit, and matter
and art, the inert, passive, feminine part has the upper hand, condemn-
ing "poor Margaret" to her biological destiny. Years before, in a letter
to her mother, Sophia Hawthorne had expressed the analogous idea
that Fuller's feminism derived from her sexual and sentimental dissatis-
faction: "It seems to me that if she were married truly, she would no
longer be puzzled about the rights of woman. This is the revelation of
woman's true destiny and place, which never can be *imagined* by those
who do not experience the relation."[31]

The author of a biographical portrait of the end of the nineteenth
century, Josephine Lazarus, is equally ready to identify Rome, the place
of conjugal love and maternity, as a turning point in Fuller's life. But
from Lazarus's position of sympathy and esteem for Fuller, especially
for her role as supporter of women's rights, Rome is not where Margaret is finally forced to recognize that her search was mistaken. It is, instead, the place of her liberation:

> But even more than the wife, Margaret was the mother, and she threw
> herself into this new relation with naive, almost childlike fervor. . . .
> Thus, motherhood was the goal for her, the clue to all life's mazes. Her
> whole being was refreshed and born anew with the life of her child. Her
> letters take on a clear, fresh ring, different from anything we have heard
> before, as she prattles of his baby ways and doings; and we hardly rec-
> ognize the tragic, sybilline Margaret, whose freed, joyous spirit soars
> and sings like a bird.[32]

Many portraits of Fuller written by women in the nineteenth century
exalt the experience of maternity as the realization of a repressed femininity, while maintaining their distance from the arrogant and reductive tones of certain masculine accounts. But the union with Ossoli and
her pregnancy become important factors in Fuller's transformation
even for contemporary scholars. Chevigny, for example, interprets them
as instrumental in bringing about a healthy oneness in her separation of
mind and body: "In Italy she took a lover and bore a child, acts of

self-discovery and release which, as we shall see, tended more to complement than to conflict with her political development."[33] By becoming a mother, Chevigny maintains, Fuller gained an even more lucid political self-awareness. The temptation to read Fuller's search for a mother, for an origin, and for a sense of self as a path that culminates in success, confirmed and/or produced by her biological maternity, is strong. The constant tension toward self-interpretation in her writing seems to disappear in the pure pleasure of presence, or in the physical suffering of the body in pregnancy, in the pain for Rome's fortunes, or in her worrying over the contingencies of Ossoli or Angelino. Even the utopian mode of her Roman writings—the sense of a pressing future, a life that grows, hopes that cannot be thwarted—is easily read as picturing a final reconciliation with the feminine through maternity. But I wonder if the thesis of Fuller's course toward the maternal is not ultimately dangerous. Are we not coopting her in a sphere of domesticity whose limits she herself questioned?

How distant is the approach of feminists who emphasize her sexual liberation from that of nineteenth-century biographers? The latter elaborated various strategies of containment and explanation: Fuller the exception, the monstrosity, the half-man, not to mention the "poor Margaret" forced to repress her femininity. In their variety, all these strategies reveal a common structure that aims at neutralizing the danger Margaret Fuller posed. The oxymoronic third element, that which could disrupt sex and gender binarism, is rendered innocuous through absorption in one of the two poles, or through the category of uniqueness, which enormously reduces its potential for cultural criticism. I fear that reading Fuller's maternity as a final synthesis of self-realization implies reducing an excessive, larger-than-life woman to her biological identity. In this way, of course, Fuller ends up completely harmless.

The Contradictions of the Maternal Body

Fuller became a mother in Italy, it is true, but she had impersonated the role of mother and adopted a maternal voice as a rhetorical strategy capable of articulating a discourse for women much earlier. I am referring principally to her relationships with her students and with women who participated in the Conversations, mentioned above. But in the past she had taken over also a more concretely maternal role, closer to the kind of caretaking that biological motherhood generally entails. As the oldest daughter of a large and by no means rich family, Fuller had often assumed part of her mother's duties and tasks, especially those that involved rearing her siblings for which she alone was responsible. At her father's death she also took over the "masculine" role for the family, becoming its breadwinner, and she combined it with the one she already had as a moral and spiritual advisor, which appeared more typically feminine. As an adult she extended her capacity for caretaking—with a facility that does not coincide with the image of the severe and egocentric old maid that even now seems common—to all the children with whom she came in contact, from her sister's daughter (her namesake who shared her birthday) to Una Hawthorne, Waldo Emerson, and Pickie Greeley.

In the ambivalent portraits painted by friends, Fuller is at times depicted as arrogant, aggressive, egocentric, and domineering; at other times she is described as sensitive, attentive, and capable of listening to others. These portraits often reveal her incredible capacity to develop relationships of particular intimacy, above all with other women, children, and servants. Sometimes it is like a second portrait surfacing just beneath the first, without the authors perceiving the contradictory nature of their memories. Horace Greeley, for example, adheres to many of the prejudices of his era regarding Fuller. For him, too, she was a woman of great intelligence transformed by the regime of her father into an invalid incapable of finding the right outlet for her "natural" female desire for motherhood. Yet without realizing it, he offers us a scene that sheds light on Fuller's maternal competence:

> There was no assumption of precedence, no exaction of deference, on her part; for, though somewhat stately and reserved in the presence of strangers, no one "thawed out" more completely, or was more unstarched and cordial in manner, when surrounded by her friends. Her magnetic sway over these was marvellous, unaccountable: women who had known her but a day revealed to her the most jealously guarded secrets of their lives, seeking her sympathy and counsel thereon, and were themselves annoyed at having done so when the magnetism of her presence was withdrawn. I judge that she was the repository of more confidences than any contemporary; and I am sure no one had ever reason to regret the imprudent precipitancy of their trust. Nor were these revelations made by those only of her own plane of life, but chambermaids and seamstresses unburdened their souls to her, seeking and receiving

her counsel; while children found her a delightful playmate and a capital friend.[34]

But, of course, Greeley's view that only a child generated from her body could realize Fuller's desire for motherhood hardly comes as a surprise. In the memories of her female friends and students, Fuller's talent for transforming herself into a means through which the other comes forth and is able to narrate herself clearly emerges. Sarah Freeman Clarke (the sister of James), who at first instinctively resisted Fuller, wrote the following of her:

> Though she spoke rudely searching words, and told you startling truths, though she broke down your little shams and defenses, you felt exhilarated by the compliment of being found out, and even that she had cared to find you out. . . . Many of us recoiled from her at first; *we feared her too powerful dominion over us, but as she was powerful, so she was tender; as she was exacting, she was generous.* She demanded our best, and she gave us her best. To be with her was the most powerful stimulus, intellectual and moral. *It was like the sun shining upon plants and causing buds to open into flowers. This was her gift, and she could no more help exercising it than the sun can help shining.*

In this passage, Fuller almost acquires the features of a mythical mother. She is, like Demeter, exacting and generous, powerfully dominant—to the point that the daughter fears she might be annihilated—and the very soil allowing the growth of the young one. In *Reminiscences,* her autobiography, Edna Dow Cheney speaks of Fuller in a similar tone: "Whatever she spoke of revealed a hidden meaning, and everything seemed to be put into true relation. Perhaps I could best express it by saying that I was no longer the limitation of myself, but I felt that the whole wealth of the universe was open to me. . . . She did not make us her disciples, her blind followers. *She opened the book of life to us and helped us to read it for ourselves.*"[35] If only biological motherhood counted, then vicarious forms of motherhood cannot be compared to the real thing, one might say. But if her contemporaries saw Fuller as an incomplete woman, without a husband or children, and could think of her as a "mother" only when she finally had her own pink bundle in her arms, should we be applying the same paradigm? The feminist narrative that assumes that a pivotal change took place in Fuller's life in Rome and links it to her maternity, even though it emphasizes her new ability to listen and respond to her bodily needs, again strikes me as surprisingly similar to the one produced by advocates of domestic ideology.

Before going any further, however, let me add something about biology, that is to say, about the concrete physical experience that Fuller was living in Rome, which seems to me much more problematic than has been so far recognized. The first consequence of her pregnancy was probably not—it could not be, given the circumstances—the pleasure of wholeness but the extreme discomfort of being confined to bed. Motherhood was accepted at a certain point, but its first effect was the limitation of Fuller's freedom of movement. She was not able to write and had to reduce her public appearances. Then she was forced to leave Rome, the historical theater in which she wanted to play her part. She was also gripped by a number of fears, including those of social censure, childbirth, and her constraining financial situation. In addition, she was alone, bored, and far from both her mother, whose presence perhaps she desired as never before, and those social relationships that were vital for her. As her letters reveal, at a certain point she saw death as the only way out of what seemed to her a "nightmare," and then feared it when the moment of birth was near.

But these were transitory states of mind, which she overcame when the pregnancy ended. In the first months after childbirth she seemed to approach a condition of joyful fusion with the baby, but this changed when she returned to Rome and was seized by worries, doubts, and fear for her son, who had been left in the care of strangers. The letter to her sister Ellen Channing in December of 1849, in which she traced that first year of motherhood, offers a different perspective on her experience as a mother. From it emerges a profound anxiety, an internal conflict that in all probability she had no way of resolving because it was tied to one of the strongest taboos of our society and hers. I am referring to the possibility that women can easily experience motherhood as an unbearable sacrifice of their ambitions, and that their own desires may not necessarily disappear when faced with the child's. The letter is worth quoting at length because it adds another crucial detail to the portrait:

> Still all this I had felt before in some degree [the love for a man]. The great novelty, the immense gain to me is my relation with my child. I thought the mother's heart lived in me before, but it did not. I knew nothing about it. Yet before his birth I dreaded it. I thought I should not survive, but if I did, and my child did, was I not cruel to bring another into this terrible world. I could not at that time get any other view. When he was born that deep melancholy changed at once into

rapture, but it did not last long, then came the prudential motherhood, then came Mrs. Edgeworth, Mrs. Smith. I became a coward, a caretaker not only for the morrow but impiously faithless twenty or thirty years ahead. It seemed wicked to have brought the tender little thing into the midst of cares and perplexities we had not feared in the least for ourselves. I imagined everything: he was to be in danger of every enormity the Croats were then committing upon the babies of Lombardy. The house would be burned over his head, but if he escaped, . . . his father was to be killed in the fighting, and I t[o] die of [ ].[36]

Fuller, like her friends, seems to regard biological motherhood as the real thing, to which nothing can compare: "I thought the mother's heart lived in me before, but it did not. I knew nothing about it." Yet between the lines another story peeps through: "I became a coward." At sixteen, in a letter to Susan Prescott, she had asked with contempt and a confidence in her power to defy petty rules typical of male adolescents at the time, "Now tell me, had you rather be the brilliant De Stael or the useful Edgeworth?"[37] But now she has to come to terms with the fact that a part of her *is* Mrs. Edgeworth. That, in some respects, she even enjoys being the useful Edgeworth, as much as she hates this paralyzing reduction of her social horizon to her unconventional family. Not only is motherhood a nightmare and not, as the ideology of true womanhood would have it, the completion of self, but it also makes one a coward without hopes for the future.

Margaret Fuller had transferred the utopian discourse of American democracy to Europe and in particular to Italy. Now we are left to wonder how she was able to live with the emergence within her of catastrophic fantasies, how she experienced the uncontrollable contraction of a collective political horizon to the exclusively private, personal dimension of a mother worried for her son. The profound conflict Fuller lived, in other words, has to do with the political and social role that she had made hers in Italy. That role now appeared threatened by motherhood, which obliged her to stay near her son, under the assault of a maternal body whose desire for fusion with the child approached the annihilation of self.

Motherhood, then, seemed to force her both externally and internally to renounce any form of autonomous subjectivity. Fuller guiltily managed to summon sufficient reasons for her to leave Angelino in Rieti and return to Rome, but she dreamt of him dying and was consumed with anxiety: "I yet often seemed to hear Angelino calling to me amid the roar of the cannon, and always his tone was of crying" (*M* 2: 301). Perhaps as a strategy of resistance, she identified her own situation with that of the besieged city that must watch helplessly as her sons die. As a strategy that alone could justify her decision to return to Rome, she impersonated the Mater Dolorosa—the figure of a superior, collective motherhood that assumes within itself the pain of all mothers forced to sacrifice their sons to the cause. Fuller identified with the mothers of ancient Rome who incited their sons to return victorious or spread out on their shields. But her effort at sublimation failed. In her letter to Ellen, she goes on to express in ambivalent words that unthinkable thought that she would be free only if her child were dead: "It seemed then I was willing he should die." Of course, she wishes death for her child only because she wants to save him from a more terrible fate. Yet the thought is now there, on paper. At the same time, she cannot think of living without her child: "But when I really saw him lingering as he did all July and August between life and death, I could not let him go unless I could go with him. . . . I resolved to live day by day and hour by hour for his dear sake and feed on ashes when offered."[38] The desire for union with her son, at least for the moment, has won, and the presence of Angelino gives her a sense of wholeness that takes the place of every ambition in the public sphere: "What a difference it makes to come home to a child!—how it fills up all the gaps of life, just in the way that is most consoling, most refreshing! Formerly, I used to feel sad at that hour; the day had not been nobly spent, I had not done my duty to myself and others, and I felt so lonely!" (*M* 2:304).

She decided to leave Rome and then Italy for the United States in search of a tranquil place for her son to grow up in. Her worries about how her friends would welcome her and her child, and especially Ossoli (who was so different from them, so intellectually unarmed, and rich only in his capacity for love, which they would not understand), come up repeatedly in her letters. Her desire for a private domestic life centered on her husband and son comes up as well:

> My relation to Ossoli has been like retiring to one of those gentle, lovely places in the woods—something of the violet has been breathed into my life, and will never pass away. It troubles me to think of going to America. I fear he will grow melancholy-eyed and pale there, and indeed nothing can be more unfit and ill-fated outwardly than all the externals of our relation. I can only hope that true tenderness will soothe

some of them away. I have, however, no regrets; we acted as seemed best at the time. If we can find shelter for our little one, and tend him together, life will be very precious amid very uncongenial circumstances. I thought I knew before what is the mother's heart, I had felt so much love that seemed so holy and soft, that longed to purify, to protect, to solace *infinitely;* but it was nothing to what I feel now, and that sense for pure nature, for the eager, spontaneous life of childhood, was very partial in me before. . . . I should not be sorry to leave Italy till she has strength to rise again, and stay several years in America. I should like to refresh my sympathy with her great interests and great hopes. I should like to do anything I could for people there; *but to go into the market, and hire myself out, will be as hard as it never was before;* my mind has been very high-wrought, and requires just the peace and gradual renovations it would find in still, domestic life.[39]

With this quote I do not wish to support the thesis that Fuller had reconciled herself to the domestic ideal, which she had always seen as suffocating, and was prepared to return to America to become a defender of the sacredness of the home. On the contrary. Many have speculated on her writing after her return to the United States. I would like, more than to read the story of the Roman Republic or her travelogue, to see what type of discourse she would have elaborated as she sought to deal with the conflict between her overwhelming desire for a private life and the equally compelling desire to assume a public role. The latter also would have been a concrete need, forced as she would have been by circumstances to leave the care of their child to Ossoli (perhaps with the help of Margarett Crane), and dedicate herself to the task of being the family's sole breadwinner. A courageous and anticonformist discourse about the various conflicts arising from motherhood, as only the likes of Fuller could have given us, would perhaps have rendered less painful the lives of many women who came after her. I think of Charlotte Perkins Gilman who, because of the same conflict, struggled with depression all her life, not only after childbirth but also after her divorce and her decision to leave her daughter with her husband in order to dedicate herself to the political role of mothering the future society. Things went otherwise. Charles Walter Stetson, Gilman's first husband, commented in his diary that Charlotte had started a course of reading on women, but it seemed only to worsen her state, causing her finally to burst into tears. Among these texts was *Woman in the Nineteenth Century*.[40]

Notes

1. The excessive tendency toward biography in the studies dedicated to Fuller was already noted in 1984 by David M. Robinson ("Margaret Fuller and the Transcendental Ethos: *Woman in the Nineteenth Century*," *PMLA* 97, no. 1), who attributed it to the late twentieth-century evaluation of her, which was based more on an interest in transgressive female figures distinctly different from the nineteenth century's feminine ideal than on a greater contemporary sensitivity toward her writing. That the orientation of the criticism is changing is indicated by the publication in the nineties of new editions of out-of-print texts, such as *Summer on the Lakes*, edited by Susan Belasco Smith, and a collection of Fuller's articles for the *Tribune*, edited by Judith Mattson Bean and Joel Myerson.

2. Christina Zwarg, *Feminist Conversations: Fuller, Emerson, and the Play of Reading* (Ithaca, N.Y.: Cornell Univ. Press, 1995), 1 (emphasis mine).

3. Zwarg refers explicitly to Bell Gale Chevigny and Larry Reynolds, who see the unfolding of a different awareness in Margaret Fuller during her Italian experience. On this subject see Zwarg's introduction in *Feminist Conversations*, 1–31, and the chapter dedicated to Fuller's essays on America for the *New-York Daily Tribune*, 189–97. Zwarg's study is based instead on the hypothesis that from the beginning Fuller's principal form of intellectual action was cultural criticism exercised through *reading*, and she rejects the traditional idea of Fuller's dependence on Ralph Waldo Emerson, transforming their letters into a sort of conversation in which it is the woman who acts as guide, intellectual trainer, and first addressee of ideas on which the philosopher will later elaborate in his essays. (From this perspective Emerson's famous comment upon learning of the death of his friend in a shipwreck, "I have lost in her my audience," assumes a less presumptuous, however egocentric, tone.)

4. Actually, Hawthorne limits himself to reporting what the American sculptor Mozier, who had had a close relationship with Margaret in Rome, had told him. But in the context of his malevolent portrait of "poor Margaret," as he calls her, this information is another detail in a mosaic that tends to offer an image of Fuller modulated on the concept of falseness. See Hawthorne, *The French and Italian Notebooks*, ed. Thomas Woodson (Columbus: Ohio State Univ. Press, 1980), 156.

5. Zwarg, *Feminist Conversations*, 11.

6. I am thinking, for example, of recent essays whose authors (Jeffrey Steele, Annette Kolodny, Sandra Gustafson, among others, besides Zwarg) agree on the hypothesis that the peculiarities of Fuller's writing—which many women readers continue to find abstract, digressive, ineffective—depend on her search for a feminist means of discourse within and beyond the boundaries of logic-centered language.

7. Adriana Cavarero, *Relating Narratives: Storytelling and Selfhood* (London: Routledge, 2000), 42.

8. Cavarero, *Relating Narratives*, 67, 70, 74. Cavarero sets the scene in New York. In Liz Stanley's account in *The Auto/biographical I: The Theory and Practice of Feminist Auto/Biography* (Manchester: Manchester Univ. Press, 1992), it probably occurs in England, where Stanley lives and teaches.

9. On the problem of the identification of the biographer with her own subject, see Bell Gale Chevigny, "Daughters Writing: Toward a Theory of Women's Biography," *Feminist Studies* 9, no. 1 (Spring 1983): 79–102. Cavarero warns of the empathetic trap that every scene of narrative reciprocity risks sparking, or rather the possibility that the recognition of oneself in the story of another produces an identification that envelops and cancels the other's uniqueness (see Cavarero's chapter "The Necessary Other" in *Relating Narratives*).

10. Bell Gale Chevigny, foreword to *The Woman and the Myth: Margaret Fuller's Life and Writings*, rev. ed. (Boston: Northeastern Univ. Press, 1994). The first edition of the volume was published in 1976 by Feminist Press.

11. Ibid., xviii. The passage from Poe appears in full in Chevigny, *Woman and the Myth*, 162–63.

12. Hawthorne, *French and Italian Notebooks*, 157. As I mentioned in note 4, in his 1858 notebook entry Hawthorne reported Mozier's remarks on Fuller and her husband, but then he went on to elaborate on the American sculptor's gossip, especially on Fuller's strange choice of a "clownish husband." When Hawthorne's notebooks were first published, his wife, Sophia, elided the Fuller passage. The entry became public in 1884, when Julian Hawthorne published it in his *Nathaniel Hawthorne and His Wife*, and provoked a passionate feud between Fuller's friends and her detractors. Julian carefully edited the entry to add objectivity, omitting his father's negative evaluation of Mozier's character as well as his prurient comments on Fuller's sexuality. Thomas R. Mitchell has analyzed the scandal in the context of the late-nineteenth-century making of a national literary canon in "Julian Hawthorne and the 'Scandal' of Margaret Fuller," *American Literary History* 7, no. 2 (Summer 1995): 210–33.

13. *Memoirs of Margaret Fuller Ossoli*, ed. R. W. Emerson, W. H. Channing, and J. F. Clarke, 2 vols. (Boston: Phillips, Sampson, 1852), 1:140 (hereafter cited in text and notes as *M*). This 1840 passage from her diary recounts the mystical experience Fuller had when she was twenty-one, but the questions about her identity are a memory placed imprecisely in her childhood.

14. *M* 2:7. It is superfluous here to recall all the aspects in which Fuller's talent for impersonations, her passion for the theater, and her extreme attention to social performance were revealed. Her theatricality—united with traits considered inappropriate for her sex, like the ability to dominate the conversation, the tendency to attract the attention of others, and a taste for satire and cutting remarks—has certainly contributed to her reputation, especially among her

male acquaintances, for artifice and affectation. ("She was a great humbug," writes Hawthorne. *French and Italian Notebooks*, 156.)

15. *Summer on the Lakes*, in *The Portable Margaret Fuller*, ed. Mary Kelley (New York: Penguin, 1994), 118. I find it interesting that Emerson bestowed an exotic identity on Fuller—whom he tried to keep at a distance in order to save his own serenity from her uninhibited attacks on his privacy—with an ethnic designation characterized by contemporary ideology as racially ambiguous, on the border between blacks and whites: "In the first days of our acquaintance, I felt her to be a foreigner,—that with her one would always be sensible of some barrier, as if in making up a friendship with a cultivated Spaniard or Turk." *M* 1:227. Channing, on the other hand, in his portrait modeled on the paradoxical co-presence of contrasting aspects, both physical and otherwise, writes: "Finally, in the animation, yet *abandon* of Margaret's attitude and look, were rarely blended the fiery force of northern, and the soft languor of southern races." *M* 2:36.

16. Since the publication of *Memoirs of Fuller*, the story of Mariana has been considered to be based on an episode that happened to Fuller at the school of Susan Prescott. Some scholars like Mary Kelley have recently questioned whether the story represents a concrete autobiographical fact and tend to consider it as Fuller's retrospective interpretation of her peers' and teachers' disapproval of her exuberance. In an 1830 letter to Susan Prescott, Fuller recalls a painful episode that the teacher helped her overcome. *The Letters of Margaret Fuller*, ed. Robert N. Hudspeth, 6 vols. (Ithaca, N.Y.: Cornell Univ. Press, 1983–94), 1:160. On a couple of occasions she refers to the story as autobiographical, but that does not exclude the possibility that Mariana is more than anything else "a metaphor for extracurricular lessons Fuller mastered at no small cost." Kelley, introduction to *Portable Fuller*, xiii. Charles Capper, on the other hand, though emphasizing that the account is fictional, notes the similarities between the personality of Mariana and that of Fuller and hypothesizes that the fragment actually refers to some traumatic event at school. The most recent biographies interpret Fuller's parents' decision to remove her from Dr. John Park's prestigious and rigorous Boston Lyceum for Young Ladies and enroll her at Susan Prescott's more conventionally "feminine" female seminary in Groton as an attempt to rein in Margaret's aggressiveness and competitiveness, which were alienating her from her peers. Both Capper and Joan von Mehren attribute the choice to paternal concern regarding the effects that disciplined study had had on Margaret. While von Mehren tends to present it as a sort of belated regret on Timothy Fuller's part, Capper underscores the role of Margaret's mother, who in numerous letters to her husband complained about Margaret's disrespectful and impudent behavior and of her own inability to control her. Capper, *Margaret Fuller: An American Romantic Life*, vol. 1, *The Private Years* (New York: Oxford Univ. Press, 1992), 57–83; von Mehren, *Minerva and the Muse: A Life of Margaret Fuller* (Amherst: Univ. of Massachusetts Press, 1994), 24–27.

17. Fuller, *Summer on the Lakes*, 123. The scene of Mariana's "healing" through the recounting of another woman's painful story, a true illustration of the feminine narrative relationships of which Cavarero speaks, deserves to be cited in full: "'Let me trust you, let me tell you the griefs of my sad life. I will tell to you, Mariana, what I never expected to impart to any one.' And so she told her tale: it was one of pain, of shame, borne, not for herself, but for one near and dear as herself. Mariana . . . heard the story to the end, and then, without saying a word, stretched out her hand for the cup." *Summer on the Lakes*, 125.

18. Fuller, *Summer on the Lakes*, 126.

19. Miranda appears in *Woman in the Nineteenth Century*. The reference to her "masculine" culture and to a magnanimous paternal figure who reared her as a person and not as a woman has of course authorized the autobiographical reading of Miranda; nevertheless, it must not be forgotten that Fuller painted a much less benevolent portrait of her father in her "Autobiographical Romance." In addition, in *Woman in the Nineteenth Century* the presence of a narrative voice that recounts Miranda's story and speaks with her renders the interpretation of the passage more complex.

20. *M* 1:11–42. On the role of mourning and its elaboration in the life and writing of Fuller, see the introduction to *The Essential Margaret Fuller*, ed. Jeffrey Steele (New Brunswick, N.J.: Rutgers Univ. Press, 1992).

21. An excerpt was published for the first time in Chevigny, *Woman and the Myth*.

22. Douglas, "Margaret Fuller and the Search for History: A Biographical Study," *Women's Studies* 4, no. 1 (1976): 54.

23. *Woman in the Nineteenth Century*, in *Portable Fuller*, 251; *M* 1:139, 1:140. Thanksgiving was not yet a national holiday (it was instituted by Abraham Lincoln following a campaign promoted and supported by Sarah Josepha Hale in *Godey's Lady's Book*), but it was clearly a celebration of the founding of the country.

24. Fuller, *Woman in the Nineteenth Century*, 244, 245.

25. Capper, *Margaret Fuller*, 29–32; von Mehren, *Minerva and the Muse*, 11–13.

26. Capper, *Margaret Fuller*, 24–83.

27. Douglas, "Fuller and the Search for History," 44.

28. Among the scholars of the seventies and eighties, Ann Douglas is the one who separates Fuller most decisively from the feminine cultural tradition of the domestic and sentimental, placing her in the "masculine" side of social criticism and history. Given the generally negative opinion of the effectiveness and quality of her writing, shared by Douglas, it must follow that Fuller appropriates a "masculine" discourse which she is however unable to dominate. For a revision of this idea, in which her debt to contemporary sentimental rhetoric is examined, see Sandra M. Gustafson, "Choosing a Medium: Margaret Fuller and the Forms of Sentiment," *American Quarterly* 47, no. 1 (1995): 34–65.

29. Unfortunately information on Fuller's teaching method and especially her Conversations is scarce and secondhand except for scattered references in her letters (in particular the one to Sophia Ripley, August 27, 1839) and in the essay "Bettine Brentano and Her Friend Günderode." On this subject, see Capper, *Margaret Fuller,* 290–306; Annette Kolodny, "Inventing a Feminist Discourse: Rhetoric and Resistance in Margaret Fuller's *Woman in the Nineteenth Century,*" *New Literary History* 25, no. 2 (1994): 355–82; Gustafson, "Choosing a Medium."

30. Letter of April 14, 1850, quoted in Chevigny, *Woman and the Myth,* 400n43.

31. Greeley, *Recollections of a Busy Life* (New York: Ford, Brown, & Co., 1896), 176; Hawthorne, *French and Italian Notebooks,* 156–57; letter of July 1843, quoted in Chevigny, *Woman and the Myth,* 231.

32. Josephine Lazarus, "Notable Women: Margaret Fuller," *Century* 5, no. 6 (April 1893), 923–34.

33. Chevigny, *Woman and the Myth,* 367.

34. Greeley, *Recollections,* 178–79.

35. Sarah Freeman Clarke, in Thomas Wentworth Higginson, *Margaret Fuller Ossoli* (Boston: Houghton Mifflin, 1885), quoted in Chevigny, *Woman and the Myth,* 87 (emphasis mine); Edna Dow Cheney, *Reminiscences* (Boston: Lee & Shepard, 1902), quoted in Chevigny, *Woman and the Myth,* 230–31 (emphasis mine).

36. December 11, 1849, *Letters of Fuller,* 6:292.

37. Letter of May 14, 1826, in *Portable Fuller,* 480.

38. December 11, 1849, *Letters of Fuller,* 6:293.

39. To [?], November 29, 1849, *Letters of Fuller,* 6:283 (emphasis mine).

40. Charles W. Stetson, *Endure,* ed. Mary A. Hill (Philadelphia: Temple Univ. Press, 1985), 352.

II

Italy as Text and Context

5

Mutual Interpretation

Margaret Fuller's Journeys in Italy

BELL GALE CHEVIGNY

Had Fuller fulfilled her youthful dream, she would have accompanied Harriet Martineau to Europe in 1835 when she was twenty-five. But her father's death on the eve of her trip caused a delay of eleven years, years of transformative experience both in Europe and in Fuller. Arriving in time for the great social changes of 1846–50, she was equipped like no contemporary American to understand and interpret them fruitfully to her compatriots. Now she traveled as an accomplished teacher, creator of groundbreaking Conversations for women, analyst of gender relations, translator, editor, travel writer, literary and social critic, and journalist. All this meant that Fuller brought to Europe a richly informed curiosity and commitments to human fulfillment, social equality and justice, and an expansive ideal of democracy. More particularly, her lifelong study of consciousness and its growth made her both uniquely sensitive to changes in European society and susceptible to further emotional and political evolution. After exploring Fuller's understanding of the social origins of consciousness, a process she called "mutual interpretation," this essay examines how this understanding shaped her early career and her responses to events in Italy, both personal and public.

While Fuller shared the Transcendentalist faith that the self is spiritual and participates in universal truths, she had also learned that all knowledge is shaped and limited by our personal experience and our historical moment and place. Fuller's critical intelligence and questing spirit owe much to her struggle as a young woman against her time's rigorous assumption of essential gender differences. Again and again, she counterposed the claims of womanhood and mind, womanhood and action, refusing to foreswear any of these. Her sense of conflict between equal and warring values fed her intellectual predilection to reconceive issues in dialectical terms.[1] To be sure, she was not always consistent, yet her work argues that for the growth of the individual soul, its greatest asset was its complexity—its multiplicity and contradiction. She feared failure, rejection, and even pain less than missing the opportunities they offered to deepen understanding. She understood that our human capacities are malleable and grow if we welcome other perspectives and engage them dialectically, letting them clash and mingle with our own.

An exploration of the implications of mutual interpretation, a supple term favored by Fuller in a wide range of contexts, helps us to cut into her unique receptivity and the ambitious trajectory of her life. Fuller moved toward individuals, groups, and causes with especial alacrity when this dynamic engagement could be brought into play. This career student/teacher was as interested in the ways we blind ourselves as in the ways we see and learn. Alternative perspectives can illuminate, check, and complicate our initial sense of things. "Interpretation" takes various forms, and "mutual" juggles its many senses—reciprocal, joint, shared, and common—as it refers to friendship, travel, journalism, political consciousness, and domestic intimacy. Never defined except by context, mutual interpretation is a dynamic concept, both a disposition of mind and a practice. It variously denotes responses she sought in personal relationships, criteria for cross-cultural understanding, stimuli for the empowerment of women and popular education, goals for social policy, and standards for a deeper international democratic commitment.

Fuller's psychology is rooted in its appreciation of mutuality. She knew herself best relationally: "I need to be called out," she wrote, "and never think alone, without imagining some companion."[2] Further self-knowledge demanded knowledge of the other. Such knowledge was best obtained through a double move like that of empathy—a combination of identification and distinction. "Man is nothing but the desire to feel himself in another," wrote the German author Bettina von Arnim, whom Fuller translated; Fuller would have assented, with this addition: "and the wisdom to discover the uniqueness of that other." The vibrant discovery of likeness and difference yields more faithful perception of the other and sets in motion a re-vision of oneself, which can in turn offer the other a freshly challenging mirror. Mutuality is most available to persons with some affinity or sympathy, and unequal relations preclude it. Fuller was peculiarly sensitive to the misinterpretations of the powerless by the powerful.

In her Massachusetts years, Fuller honed these intuitions in personal relations. "Mutuality" named her ethos of friendship, encompassing reciprocity, openness, equality, and joint experiments; and "interpretation" was a friend's chief obligation. Friendship required the growth of both, and interpretative dialogue—never complete, always in process—promoted it. Friends, she suggested, did not confront one another as physical mirrors, presenting static images in infinite regress; rather, each advanced the interpretation of the other, often literally by projecting the interpretation into the future. Friendship was collusion in prophetic activity—one helped the other to discern "the law of one's being." She met others with what she called "enthusiasm"—a heady but exacting drive to define and advance intimacy—to which few were equal. Differences between individuals, what she and Emerson called the "'foe' in your friend,"[3] excited her to keener understanding but made him withdraw. And Fuller's tendency to impose her ideal on the object of her attentions was not always reciprocated.[4]

Mutual interpretation served Fuller better in her encounters with classes or cultures different from her own. Respecting otherness, the wise traveler, she argued, divests herself as best she can of preconceptions, and seeks to read the alien terrain on its own terms, to find the law of its being. "It is always thus with the new form of life," she writes of the Midwest in *Summer on the Lakes, in 1843*, "we must learn to look at it by its own standard" (*WM* 319). That standard can be learned only in meaningful contact. This comes partly from physical immersion (thus Fuller sought -far too briefly, as she knew—to mix with Native Americans) and partly from engaging the idioms of others. In an attack on cultural imperialism, she put it succinctly (man here meaning human being): "Would you speak to a man? First learn his language" (*WM* 344). When we attend with an open mind, she suggested, we find Native American practices critically interpreting our own; Native American ecology and respect for the land, for instance, reflect on Yankee wastefulness.

A condition and consequence of respecting otherness is heightened attention to the cultural and ideological assumptions one brings to the encounter. Fuller dramatizes this brilliantly in *Summer on the Lakes*, describing how, on her first visit to Niagara Falls, her mind was flooded with images, "unsought and unwelcome," of "naked savages stealing behind me with uplifted tomahawks" (*WM* 317). Finding herself haunted more by colonialist fantasies than by real Native Americans alerted Fuller to the difficulty of "serving as anything other than a standard-bearer for . . . colonial imperatives."[5] The form of *Summer on the Lakes*, juxtaposing her own experiences with citations of white experts, challenges readers to attend to ways they, too, are inscribed by colonial ideology. A poem that closes the volume urges mutuality on the reader: "read me, even as you would be read."

It may be argued that the very absence of mutual interpretation between men and women in her time galvanized Fuller to write *Woman in the Nineteenth Century* (1845). Human evolution itself is for Fuller a joint work-in-progress in which woman's creativity and vision have had much too little scope. "The idea of man, however imperfectly brought out, has been far more so than that of woman," she writes. "She, the other half of the same thought, the other chamber of the heart of life, needs to take her turn in the full pulsation . . . ; improvement in the daughters will best aid in the reformation of the sons of the age."[6] Until woman "unfolds such powers as were given her when we left our common home," human experience is distorted for both sexes. Disabled by disproportionate power, men can neither represent nor interpret women: "not one man in the hundred million," she writes, "can rise above the belief that woman was made *for man*" (*WM* 247). Woman's dependence on man had likewise "prevented either sex from being what it should be to itself or the other."

For woman to "take her turn," she had first to discover her self-dependence. To promote this goal, Fuller offered three kinds of female mutual interpretation. *Woman in the Nineteenth Century*, culling history, mythology, and literature for female interpreters of woman's potential, embodies mutual interpretation. And her argument is that woman can become her own best interpreter, if she prizes her multiplicity, her incorporation of both sides of the "great radical dualism," what Fuller's peers called the masculine and feminine and she termed Minerva and Muse. By engaging her internal dialectic and, in this crisis of history, giving precedence to the Minerva in her nature, woman might become "a radiant sovereign self" and further human evolution. Finally, Fuller's own Conversations for women, conducted in Boston in the early 1840s, represented an organized and systematic form of mutual interpretation.

Very different kinds of mutual interpretation underlay Fuller's objectives in journalism. She characterized her literary endeavors at Horace Greeley's *New-York Daily Tribune*, where she was employed beginning in 1844, as aiding in "the great work of mutual education. . . . ; I never regarded literature merely as a collection of exquisite products, but rather as a means of mutual interpretation" (*L* 5:359). In a review of poems by William Thom, she criticized elitist biases, insisting that literature should be "the great mutual system of interpretation between all kinds and classes of men. It is an epistolary correspondence between brethren of one family," embracing the work both of "nature's nobleman" and the prisoner who writes in "soot and water."[7] The American literature we need, Fuller argued, will cut across ethnic as well as class lines. "What suits Great Britain . . . does not suit a mixed race, continually enriched with new blood from other stocks the most unlike that of our first descent" (*WM* 186). Fuller did not confuse genius with talent; she always sought to enlarge her compatriots' access to great figures like Dante, Goethe, and Shakespeare. And she surveyed current European literature to encourage Americans' cosmopolitan taste. But she also put diverse native works into dialogue with each other in an incipient mapping of a literature that bridged class, racial, and ethnic divides.

The goal of mutual interpretation similarly informed her social criticism for the *Tribune*. While adopting Greeley's essentially liberal Whig agenda—opposition to imperialism, the death penalty, the Mexican War—she also went beyond it in embracing Democratic support of European revolutions.[8] Fuller was drawn to explore the living conditions of women and marginal groups like prisoners, the poor, the mentally ill, Jews, Irish immigrants, and slaves (with a review of *The Narrative of the Life of Frederick Douglass*). Her reaching out to include many kinds of people and experience while protesting failures of democratic policy contributed to her evolving feminist and democratic vision. Her translations from immigrant newspapers (including possibly the earliest mention in the U.S. press of Marx and Engels) and her attention to struggles against European autocracy gave the question of U.S. fidelity to its mission additional urgency.[9] Increasingly opposed to the expansionist doctrine of "manifest destiny" as enacted in the Mexican War, Fuller envisioned a national destiny more committed to equality and an inclusive democracy at home and an international democratic movement. With this eclecticism, this myriad outreach, Fuller was reinterpreting herself as a committed and activist intellectual. By expanding her readers' social consciousness, she was encouraging them to demand an elastic and emancipatory democracy, to respect and protect the rights of all, and to resist U.S. imperialist gestures. The shared conception, or radically democratic ideological consensus, that Fuller hoped to forge with her readership is yet another sense of mutual interpretation.

When Fuller did at last go abroad in 1846 as the *Tribune*'s foreign correspondent, she had thus already given much thought to the importance of sympathetic interaction with other consciousnesses, other social classes, and other cultures. Indeed, while still in New York City, she had begun traveling—literally to the prisons of Sing-Sing and Blackwell's Island and figuratively across the social divides her writing sought to reduce. Such dual voyaging accelerated and gained a sharper social focus when her travel to other societies provided her with social alternatives to her homeland and its political consciousness. In Great Britain and France, for example, she reported on public baths, public laundries, workers' schools, and day-care centers that might be adopted at home.[10] More tellingly, Europe shocked her into deeper class awareness. "Poverty in England has terrors of which I never dreamed at home," she wrote, yet we know that she had visited the slums of New York's Five Points (*SG* 88). Ideological growth explains the change. What her deep-seated adherence to U.S. democratic rhetoric had made her perceive as inequity at home, European traditions of social criticism made her begin to conceive in revolutionary terms. America's myth of itself insisted on harmonious classlessness, while European awareness of class made the notion of class struggle inescapable.[11] How consistent or sophisticated her class awareness became we cannot know in the absence of her final manuscript on European revolutions. But it led her to celebrate as "glorious" Paris's social revolution of February 1848 and to hold it up as a mirror to her countrymen so that they might "learn in time for a preventive wisdom . . . the real meaning of FRATERNITY, EQUALITY . . . , [and] learn to reverence . . . the true aristocracy of a nation, the only real nobles . . . , the LABORING CLASSES."[12]

Fuller would write this from Rome; she neither witnessed the Paris uprising nor considered it at length in any surviving manuscript. Though her writings are punctuated with allusions to a more far-reaching critique than that of either the French social visionary Charles Fourier or the Italian republican champion Giuseppi Mazzini, the richest example of mutual interpretation would center on her personal engagement with Italy and the Italians.

Three influential encounters—with the exiled Mazzini in London, the Polish poet Adam Mickiewicz, and the novelist George Sand in Paris—readied her to hit the ground running in Italy. Embodying her principle of mutual interpretation, each held up an interpretative mirror that enlarged her consciousness—of Italy's suffering and hopes, of her right to passion, and of what she called "acting out her nature" by following her desires. Meeting Sand, whose work Fuller had long championed, though with regret for her moral lapses, was a drama of personal mutual recognition and reinterpretation. "Il me fait de bien de vous voir," Fuller said in all accuracy. Sand's "expression of goodness, nobleness, and power"; of "large and so developed" character; and of "rich," "prolific," and "ardent" "genius" personified the comfortable fusion of man's mind and woman's heart that Fuller had always longed for. And Fuller's stress on Sand's womanhood—"I liked the woman in her . . . very much: I never liked a woman better"—suggests that Sand's presence was reinterpreting "woman" for her, confirming woman's right to exploit all her talents. Sand's multiple liaisons were thus reinterpreted: "She might have loved one man permanently," Fuller wrote, had she found one to "interest and command her throughout her range"; failing that, she had "naturally" and often changed lovers. Sand "needs no defence," Fuller concluded, "but only to be understood, for she has bravely acted out her nature." Fuller later explained her own liaison with Giovanni Ossoli in the same language: "for bad or for good, I acted out my character" (*WM* 361–62, 487). She had followed her own injunction and read Sand as she would be read.

In Italy at last in the spring of 1847, Fuller found the place and people suited for her most sustained experiment in mutual interpretation. "The Italians sympathize with my character and understand my organization as no other people ever did," she reported. On another register, she added: "Italy receives me as a long lost child, and I feel myself at home here" (*L* 4:299, 4:293). Her entry into Rome was a psychological homecoming: she was returning to the scene and people of her earliest study, performed as a child with her long-lost, much mourned, father. Her reading of Roman heroes, undertaken initially to please her father, had shaped her character and colored her dreams. "I kept their statues as belonging to the hall of my ancestors," she had reflected at thirty, "and loved to conquer obstacles, and fed my youth and strength for their sake" (*WM* 41). This complex intimacy—father and child and difficult dream—was stirred to life by her being in Rome, with the difference that she was now grown and freer to continue to grow than she had ever felt in her father's custody. Rome—as she later wrote of Mazzini—was the natural haven of "orphans of the soul."[13] Thus, even before she felt Ossoli's love or engaged the Italian people, Rome released Fuller's capacity for love, happiness, and even rapture as no other place had done. To understand her Roman experience—her feeling for the city, its denizens, and its social struggle—we must see them as suffused by her enlarged emotional responsiveness. Where love earlier had made Fuller volatile and extravagant, it seemed now to make her more steady and clear-eyed. All manner of Roman experiences contributed: she wrote often, for example, of St. Cecilia, whose image conveyed "the sense of an inexhaustible love—the only love that is much worth thinking about" (*SG* 241). Her intellectual life and her political analysis, even when fierily indignant, were informed by her fresh access to love.

Still eight separate states in 1847, Italy was suffused with nationalist fervor. Some of Fuller's closest Italian friends supported the priest Vincenzo Gioberti, who proposed a loosely federated Italy under a liberal pope, but she and Ossoli shared Mazzini's dream of a unified republic. Yet Fuller was moved by the early liberalism of the new pope, Pius IX, manifest in his proclamation of amnesty for political prisoners and his creation of a civic guard, and she watched closely to observe his interpretation of Italy's fate.

In June 1847 she resolved to break away from her companions' tour and make a home in Rome, seeking explicitly "to know the common people" and "to live with their life" (*L* 4:276, 4:277). Only in this way, she believed, could she achieve the mutual social interaction that she so highly valued. "We have just had glorious times with the October feasts, when all the Roman people were out," she wrote to her brother Richard that autumn; "I am now truly happy here really in Rome, so quiet and familiar." Her vantage point had shifted, quite literally, from lofty alienation to engagement on the ground, "no longer, like the mob, a staring sight-seeing stranger riding about finely dressed in a coach to see the Muses and Sibyls" (*L* 4:310). With deliberate irony, this misled elite with its uniform responses becomes for Fuller a "mob." To learn how to live economically and speak demotic Italian (in Florence the intellectuals spoke French), she sought immersion in the local life. She reveled in the prospect of an unlimited stay in "this country, dream of my heart and realization of my mind." "To any one who can feel," she added, "it must be torture merely to travel to Italy and give a passing stare at the beautiful body without ever having time or peace to come in contact with its soul" (*L* 4:305–6). Having "experienced the different atmosphere of the European mind," she reflected, "I suffer more than ever from that which is peculiarly American or English," and she sought a "divorce" from it (*L* 4:310). The "divorce" was accelerated both by her growing intimacy with Ossoli and her emerging desire to become a from-the-bottom-up historian of the Italian struggle.

Fuller's internal travel had resulted in a drastic relocation, an apparent shift of loyalties and identification regarding both class and nationality. (Her process of "naturalization" would intensify and become a double-entendre when, pregnant by Ossoli, nature itself was Italianizing her body.[14]) But in fact, her growing Italianization deepened and sharpened her Americanness; the metaphor we want is dual citizenship of an unusually interactive kind. In a sense, Fuller Italianized herself for America. Her "divorce" from things "peculiarly American" would enable her to discover how Italian and American concerns were actually married, and to better identify America's peculiar needs. While her *Tribune* dispatches, as Larry J. Reynolds and Susan Belasco Smith show, took the form of a romantic and progressive history of the Italian struggle governed by the idea of democracy (*SG* 27–28), Fuller's lifelong preoccupations with ideology, perception, and knowledge provide a lively subtext. In this subtext she pursues three processes: Americans' learning to see contemporary Italy on its own terms, Italians' learning habits of independent citizenship, and her own capacity to discern both of these. Through mutual interpretation, these processes illuminate one another.

"Rome is an all hacknied theme and by the most accomplished pens," Fuller had written (*L* 4:156). Americans' travel to Rome was vastly more inscribed than travel to Niagara and Indian country, and again Fuller, in applying her method of mutual interpretation, had to learn to move beyond conditioned responses. One response was epitomized by James Fenimore Cooper's 1838 formulation: "The Roman glorifies himself in what his ancestors have been, the American in what his posterity will be."[15] Fuller's experience, by contrast, would lead her to reverse both propositions; she gradually came to expect that Italy's past greatness might be superseded by its imminent future, while America's future seemed threatened by current betrayals of its past promise.

At first she occupied herself in discovering how to see Italy on its own terms, that is, in the context of daily life in the off-season. In effect, Rome itself taught her how to read the city, tempting her to walk without object and make spontaneous discoveries, which she then read about in the evenings. She rejoiced in closing the gap between experience and knowledge. "I study with delight," she wrote to her mother, "now that I can verify everything" (L 4:313).

By December 1847, she had also learned to see beyond "the pitiful, peddling, Anglicized Rome" and to sort out and reconstruct the city's historical layers, which had been "at first so painfully and discordantly jumbled together." With this historical perspective on the city, she first discerns traces of ancient Rome and then, when she concentrates, "the superstructures vanish, and you recognize the local habitation of so many thoughts," she writes. Kings, consuls, tribunes, and emperors flood her mental vision as they did when she was a child, and "the warriors of eagle sight and remorseless beak, return." Then, fighting her Protestant prejudices through intense study, she learns to discern in papal Rome "growths of the human spirit" instead of a seeming "senseless mass of juggleries." Finally she discerns "bright hopes" even in the oppressed darkness of modern Rome (SG 168–69). The palpable historical layering of Rome taught her to think comparatively, to mutually interpret present and past. Her likening of figures like Saint Peter and the fourteenth-century Roman leader Cola di Rienzo to contemporary figures suggests that history is layered like Rome's topography, or that its movement is spiral, returning to echo a past moment, yet with a difference.

The conceit of three Romes continually informs her meditation on a city that grew "not out of the necessities of commerce nor the luxuries of wealth, but first out of heroism, then out of faith" (SG 285), and a third time, implicitly, out of both. Later she would find this third Rome more promising than any other (SG 157, 209). Still later, she noted that Mazzini, entering the Roman Republic, called Rome "the single city . . . privileged by God to die only to rise again greater than before"; he too invoked three Romes—of the emperors, the popes, and the people (SG 263).

Unfortunately, Fuller found that her own fruitful "abandonment to the spirit of place" was "impossible to most Americans; they retain too much of their English blood; and the traveling English, as a tribe, seems to me the most unseeing of all possible animals."[16] In her taxonomy of Americans abroad, Fuller studies what makes the difference in her compatriots' capacity to see. The "servile" American overvalues Europe, the "conceited" American sees nothing there of value, while the "thinking" American is a mutual interpreter, a comparativist like Fuller herself. A kind of dialectical gardener, he is eager to collect abroad "seeds of the Past" that will withstand a "new culture" at home and as hybrids attain new stature. And in order to "know the conditions under which he may best place them in that new world," this exemplary American "does not neglect to study their history in this" (*SG* 165; *WM* 435–37).

Fuller viewed the sculptor Horatio Greenough, who took part in Florence in celebrating Pope Pius IX's 1847 decision to permit creation of a Civic Guard, as such a thinking American "who penetrates beyond the cheats of tradesmen and the cunning of a mob corrupted by centuries of slavery, to know the real mind, the vital blood, of Italy."[17] Characterizing the oppression of Italians as slavery enables Fuller to compare reactionary ideology in the United States with that in Italy: "many Americans in Italy," she writes, "talk about the corrupt and degenerate state of Italy as they do about that of our slaves at home. They come ready trained to that mode of reasoning which affirms that, because men are degraded by bad institutions, they are not fit for better" (*SG* 159; *WM* 433).

Here is a quintessential instance of the dialectical working of mutual interpretation. Recognizing that the same arguments are used against emancipation of Italy and emancipation of blacks at home, and that the causes of "tyranny and wrong are everywhere the same," she criticizes America with new vehemence as "the darkest offender, because with the least excuse," in betraying its highest principles. The Italian struggle, in short, operated for Fuller as a mirror magnifying her homeland, in the process deepening her belated appreciation of the abolitionists (*SG* 165–66; *WM* 438).

In 1848, as a series of revolutions exploded across Italy, France, Austria, and Germany, she found that the spirit of America was more alive in Europe than at home. "My country is at present spoiled by prosperity, stupid with the lust of gain, soiled by crime in its willing perpetuation of slavery, shamed by an unjust war," she wrote, while "in Europe, amid the teachings of adversity, a nobler spirit is struggling. . . . This is what makes my America" (*SG* 230; *WM* 452). This conceit of a portable "America" of the mind, distinct from the reality of the actual United States of the 1840s, signaled her dismantling of a hierarchy grounded in the myth of America's unique destiny; she urged instead an egalitarian cosmopolitanism, which would reposition America morally as one nation among many. The emphasis of Fuller's dual citizenship had shifted; no longer studying Italy to instruct America, she now is committed to tracing the growth of democratic impulse and capability in Italy.

Italians having seized the moral lead from America, Fuller's task as historian of the Italian struggle gained new impetus. Mutual interpretation, in addition to its value in interpersonal and cross-class relationships, and in discerning the impact of Rome's past on its present, now also became a tool of comparative political and social analysis. Fuller now undertook to demonstrate that the Italian people, like American slaves, though "degraded by bad institutions," are "fit for better." Her lifelong interest in social experiment and holistic education had readied her to embrace this challenge. Hence "the people" take center stage in the dispatches. As Reynolds and Smith argue, the romantic historian has a formal need for a heroic protagonist, and her commitment to Mazzini's cause and rhetoric further heightened her interest in "the People" (*SG* 30). Finally, her privileged knowledge and experience, through Ossoli, of that innovative proving ground of popular sovereignty, the Civic Guard, made the people a natural and desired object of study.

In this way Fuller took on a role that in some respects anticipates the suggestive description of the organic intellectual that Antonio Gramsci would later frame in his *Prison Notebooks*.[18] Both shared a comprehensive philosophy that privileged experience over theory and process over product. Gramsci preferred "organic" intellectuals (members of an emergent social class who elaborate that class's self-consciousness about culture, politics, and economics) to "traditional" elitist intellectuals (who so long represented the dominant social group that they fancy themselves autonomous). In the American West and in New York, Fuller had already abjured the contemplative role to become (in Cornel West's formulation) "part of a social movement by nourishing and being nourished by the philosophical views of oppressed people themselves."[19] With Italians, however, her identification became more pronounced than with any other group except women. A transnational organic intellectual, she practiced a mutual interpretation that would reinforce the

Italians' growing national consciousness while feeding an emerging radical democratic and internationalist consensus in America.

This was no easy task. Americans' ideological fixation on Rome's past greatness blinded them to its contemporary struggle and, more fundamentally, to the role of the Italian people as agents in that struggle. As Brigitte Bailey observes, Italy was "constructed by American tourists as a posthistorical, feminized, and aesthetic realm—outside and opposed to the modern world of rational, masculine agency and progressive history."[20] The reigning representation of Italians in picturesque genre sketches, as lacking in agency as the landscape they adorn, was so inscribed in the American gaze that even supporters of Mazzini and Italian unification illustrated their texts with such images.[21]

While Fuller's aesthetic appetite remained intact, her capacity to see Italians as agents grew steadily during her years in Rome, and indeed her aesthetic excitement increasingly derived from popular expressions of political initiative. What she calls "that beautiful poetic manner peculiar to this artist people" drew her attention when it indicated a growing capacity for independence (*SG* 158; *WM* 433). This growing capacity appears both in traditional festivities, where, Fuller writes, "the thought, the feeling, the genius of the people have had more chance to expand, to express themselves . . . than anywhere else" (*SG* 180), and in spontaneous celebrations, for instance, of the pope's 1847 reforms. Fuller writes of "the continual hymn in the streets of Florence, in honor of Pius IX," of "extempore concerts" and "rejoicings at the theaters."[22] In Rome she detailed the people's adaptation of the traditional carnival feast of the *moccoletti* (tapers) to celebrate revolutionary victories in 1848: instead of competing to extinguish the tapers, they held them aloft, while "clanking chains, emblem of the tyrannic power now vanquished by the people" (*SG* 210–11).

Mutual interpretation had its limits. Fuller's respect for the Italian people developed gradually and not altogether consistently. In her first Italian dispatches, Pius IX seemed to be Fuller's "heroic protagonist" almost more than the people. Although never failing to note the irreconcilability of "Reform and Priestcraft" (*SG* 205), Pius IX's early reforms moved her, as they did the Italian people, to believe in his inherent goodness. His bounty touched her orphaned spirit, and she wrote: "It makes me very happy to be for once in a place ruled by a father's love" (*SG* 169). While she never believed that the moderate Giobertian approach would "suffice to lead Italy to her goal," she nevertheless saw it as "an onward, upward road, and the people learn as it advances" (*SG* 160). Hence, she wrote of the people's early enthusiasm for the pope: "I saw with pleasure their childlike joy and trust" (*SG* 155; *WM* 432). The term "childlike" was less condescending for Fuller than it might seem to a modern reader, especially given her own trustful yielding to Rome at this time, which she also characterized as childlike.

Moreover, she believed that popular responsiveness to the stirrings of reform represented the shaking off of slavish cynicism and a receptivity to education. Fuller consistently attributed the "ignorance of the people" to "centuries of the worst government, the neglect of popular education, the enslavement of speech and the Press" (*SG* 225). It would be alleviated by "enlightened minds . . . , elder brothers, and guardians of the lower people," especially after the creation of the National Guard, which permitted "free interchange of thought between the different classes." Meanwhile, she noted approvingly the people's learning of "prudence" and their "singular discretion" in distinguishing minor from major affronts (*SG* 157, 187). To be sure, Fuller sometimes did condescend: in the Italian countryside, though she claimed to love the people, she found their ignorance "amazing." They regarded her, she writes, as "a divine visitant,—an instructive Ceres,—telling them . . . legends of the lives of their own Saints" (*L* 5:86).

But, in early 1848, when uprisings in Milan and Venice and news of Prince Metternich's flight following a revolution in Vienna produced a wave of troops swarming north from Tuscany, Naples, and Rome, Fuller wrote of the people without a trace of condescension. In fact, despite foreigners' skepticism, the Roman people now teach her their virtues, including courage in battle and generosity in giving all they have to support the troops. Fuller delighted in the serial embarrassments of her favorite foil, a "bristling" Englishman. When Sicilian rebels gave the lie to this individual's assertion that "this people would not fight," he retorted that the Sicilians were exceptional, and that in Lombardy, Italian cowardice would be revealed. But when the Milanese also fought, the Englishman argued for the superiority of Lombards to Romans, who couldn't do without their *minestra*. Fuller then documents the Romans' marching without food (*SG* 213–14). The analogous doubt in the United States about slaves summoning courage to fight for their liberty was here implicitly addressed. (Harriet Beecher Stowe would soon assail this doubt in *Uncle Tom's Cabin* as would Thomas Wentworth Higginson, Fuller's future biographer, in an 1861 essay.)

Next, and despite himself, the pope taught the people the contradiction inherent in papal nation and nationalist pope: as nationalist, he had blessed the banners of the troops rallying to fight oppression by Catholic Austria; upon reflection as Catholic, however, he retracted his support. The shock forced the people to depend on themselves. A Bolognese boast Fuller had cited about the Italians' "vivacious genius" proved true: "We are unhappy but not stupid. . . . We can learn as much in two months as other nations in twenty years" (*SG* 157). The erstwhile "children" become keen observers of the pope's serial abandonment of his promises and even then give him the benefit of the doubt until, in November 1848, they are pushed beyond endurance.

Continuing her close observation of public events and popular response, and interpreting their larger meaning, Fuller details a series of affronts: the cardinals mislead the pope, the pope insults the people by elevating the treacherous Pellegrino Rossi to become Home Minister in September 1848, Rossi withdraws the new popular rights and calls on "the troops of the line," not the National Guard, to defend him. In narrating the assassination of Rossi on November 15, 1848, Fuller's emphasis is on restraint and unity. She frames the stabbing as a work of mutual accord between the citizens of the National Guard and the regular troops, who remained inactive and silent until evening, when they marched with the people, singing, "Happy the one who rids the earth of a tyrant." Fuller, who did not witness the scene, takes instruction from it: "I never thought to have heard of a violent death with satisfaction, but this act affected me as one of terrible justice" (*L* 5:146–47).

The next day, when the Swiss Guard fired on the people seeking to meet with the pope at the Palazzo Quirinale, the carriage of Prince Barberini with its "liveried retinue" rushed past Fuller's house to the shelter of the palazzo's courtyard. Seeing this, Fuller's servant Antonia exclaimed, "Thank Heaven, we are poor, we have nothing to fear!" This identification of poverty with safety was for Fuller the fundamental promise of this revolutionary moment. It was, she hoped, "a sentiment which will soon be universal in Europe."[23]

The pope's subsequent flight from Rome offers another invaluable lesson. "'Well, who would have thought it?'" Fuller quotes the people as asking; "'The Pope, the Cardinals, the Princes are gone, and Rome is perfectly tranquil, and one does not miss anything, except that there are not so many rich carriages and liveries.'" To this she adds: "The Pope may regret too late that he ever gave the people a chance to make this reflection." Even one of the class of "unheeding cabbage-sellers" rouses himself to scorn the pope's cowardly abandonment of his convictions (*SG* 243–44, 250). (Fuller later observes people beginning to question even the necessity of the priesthood.)

Fuller's twin themes, Americans' inaptitude and Italians' great aptitude for learning, come together in her account of the events leading up to the proclamation of the Roman Republic in February 1849. In Florence, Giuseppe Montanelli (whom Fuller deemed a leader greater than any yet in Rome) won acceptance for Mazzini's plan for a constitutional assembly. Montanelli magnanimously deferred to Rome, "a sister city, still more illustrious than ours," as the appropriate venue for the assembly. Welcoming Mazzini's thought as soon as they understood it, Romans proved themselves deserving of suffrage. "A few weeks' schooling" at popular meetings, clubs, and in conversation with the Civic Guard prepared Italian citizens to vote for the assembly "in larger proportions than at contested elections in our own country" (*SG* 255).

"I rose and went forth to seek the Republic," Fuller wrote after the February proclamation, with the joy of a woman going to meet her beloved (which the republic was for her) and the assurance of an ambassador, which she uniquely was, as a representative of the America she hoped to help bring into being. (In a future century, she announced in the *Tribune*, she herself could have been appointed ambassador.) "Over the Quirinal I went, through the Forum to the Capitol," she says, marking the monuments of papal and ancient Rome on her way to republican Rome *rediviva*. Her narrative then centers on the problem of perception. A British observer imperially dismisses the event, hoping "to see all those fellows shot yet." Fuller expects better from a thoughtful American artist passing his first winter there, but he, too, had "'no confidence in the People.' Why? Because 'they were not like our People.'" During the reading of the decree announcing the end of the papacy and the birth of "a pure Democracy" she looks to the American for "an answering glance . . . , a little of that soul which made my country what she is." But he remains impassive. "Receiving all his birthright from a triumph of democracy, he was quite indifferent to this manifestation on this consecrated spot." He is blind to the American spirit being reenacted before him because its source has withered in his complacency. Worse, he sneers that "the people" are not taking part, only soldiers. "Soldiers!" Fuller exclaims. "The Civic Guard; all the decent men in Rome" (*SG* 245, 256).

Like this representative American, the United States, too, fails to respond, sending neither an ambassador to the republic nor a token of sympathy, despite Fuller's beseeching pleas, even after French troops mount their attack in April 1849. Surrogate ambassador of a better America, she continues as historian; as nurse to Rome's defenders; and, in defeat, as prophet. Although her confidence would flag, it is initially dialectical: "Temporary repression will sow the seed of perpetual resistance," she wrote hopefully. Similarly she writes that democracy ought to "bless" French perfidy, English inertia, and the Russian invasion of Hungary: "Young Europe will know next time that there is no possible compromise between her and the old" (*SG* 306, 313).

Indeed, it would be soldiers—"only soldiers"—who would vindicate Fuller's profoundly democratic belief in the essential human drive for emancipation. "Only soldiers" in Italy would rise again to the occasion (though with more moderate political goals) in 1859. In the United States four years later, following the Emancipation Proclamation, African Americans, "only soldiers," would discover their dignity and their courage in fighting for freedom and (though not all of this would be won) for a more expansive, more radically democratic, fuller and Fuller-esque America.[24]

—⟨⟩—

Fuller did not live to see those battles, but she survived the fall of the Roman Republic at the end of June 1849 by a little over a year. In this year, Italy and its people would continue to hold up an interpretative mirror. But if the mirror was now less political, it was even more intensely emotional. Rome had given Fuller access to feeling, and though the republic fell, she carried her emotional reality out of the wreckage. First Mazzini's self-presentation during the French siege showed Fuller her limits. "Mazzini had suffered millions more than I could," she wrote. Despite his "fearful responsibility," the perishing of "his dearest friends," and his precipitous aging, he remained "full of a more fiery purpose than ever; in him I revered the hero, and owned myself not of that mould." The "noble courage" and "noble patience" of the wounded in hospital further humbled her (*L* 5:247–48).

Yet Fuller's sufferings, if less than these, were considerable. The "holocaust of broken hearts," as she called the fall of Rome, redefined her as one who suffered. Caring for the dying men in the hospital, she

wrote, she "forgot the great ideas to sympathize with the poor mothers."
More tellingly than their sons, these mothers became reciprocal reflections of Fuller herself, cut off from news of her baby, Angelino, being
cared for by a nurse in Rieti, fifty miles from Rome, yet sometimes
seeming to "hear him calling me amidst the roar of the cannon." Fuller
saw herself as a Mater Dolorosa, in anguish about her child and seeking
consolation in caring for youth who had "died worthily." But this consolation was short lived. Overwhelmed by feelings of loss, she imagined
Angelino surviving childhood only to become, twenty years later, "one
of a glorious hecatomb," sacrificed in some imagined future struggle (*SG*
264; *L* 5:258, 5:293).

When she found Angelino near death at Rieti, however, he became
the distilled focus of her suffering and offered yet another dialectical
mirror. "He still wanders feebly on the surface between the two worlds,
inclining, I fear me, most over the abyss." Near physical and emotional
collapse, she felt, "I could not let him go unless I would go with him."
After waiting a month for his first smile, she considered him a "treasure
lent" and resolved to live each hour for his sake. Her own will to survive
now depended on his well-being: "When we look on the sweet face of
our child, we think if we can keep him, we shall have courage for whatever we may have to do or endure" (*L* 5:248, 5:293, 5:266).

The recovering child would help his mother reinterpret her past and
her future, with Florence, where the Ossolis took up residence in September 1849, as the site of this final unfolding. A stopover in Perugia
boded well. Fuller wrote celebrating the beauty of the September vintage, the garlanded grapes, the fields "animated by men and women,"
and then of her new pleasure in the city, "so cheerful and busy after
ruined Rome." Florence sheltered a small but nourishing social circle,
some of whom she saw alone, and several of whom Ossoli enjoyed as
well. Taking quarters in the Casa Libri on the Piazza Sta. Maria Novella, which she loved, she rejoiced most in excursions with Ossoli—a
man happiest in woods and meadows—to the "sunny heights near Florence." As in Rome, it was a revelation to explore on foot. Roving with
responsive companions on the New England coast, in Concord, and in
the Midwest, Fuller had always recovered an expansive sense of well-
being, both animal and soulful, and she never had needed it more than
now. Angelino, taken on outings to the Cascine, a large public park,
blossomed into "rosy health." "The air of Florence agreed with him,"
she wrote, "and that made me love Florence" (*L* 5:265, 5:278, 6:70).

Whenever she gave her political feelings voice, however, what she considered the cowardice of Florence blighted her spirits. In October 1849 she expressed homesickness for the political vivacity of the Roman people before their defeat, when "the artistic genius of the people displayed itself at every moment by some refined symbol, some glorious pageant; never in any place or time was every day life so poetical." In Florence, by contrast, "simple life seems not so great." In her penultimate dispatch to the *Tribune,* in November 1849, she reported on Italian resistance elsewhere but of Tuscany she noted only the abandonment of the liberal cause, the new constraint on press, and the priests preaching against liberty. The Austrian occupation, welcomed only by "the rabble of boys in the streets, and the ladies of England," sickened her: "It is painful to see what a quantity of valuable objects the Austrian soldier has to sell. Their depredations must have been very great." And in her final dispatch, dated January 6, 1850, one finds this lapidary remark: "Tuscany is stupified." By March, however, she remarked in a letter that "the Tuscans reluct more and more at finding themselves Austrian subjects," even though "the contegno [behavior] of the Austrian troops . . . is wonderfully discreet." At a performance of Bellini's *I Puritani,* the substitution of the word "beata" (blessed) for "liberata" (liberated), she wrote, made the people hiss in the Grand Duke's presence (*L* 5:274, 5: 69–70; *SG* 319, 322). Yet even such mild acts of defiance appear to have been rare.

Political observation fades in Fuller's surviving correspondence, partly out of fear of surveillance ("we study to give no umbrage") after the police threatened their right to stay. To what extent she spent time in Florence working on her history of Italian revolutionary movements is difficult to discern. In October 1849, Joseph Mozier, an American sculptor living in Rome, proposed a quite different writing project: a series of letters from Florence. Fuller warmed to the idea—"a natural way for me to earn money," giving her indispensable exercise and "life in the open air" while replicating her "delightful" study routine in Rome, now amplified by family life. "If, after the morning care of the baby, and an hour's study we went out and at the end of our walk, saw with care and love something good, then I gave the later hours of the eve[nin]g to writing some remarks upon it, it would suit us exactly." Though Mozier apparently failed to follow through, the prospect of harmonizing writing and domestic intimacy—seeing "with care and love something good"—points to a shared plenitude rare in her experience.[25] Mutual interpretation, the goal of sympathetic understanding that had served her so well in her approach to Roman history, in understanding the turbulent Italian events of 1847–49, and in comparing American and Italian politics, now again took on for her its primal meaning: the spiritual understanding between two people, to the enhancement and enrichment of both.

In the discipline of writing private letters from Florence, Fuller staved off despair and crafted, while defining, the plenitude of her new life. Ossoli offered the solace of having shared first the dream of the republic; then the terrifying defense of Rome ("I saw blood that had streamed on the wall close to where Ossoli was"); and, finally, grief over the destruction of their hopes. As she wrote to Samuel Gray Ward, "He has suffered enough to understand what I feel, yet at the same time his disposition is so gentle and I may say in the strictest sense so pious, that it reacts easily" (*L* 5:293, 5:278). Mutual interpretation abounds between them in a dialectics of grief. Mirrored in Ossoli's irreparable loss, Fuller's own loss was tempered, shedding some of its harshness. At the same time, his capacity—through gentleness and piety—to "react," or recover, mirrored a spirit that Fuller was learning to accommodate.

Fuller so stressed Ossoli's difference from herself that his influence on her may go unnoticed. Lacking education and intellectual life, he was, unlike her, "delicate"—very reserved in verbal expression—and "retiring," marked by purity and strength of character. She distinguished Ossoli's love from the sorts she had known earlier, mixed as they were with "fancy and enthusiasm excited by my talent at embellishing subjects." Ossoli, by contrast, "loves me from simple affinity." He taught her a new idiom, a language at once deep and so quiet that she had to abandon her performative eloquence and the drives behind it in order to hear and begin to sound it. That this language was native to her childhood, if undercultivated, is hinted when she writes that no one, "except little children and mother, loved me as genuinely as he does" (*L* 6:53, 5:300). Ossoli's evocation of her mother's love (and his anticipatory love for that Margarett, her mother) met elemental longings in Margaret, and allowed her own tenderness to emerge and grow.

Fuller acknowledged how much she owed Ossoli in a November 1849 letter that alludes to her failure to meet her own heroic self-expectations during the siege of Rome: "I have been deeply humiliated finding myself inferior to many noble occasions, but precious lessons have been given, and made me somewhat better, I think, than when you knew me." The tempering of her fierce demands on her self, the conversion of humiliation into humility, even the emergence of self-acceptance, is explained in her next sentence. "My relation to Ossoli has been like retiring to one of those gentle, lovely places in the woods—something of the violet has been breathed into my life, and will never pass away" (*L* 5:283).

While "mutual tenderness" and "mutual solace and aid" sustain the couple, a growing tenderness and humility appear also in her reflections on others. She expresses candid regret for "hasty judgments" (of the English poet Arthur Hugh Clough, a supporter of the Italian Revolution) and her failure to extend unqualified support to the maligned Edgar Allan Poe or to her mother in her widow's grief. One senses an acceptance of limits, an end to the idealistic striving and straining that had always made her "anticipate" her life. She finally allowed herself the repose she desperately needed, and with it an opportunity to reflect. In her letters, exploration of feeling seems to displace the political analysis that earlier consumed her. As winter's chill recedes, visits to the Uffizi elicited this tantalizing observation: "I feel works of art more than I have ever yet. I feel the development of my own nature as I look on them; so many hid meanings come out upon me" (L 5:285, 5:289, 5:298, 6:68).

But it was Angelino whose recovery was most responsible for Fuller's own. Despite her devoted rapport with several children, Angelino inspired feelings previously unknown. Sometimes they were spiritual: "I play with him, my ever-growing mystery," she wrote, "but from the solemnity of thoughts he brings, is refuge only in God." Others were psychological: To "come home to a child," she wrote, "fills up all the gaps of life, just in the way that is most consoling, most refreshing . . . I feel infinite hope for him—seeing how full he is of life, how much he can afford to throw away, I feel inexhaustibleness of nature and console myself for my own incapa[city]." The unfolding chemistry of her relation to the baby afforded intricate reinterpretations of her past. First it reunited her with her own mother and allowed her to recuperate the nurturing power of her childhood: The baby sits on his stool as "I sat on mine," she writes to her mother, "between you and father." And Angelino mirrored and helped her to recover what she had lacked—the freedom to be a child, by eliciting a "sense for pure nature, for the eager spontaneous childhood, [which] was very partial in me before." The child's vitality and love helped her to recover from a "fatigue of soul" she had felt "even in childhood." Insofar as she was able to contemplate their return for a few years to the States, she committed herself to keeping their experience of this freedom alive there (*L* 5:294, 5:280, 5:299, 5:283, 5:278).

Fuller, however, never contemplated this return with pleasure. As Florence had reinterpreted her self-understanding and fed her emotional growth—her new tenderness, her acceptance of herself and others, her love of nature and spontaneous feeling—so did her hard-won happiness depend on the family's remaining in that city. Prizing their "interval of peace . . . as the halcyon prelude to the storm," her thoughts of change were at best stoical, and, more often, grim. Imagining her homeland, she feared for Ossoli's well-being except in the countryside or with her mother and a few "true" friends. She feared for her precarious stability: "To go into market and hire myself out will be hard as it never was before," she wrote; "my mind has been very high-wrought, and requires just the peace and gradual renovation it would find in still domestic life." She feared for the child, about whom something was not right. And the thought of the sea voyage always came twinned with thoughts of death, especially Angelino's. With uncanny prescience, Fuller mirrored the future's final interpretation of her life when she wrote at the beginning of this remarkable last year: "If he dies, I hope I shall, too. I was too fatigued before, and this last shipwreck of hop[es] would be more than I could bear" (*L* 5:299, 5:284, 5:246).

The cook of the *Elizabeth* is said to have reported that when the ship was breaking apart off Fire Island, Fuller said, "I see nothing but death before me."[26] Appreciating Fuller's need of mutuality and knowing how profoundly she had found it in Italy, we can imagine that she saw neither homeland nor "America"—that both lay behind her across the ocean and in the unrecoverable past. The shore before her neither knew her now nor promised her the growth that for her was inseparable from life itself. All that remained to her was the mutual interpretation of death.

Notes

I am grateful to the American Academy in Rome for its hospitality, enabling me to research Fuller's Italian experience in 1998 and 1999, and to Antonella Bucci for research assistance.

1. See Bell Gale Chevigny, "To the Edges of Ideology: Margaret Fuller's Centrifugal Evolution," *American Quarterly* 38 (Summer 1986): 173–201.

2. *The Letters of Margaret Fuller*, ed. Robert N. Hudspeth, 6 vols. (Ithaca, N.Y.: Cornell Univ. Press, 1983–94), 6:193 (hereafter cited in text and notes as *L*).

3. Bell Gale Chevigny, *The Woman and the Myth: Margaret Fuller's Life and Writings*, rev. ed. (Boston: Northeastern Univ. Press, 1994), 125 (hereafter cited in text and notes as *WM*).

4. Ellery Channing, for instance, was made uncomfortable by her "too ideal" expectations: "You will always be wanting to grow forward," he wrote her; "now I like to grow backward too." *WM* 107.

5. According to Susan Gilmore, "Margaret Fuller 'Receiving the Indians,'" in *Margaret Fuller's Cultural Critique: Her Age and Legacy*, ed. Fritz Fleischmann (New York: Peter Lang, 2000), 194, 221.

6. Fuller, *Woman in the Nineteenth Century*, ed. Larry J. Reynolds (New York: W. W. Norton, 1998), 12.

7. Perry Miller, ed., *Margaret Fuller: American Romantic* (Ithaca, N.Y.: Cornell Univ. Press, 1963), 215.

8. Judith Matson Bean and Joel Myerson, eds., introduction to *Margaret Fuller, Critic: Writings from the* New-York Tribune, *1844–1846* (New York: Columbia Univ. Press, 2000); *WM* 290ff.

9. In August 1845, Fuller translated Heinrich Börnstein's discussion of Karl Marx, Arnold Ruge, and Friedrich Engels; see *WM* 294.

10. Fuller's interest in these experiments was stimulated by her reform-minded Quaker friends Marcus Spring, a wealthy merchant and philanthropist, and his wife, Rebecca. Fuller, *"These Sad But Glorious Days": Dispatches from Europe, 1846–1850*, ed. Larry J. Reynolds and Susan Belasco Smith (New Haven, Conn.: Yale Univ. Press, 1991), 7–11 (hereafter cited in text and notes as *SG*).

11. Elsewhere I contrast Fuller's quietist retreat from the 1842 Dorr Rebellion in Rhode Island, a tumultuous popular uprising demanding an end to property limitations on the suffrage, with her militant support of the assassination of Pellegrino Rossi by the Italian mob to illustrate this evolution of Fuller's ideology. See Chevigny, "To the Edges of Ideology."

12. *WM* 446; *SG* 211. For Fuller's ideological growth, see Chevigny, "To the Edges of Ideology."

13. "Rome was the theme of his thoughts, but, very early exiled, he had never seen that home to which all the orphans of the soul so naturally turn." *SG* 263.

14. Her (perhaps conscious) pun when, secretly pregnant, she wrote from her L'Aquila retreat in the Abruzzi mountains about her book on revolutions, suggests a mind/body fluidity, conflation of her two creative expressions: baby and book: "It grows upon me." As mother and historian of revolution, she doubly nurtured the future of Italy. *WM* 384.

15. See William Salomone, "The Nineteenth Century Discovery of Italy: An Essay in American Cultural History," *American Historical Review* 78 (June 1968): 1359–91.

16. *SG* 132. The absurdly blind Englishman appears frequently in her dispatches, a foil to the implicit seeing American she would make of her reader. In Fuller's time, Italy and England were U.S. tourists' destinations of choice, and she strives, for her country's own sake, to turn its attention from conservative England to promising Italy.

17. Italian nationalists welcomed the Civic Guard (later called the National Guard) as the beginning of a patriotic army that could defend Rome against Austria; they also saw Pius's action as a defeat for papal advisors who opposed the Civic Guard as a potential breeding ground of antipapal agitation.

18. *Selections from the Prison Notebooks of Antonio Gramsci*, ed. and trans. Quintin Hoare and Geoffrey N. Smith (New York: International Publishers, 1983). Elsewhere I have written of Fuller acting as an organic intellectual in her New York journalism; see Chevigny, "'Cheat me [On] by No Illusion': Margaret Fuller's Cultural Critique and Its Legacies," in Fleischmann, *Fuller's Cultural Critique*, 27–41.

19. West, *The American Evasion of Philosophy: A Genealogy of Pragmatism* (Madison: Univ. of Wisconsin Press, 1989), 231. It is a provocative fact that Gramsci's notion of the intellectual's role grew out of his study of the Risorgimento, though he focused chiefly on its latter phase (1859–60), when the Moderates absorbed the Action party of Garibaldi. John M. Cammett, *Antonio Gramsci and the Origins of Italian Communism* (Palo Alto, Calif.: Stanford Univ. Press, 1967), 214. Fuller attends to those whose growing political self-consciousness led them to oppose the moderates in the earlier, and far too brief, period. Her "membership" in this group was, of course, based on ideological sympathy.

20. Bailey, "Representing Italy: Fuller, History Painting, and the Popular Press," in Fleischmann, *Fuller's Cultural Critique*, 232.

21. Bailey cites the art critic Henry Tuckerman and the *United States Magazine and Democratic Review* in this regard. Ibid., 230.

22. *SG* 159–60. Verdi's series of operas about tyrants so filled the air, allegorizing, orchestrating, and accompanying events, that she complained "there is little hope of hearing in Italy other music than Verdi's." *SG* 180.

23. *L* 5:147. Later, in fact, when the Roman Republic was under siege, Fuller would write that she could go from one end of the city to the other, among the poorest denizens, "alone and on foot," for political dignity had rehabilitated even the criminals: "[The Roman's] energies have true vent; his better feelings are roused; he has thrown aside the stiletto." *SG* 284.

24. Fuller makes the equation again in July 1849, asking W. H. Channing, who had "felt so oppressed in the slave states," to "imagine what I felt at seeing all the noblest youth, all the genius of this dear land, again enslaved." *L* 5:247.

25. *L* 5:278. See *SG* 34, on the rejection of her book idea by London publishers, September 5, 1849; *SG* 3n, on the announcement of its near completion in the *Boston Republican* in January 1850; and *L* 5:278 and 5:283: "I had a promise of employment here, but the promiser seems to have forgotten it."

26. Fuller, *At Home and Abroad, or Things and Thoughts in America and Europe*, ed. Arthur B. Fuller (1856; repr., Port Washington, N.Y.: Kennikat Press, 1971), 446.

6

The Unbroken Charm

Margaret Fuller, G. S. Hillard, and the American Tradition of Travel Writing on Italy

JOHN PAUL RUSSO

The earliest American tradition of travel writing on Italy was actually a New England tradition, and it grew out of the fact that so many New Englanders followed one another to Italy in the first half of the nineteenth century, leaving a wealth of journals, letters, travelogues, newspaper articles, aesthetic commentaries, poems, fiction, and anecdotes. On a spring day of 1833 Emerson counted fifteen Bostonians in Rome's Piazza di Spagna. In 1852 fourteen Lowells were visiting Rome; James Russell Lowell said he was "going abroad to become acquainted with his family."[1] Many travelers aimed to recover the lessons of an old country for the purpose of educating a young one. With their eclectic intellectual roots in the quasi-aristocratic, neoclassical eighteenth century as well as in the neoromantic, broadly bourgeois tradition of self-culture, they placed instruction above entertainment, though they knew their message of cultural improvement had a better chance of success if it were leavened with pleasure.

Washington Allston followed up his studies at Harvard with a long period in Italy (1804–8), gathering impressions and deepening his knowledge of the classical world. He would write the first novel by an

American with an Italian setting (*Monaldi*, 1822; pub. 1841); "profoundly influenced by his experience there, Allston more than any other American may be said to have introduced that country [to Americans]."[2] Though in 1814 George Ticknor complained of being unable to locate a single Italian grammar in Boston, the Boston Anthology Club was stimulating interest in Italian studies through its *Monthly Anthology* (1803–11). The founding of the Boston Athenaeum in 1807 furthered these goals; its holdings of Italian travel books would become so extensive that shelf sections would be labeled by individual cities and towns, a proud reminder of Italophilic Boston in the past two centuries. The first issue of the *North American Review* in 1815 contained a spirited defense of the Italian language against the Abbé Prévost's attack.[3] Jared Sparks, the future president of Harvard, lamented the exclusion of Italian "from the catalogue of acquirements necessary for an accomplished scholar" and promoted it over French: the Italian language is "vastly better adapted to every species of composition, than the French . . . it has more dignity and strength, a greater felicity of expression, and infinitely more sweetness and harmony."[4] The *North American Review* from its first issue in 1815 to 1850 and the *American Quarterly Review* in its brief career (1827–37) published more essays and reviews on Italy than on any other European country except England. George Bancroft and William H. Prescott were in Italy between 1817 and 1821, not as Grand Tourists, but as students of its culture. Doubtless Italy impressed them with a sense of sweeping historical panoramas, which would inform their own monumental works.

Epitomizing the tradition up through the 1850s, Henry Wadsworth Longfellow, James Russell Lowell, and Charles Eliot Norton are the Big Three against whom Margaret Fuller and G. S. Hillard may be compared and contrasted. Essentially, the Big Three pose a series of structural oppositions between Italy and America: aristocratic, hierarchical, traditionalist culture vs. modern, democratic, industrial society; Catholicism vs. Protestantism; individuality vs. Tocquevillian leveling; the free, spontaneous, expressively theatrical, and anarchic vs. the artificial, the socially imposed, and the increasingly rationalized and administered (under the guise of capitalist freedom); female vs. male; leisure or (indolence) vs. work (and time keeping); past vs. future.[5] In their definition of the natural, they assign a high value to pleasure, anticipating by several generations the harsh critique of the "genteel tradition" in American culture by George Santayana and Van Wyck Brooks.[6] "There are always two aspects of Italy,—" writes Norton in a classic statement on the conflict; "the one which makes its appeal to the poetic imagination": this is the land of smiling nature and magnificent art, of "splendour" and "poetic and historic associations which add a deeper charm to the beauty of the scene." The other Italy captures our "immediate sympathies, with a sense of the pathos of the lives" of the people, with the "squalor" in its towns and cities, and with a culture in intellectual and social decline. The two Italies "conflict with each other" but, he adds, "each intensifying the other."[7] The antitheses stood out in high relief.

The New Englanders write as exiles from themselves, from a buried life to which, as they think, Italy will help gain access. They connect the discovery of Italy with self-discovery. A psychic topography of extremes and contradictions, an Other that strangely mirrored aspects of themselves, Italy brought to the surface deep-seated fears and desires as its visitors attempted to come to terms with themselves and achieve unity in their intellectual and emotional life. Because the country is so ancient and, just as importantly, continuous in its historical deposits down to the present time, it mixes life, death, and rebirth in ways that are suggestive and homologous to an individual life. It is hardly fortuitous that "Renaissance" and "Risorgimento," the two concepts most often identified with modern Italy, contain the rebirth metaphor. For this reason Italy is like the golden bough in Virgil, a safe-conduct pass enabling the travelers to cross from one world to the other. Norton's wish, "If I ever come back, may I be born Italian," expresses a death-and-renewal theme common to American travelers in Italy.[8] He had retrieved the historical past of his culture, as it were a voyage to the classical underworld; coming to terms with the past, and amid a rich plenum of sensory experience, he felt reborn mentally and emotionally, and in touch with the deeper currents of his life, expressed in terms of "coming back" or returning home. "It was with a homesick sinking of the heart that I left Italy," confesses Norton; imagining himself back (home) in New England, he is "homesick" for Italy.[9]

In a similar vein Lowell writes that "there is no country, perhaps, with which we are so intimate as with Italy," where *intimate* (from the Latin for "innermost," "secret") suggests a very close relation, bordering on awe (as in Wordsworth's "Intimations of Immortality") and not excluding the dark side of existence. In a grove of giant olive trees, perhaps a thousand years old, he sees and hears in their "wildest contortions," as in Dante's forest of suicides, the "fearfully human." The Romantic distinction between self-enhancing solitude and painful, alienating lone-liness enables Lowell to elaborate upon a familiar topos: the "solitudes of Rome . . . are without a parallel; for it is not the mere absence of man, but the sense of his departure that makes a profound loneliness." Yet there is not only death, but also renewal: an American is "at home in Rome" but at the same time feels "more intensely American every day"; the sense of difference collapses as the underlying wholeness is per-ceived. Lowell's many references to Italy as an "Eden" convey the sense of a prelapsarian garden where one "rejoices in the recovery of his own individuality," that is, one's "natural self."[10] In "Cambridge Thirty Years Ago" Lowell recalls his quaint, provincial background and de-clares in an *ésprit de synthèse* that "an orbed and balanced life would re-volve between the Old and the New [Worlds] as opposite, but not antag-onistic poles."[11] While the spheral image expresses the ideal of a rounded education and varied life, there is a utopian coloring in the *not* antagonis-tic poles. He wants the best of both worlds, though surely the author of the *Bigelow Papers* knew that equilibrium, wholeness, and self-knowledge are won by closer understanding of the extremes and the dialectic inter-play between them ("each intensifying the other").

The New Englanders returned home feeling restored to them-selves; their Italian sojourns had provided the balance they found lack-ing in America; and they had been given the central clue to their educa-tional mission.[12] For all three writers, Italy is so old that it makes them feel, by contrast, like children; but on the other hand, Italy is the child-hood of the West and its present inhabitants are themselves the chil-dren, and the adults are the Americans and foreign travelers like them. In this sense, Italy stands apart from England, France, or Germany, each of which played a leading role in shaping modernity after the Renaissance. Though the writers admired the medieval Italian com-munes for their independence and economic aggressiveness and ex-tolled the Renaissance achievement in art and literature, they found present-day Italy sadly wanting in the virtues of commerce, efficiency, political nerve, republicanism, and domesticity. The very idea of the modern Italian struck them as oxymoronic. Yet if Italy was not the land of modernity, it furnished them with experience on the pulse by which they could examine, condemn, and resist what they regarded as the evils in modernity: the loss of individuality and ironing out of difference, vul-gar materialism, bigness, the rush of time, the artificiality and crudity of manners. When Italy finally unified itself, attempted to modernize, and

unveiled its Washington in the heroic, anticlerical, republican Garibaldi, these Americans who previously protested Italian tyranny, poverty, indolence, superstition, and vice turned about and longed for pre-
Risorgimento Italy. They hated aspects of it, they attacked it, yet they
preferred it.

George Stillman Hillard (1808–79) approached Italy in an objective
spirit, well suited to his writing a comprehensive guide. After graduating
from Harvard, he embarked on a career in law and letters, but a high-
pitched voice prevented his making his mark in the age of American
oratory. A Jacksonian Democrat, he served in the Massachusetts House
and Senate, and held down the Boston office of his radical classmate
and law partner, the abolitionist U.S. Senator Charles Sumner. When
Hawthorne, of whom he was the close friend and personal attorney, was
in financial straits, he came to his aid by raising a fund among Boston
literati. Hawthorne admired the "classic refinement of Hillard's culture."[13] In 1872, in failing health, he was chosen first dean of the Boston
University law school. In its time his *Six Months in Italy* (1853), in two volumes (887 pages), was "probably the most popular book about Italy
written by an American"; it went through twenty-one editions before
1900.[14] John Lothrop Motley said that "nothing can be more scholarly
and elegant than the whole expression of his book"; "his pages have the
effect of finely coloured photographs of the scenes he has visited."[15]
Today it ranks as among the finest travelogues in English in the past two
centuries.

Six Months in Italy covers more ground than the work of Hillard's
fellow Italophiles. While the Grand Tour provides him with a mighty
frame (Milan, Venice, Florence, Rome, Naples), he is far more ambitious in branching out to the smaller cities and towns (Verona, Parma,
Arezzo, Lucca, Todi, Pisa): "Life, indeed, is short, and art is long, and
all things cannot be seen; but thrift and resolution can do much, and let
[travelers] not fail to see Perugia and Assissi [*sic*]."[16] His interests included religion, economics, agronomy, and hospitals as well as art,
architecture, and popular culture. A monograph-length study of travel
writing on Italy, which concludes the book, is the first of its kind in
English, as if he wanted to place himself in the line of (mostly) northern
European visitors to the south.

In a tour extensive even for six months, the tireless Hillard warns
against mental exhaustion in one of his typically homespun metaphors:
"As an overcrowded trunk cannot be shut, so an overcrowded mind

falls short of its natural capacity of retention. . . . Choose what seems most interesting, and let the rest go" (*SM* 1:100). Happily for posterity, Hillard would not let things go. Thus, on Rome and the Campagna, almost half the entire work, he advises not to hurry with epigrammatic force: "The Rome of the mind is not built in a day" (*SM* 1:203). His polished, lawyer-like paragraphs are arguments studded with facts. He encouraged preparing for Italy by a course of reading on winter nights: "the more learning the better; but a little is not dangerous" (*SM* 2:454). With its sententiousness, alternation of Latinate and Anglo Saxon diction ("natural capacity of retention," "let the rest go"), energetic movement, alliteration, balance, and antithesis, his style shows the influence of Samuel Johnson (perhaps the strongest on any American style). He conducts his readers as if they were Rasselas and Nekayah touring Cairo:[17] "many things must be forgotten, in order that a few may be remembered" (*SM* 1:249); the Trevi Fountain "sounds worse in description than it looks to the eye. . . . we begin with criticism, but we end with admiration" (*SM* 1:413); "let no one, therefore, who is meditating such a journey be discouraged by the amount of what he cannot do; but rather take encouragement from the thought of how much can be done" (*SM* 2:454).

Hillard reaffirms the central themes of the New Englanders on Italy: the sense of plenitude, spontaneity and love of play, sobriety, realism, individuality, lack of hypocrisy, natural vivacity, and courtesy even among humble *contadini*. As he says, "that unconscious enjoyment of the mere sense of existence, which . . . was to the benevolent mind of Paley the most convincing proof of the goodness of God, is stamped in expressive and unmistakable lines upon the general Italian face" (*SM* 1: 48). Hillard also echoes the Italophilic contempt for customs officials, thieving coach drivers, "dirty inns, bad dinners, comfortless sleeping-rooms, bells that will not ring, servants that will not come, and horses that will not go"; an Englishman "exchanges quiet efficiency for noisy inefficiency" (*SM* 2:272). The numerous beggars, the "dark shadows which haunt all the bright points" (*SM* 1:190–91), appall his humanitarian conscience. Moreover, as William Vance comments, he is "almost unique in American travel books of the period" for his study of the agricultural conditions of the Campagna.[18] The politically liberal Hillard deplores the current scene, examining the historical origins of the latifundia, land management, absentee ownership, middlemen, depopulation, and malaria; and he condemns the "grasping spirit of the favored classes" (*SM* 2:76), the "enormous capitalist" (*SM* 2:73). For contrast, he points to Boston's relation to its thriving suburbs. "We have no right to look upon a landscape only as a picture, or to view it merely as a harvest-field for dreamy emotions" (*SM* 2:72). Again, his lawyer's eye did not fail him.

Limited contact with Italians not connected to the business of traveling prevented Hillard, no less than his predecessors, from breaking through some of the stereotypes. The Italian nature is "rich in the various modifications of sympathy, but poor in the products of principle" (Johnson again); "amiable, vivacious, good-natured," with "instinctive sympathy," yet "passionate and vindictive" (*SM* 2:237). Like most American travelers, he did not move outside Anglo American circles, mixing with "agreeable English society" (*SM* 1:175) in Florence but not with the Florentines, and remarking on English children in the Boboli Gardens, not Italian ones. Like many Anglo Americans, he would choose Florence (for its supposed bourgeois coziness) above all Italian cities as a place of residence (*SM* 1:182). In Naples the image of the adult Italian as the natural child takes on a negative coloring. The lower classes resemble the "inmates of nursery," "grown-up children," "civilized savages"; their only verb tense is "the present" (*SM* 2:181–83)—they yield to impulse.

Insufficiently knowledgeable of the medieval period, the classically trained Hillard sees only a deep gulf separating ancient Rome and modern Italy ("strength to softness, power to emotion," the "masculine" Latin language to "feminine" Italian [*SM* 2:267]), and not continuity and preservation.[19] Oddly, Hillard does not mention John James Blunt's *Vestiges of Ancient Manners and Customs, Discoverable in Modern Italy and Sicily* (1823), and it was almost too soon for him to have taken advantage of the rising interest in the middle ages. "In Italy, strangers seem to be at home, and the natives to be exiles" (*SM* 1:184). Had he understood the natives better, however, he would have realized that they are not "exiles" in their own land, uncomprehending of their heritage of classical paganism and Christianity and (what he likely means) unworthy of it. Rather, the contemporary Italians are the only possible piece that fits the historical puzzle. Yet, like the Big Three, he is right that many foreigners found themselves "at home."[20] In the heyday of the Empire, thinks the Anglophilic Hillard, the English are the "legitimate descendants of the old Romans" and "stalk over the land as if it were their own" (*SM* 2:267–68). In 1851 William Ware, a fellow Bostonian, said that "the old Roman, in truth, survives not in any of the Italian family; and if any where on the face of the earth now, in the modern Englishman." A few years later, Lowell would say that "we [America] represent more truly the old Roman Power and sentiment than any other people.[21]

"Vulgar Protestant cant" (*SM* 2:144) over Roman Catholic clergy and festivals offends Hillard's tolerance. Travelers are urged "to look upon pope, cardinal, and monk, not with a puritan scowl, but as parts of an imposing pageant, which we may contemplate without self-reproach, though without approving" (*SM* 1:204). The English are scolded for their "countenance of irreverent curiosity," "careless deportment," and "inveterate staring" in churches (*SM* 2:270); Hillard's Anglophilia was obviously not uncritical. He denounces the "sneering protest" against the "mummeries of superstition" (*SM* 1:332) and ridicules those economy-minded Protestants who wander through a noble church worrying that something might have to be paid for to be visited. He argues on behalf of the ritualism and public quality of Italian religious life: "the Romish Church, especially, is wiser in providing so much more liberally for that instinct of worship which is a deep thirst of the human soul." The boxed pews of New England churches are synecdochic of social hierarchy, personal coldness, and privacy compared to the inviting, spacious interiors of the Italian ones that permit easy mixing (*SM* 1:330–32; cf. 2:190, 230). Also, the Italian churches are much more frequently open.

Hillard's taste was formed before the massive cultural shift pioneered by Ruskin and the Pre-Raphaelites (the Brotherhood was founded in 1848, the very year Hillard was in Italy). Though Hillard respected *Modern Painters*, it failed to open his eyes.[22] Generally he adhered to the standard and taste of his times, without, however, succumbing to dryness and rigidity or losing his distinctive voice. On his view, Greco-Roman classicism is succeeded by a long blank; then Giotto; then another blank, with a few exceptions; then, the peaks of Italian art, Raphael and Michelangelo, and their successors; then gradual decline in the seventeenth century. After insightful pages on classical sculpture in Florence and the Vatican, he skims over medieval art and architecture.[23] St Mark's in Venice is a "strange jumble" whose interior is "too crowded and too dark" (*SM* 1:41), and San Zeno in Verona "left no impressions" (*SM* 1:89); these are two of the most important churches in Ruskin. Ghiberti's Baptistry Doors, declared worthy of being the "Gates of Paradise" by Michelangelo, are the "inadequate result of forty years of labor" (*SM* 1:132), and Luca della Robbia's glazed terra-cotta ceramics suggest

"soup tureens and tea drinking" (*SM* 1:165). There is too much Quattro-
cento love of the concrete detail. His observation that the "exclusive ad-
mirers of Christian art . . . the Pre-Raphaelite school . . . value an angular
virgin whose limbs look as if they had been cut out of tin, beyond the best
forms of Guido and Domenichino" (*SM* 1:364) reveals an entire aesthetic
or rather two competing aesthetics. In Heinrich Wölfflin's terms, Hillard
prefers the "chastened flow of line," broad volumetric masses, vitalized
spaciousness, economy of detail, inevitability, and compositional integrity of High Renaissance artists over the "abrupt intricacy" of line, angu-
larity, flat planes, realism, wealth of incident and "anarchic" detail, and
"multiplicity" of earlier Italian artists; in terms of Adrian Stokes, Hillard
prefers modeling over carving.[24] Raphael's *Entombment of Christ* (1507) is
the painting at which the Pre-Raphaelites drew the chronological line.[25]
For them, it was the end; for him, the beginning. Yet he leaned to the
Pre-Raphaelites and called it the "gem" of the Borghese, while they "esteem it one of Raphael's highest efforts, and one of the last expressions
of his uncorrupted pencil." Perhaps his admiration owed something to
Ruskin and the Pre-Raphaelites after all, because he clearly distinguishes
himself from more traditional critics who judged the painting "stiff and
feeble, at least in comparison with the artist's later works" (*SM* 1:364).

Set pieces on Michelangelo's Medici Chapel and the Sistine Ceiling,
Raphael's Stanze and *Transfiguration* ("at the head of all the oil-paintings
in the world" [*SM* 1:254]), and Titian's *Assumption;* his chapters on
Roman fountains, palazzi, and the Colosseum; the museum of classical
antiquities in Naples: these passages show Hillard at his best as a travel
writer. He is insightful on classical sculpture such as the Niobe; having
studied J. J. Winckelmann and Gotthold Lessing, he offers an original
explanation of why the Laocoon group aroused such controversy — not
because it epitomizes spatial over temporal art, but because "it stands
upon the very line by which the art of sculpture is divided from poetry
and painting" (*SM* 1:238). Hillard does not like sculpture that is overly
mimetic or tells a story: "when a statue becomes too expressive it ceases
to be statuesque and begins to be picturesque" (*SM* 1:353). The Apollo
Belvedere reveals limitations: "a little of the fine gentleman," "not
enough of the serene unconsciousness of the immortal Gods," less of the
"simple grandeur" of other Greek masterpieces (an allusion to Winckelmann's ideal of the Greek, "noble simplicity and tranquil grandeur")
(*SM* 1:237). He spends most effort explicating the Dying Gaul without
so much as mentioning another piece in the same room, the Marble

Faun, which was to attract Hawthorne ten years later. Hillard may not enlarge the taste of his audience; yet he enriches the taste they already have.

Baroque art receives a conventional disparagement, as Hillard disapproves of three main themes: *violence:* the grasping of the mother's hair is "too violent," her lips "too revolting" in Guido Reni's *Massacre of the Innocents* (*SM* 1:98); *theatricality:* Bernini's baldacchino resembles "a colossal four-post bedstead without the curtains" (*SM* 1:218);[26] and *sentimentality:* "Carlo Dolce is a painter against whom one gets in time to feel a sort of personal spite" (*SM* 1.154–55). Reservations creep into mostly laudatory readings of Andrea del Sarto, Correggio, and the Bolognese school; the Carracci "want vitality" (*SM* 1:99). Against Ruskin, he pleads the case for Domenichino's *Last Communion of St. Jerome*, much admired in the nineteenth century, in terms of the neoclassical antithesis of genius and art: "the fire of genius never burns along his lines; but skill, taste, correctness, judgment, and decorum always wait upon his pencil" (*SM* 1:255). The *Apollo and Daphne* and *David* of the young Bernini have the "natural vigor of his genius" ("*at least* equal to that of Chatterton in poetry"! [my italics]); later works such as the *St. Theresa* and the Chair of St. Peter's show "bad taste and corrupting patronage" (*SM* 1:393). His *Pluto and Proserpina* is both "violent" and "theatrical" (*SM* 1:387); the Fountain of the Four Rivers is "one of the heaviest sins against good taste that ever was laid upon the much-enduring earth" (*SM* 2:45). With his *Venus* Canova aimed for something "more beautiful than beauty" and ended in "affectation": a "veteran belle" hides a blush with a fan, while pecking through the sticks to "observe the effects" (*SM* 1:155). But Hillard admires Canova's statue of Pauline Bonaparte, and comments favorably on the work of Hiram Powers and Horatio Greenough. Hillard is weakest on architecture, especially the baroque: "in the middle of the seventeenth century architecture had reached its lowest state of degeneracy, under the corrupting influence of Borromini" (*SM* 1:359). Yet these are among the most important decades in the history of Italian architecture: Bernini, Longhena, Guarini, Da Cortona—and Borromini.

It would be unfair to hold Hillard's critique of baroque art and architecture against him. Antibaroque sentiment became practically universal in European taste after Winckelmann, and especially in the post-Romantic period. Lowell went through San Luigi without so much as mentioning Caravaggio's Saint Matthew paintings. As late as 1907 Camillo von Klenze blasted the "meaningless grace" of Bernini; he dated the shift away from the taste for the baroque to the final decades of the eighteenth century.[27] Only Jacob Burckhardt toward the end of his career argued for a reassessment of the baroque, which commenced with his pupil Heinrich Wölfflin and Cornelius Gurlitt in the 1880s.[28]

However much they embraced the Risorgimento, the New Englanders remained ambiguous on the subject of technological modernization in Italy. Lowell was delighted by Pius IX's decision against building a railroad from Rome to Civitavecchia: "one would not approach the solitary emotion of a lifetime, such as the first sight of Rome, at the rate of forty miles an hour."[29] Norton complained that the train whistle behind Santa Maria Novella sounded like the one in Fitchburg, Massachusetts. In the first volume of *The Stones of Venice*, which appeared in 1851, two years before Hillard's book, Ruskin decried the 220-arch railway bridge connecting Venice and the mainland for ruining the panorama. However, Hillard defends the bridge in practical, political, and aesthetic terms. It is the "artery by which the living blood of today is poured into the exhausted frame of Venice"; it proves how "wealth and genius are spent in lightening the burdens of common life; the growth of an age of schools, hospitals and almshouses, in which the privileges of the few are giving ground before the rights of the many"; and it extends the "pleasures of travel" to a "continually increasing class" (*SM* 1:86–87). These observations stand out since Hillard rarely mentions politics and never refers to the Roman revolution of 1848, which he had witnessed. Aesthetically, the bridge is also "noble," is "grander from its very incongruity." The "great results and achievements of modern civilization" have "a certain feeling of their own" —he is groping toward the technological sublime, but that bridge will never get there. In sum, the railway bridge that links Venice to the coast connects "the past with the future" (*SM* 1:86–87). The train to Pompeii likewise juxtaposes two different worlds (*SM* 2:125).

Taken together, the travelers' remarks illustrate the changing attitude toward time, of which the train had become the modern symbol: speed, schedules, punctuality, and the rational organization of time. Hillard reports how the train saved him a potentially wasted day. At 10:30 a.m. he went from Livorno to Pisa, spent an hour in and around the cathedral, took the train to Lucca for the afternoon, then retraced his steps and was back in Livorno at 6:30 p.m. That the train was manufactured in Philadelphia was "a small dividend contributed in the shape of the useful arts, by the new world, towards paying of that great debt of gratitude which all mankind owes to Italy for what it has done in the fine arts" (*SM* 2:339). Yet the day's impressions produced blurred pages. The emphasis falls on the schedule out of which he makes a kind of game. He ignored Della Quercia's tomb sculpture of Ilaria del Carretto (1408) in the cathedral of Lucca; had he noticed, he would have mentioned it—he speaks of other works there and had read Ruskin's unforgettable description in *Modern Painters* II (1846). The whole focus on speed, schedules, and locomotion adumbrates a broad theme in twentieth-century travel writing, which concerns itself more with the technical means as opposed to the ends of travel.

Hillard's sense of time contrasts with what he and his fellow Americans find so characteristic of Italians: their love of leisure (or in Fuller's phrase, being "indolently joyous"), appealing to the extent that it does not become outright laziness.[30] "Time is of no value, and the whole movement of life is adagio" (*SM* 2:101), writes Hillard; the people of Terni "strolled about in a leisurely way, as if they had a great deal more of the capital of time than they knew how to invest" (*SM* 2:314); oral culture requires "abundant leisure" (*SM* 2:230); and so forth. When he compares the villagers of the Alban Hills with those of rural New England, time as organization and gadgetry is a key factor: "in handiness and management, in labor-saving contrivances, in the adaptation of means to ends, in economy of time and labor, [the Italians] are lamentably, ludicrously deficient" (*SM* 2:238). Still, Hillard approaches the question from both sides, as when he lounges at a cafe in St. Mark's Piazza: "a week of such evenings leaves very pleasant recollections behind" (*SM* 1:47). At such a table, in what Napoleon called the drawing room of Europe, he may have recollected the noisy streets of downtown Boston: "it was agreeable to one coming from our restless country to breathe for a while the soothing atmosphere of repose—to see men sitting quietly in their chairs, and evidently not struggling against an impulse to whittle at the arms by way of safety-valve to their nervous unrest" (*SM* 1:47). Yet Hillard is no Lambert Strether after his conversion, such pleasure being virtuous only if it rewards "discipline" and "struggle" (*SM* 1:47).

One consequence of modernization that Hillard noticed in the Italy of the 1840s was the weakening of individuality and particularism. The "racy traits of life and character which so much impressed the travellers of a earlier period, are fast disappearing" (*SM* 2:174). The *lazzaroni* in Naples are gone, owing to the "greatly extended net-work of communication between Naples and the rest of Europe, by means of the increased facilities of travel" (*SM* 2:174). "Are gas lamps, cheap calicoes, and railways inconsistent with Titians and Sansovinos?" (*SM* 1:57). Perhaps so: Hillard disliked foreigners' bourgeois bonnets with their "bold staring front and incongruous ornaments" in contrast to the "beautiful headdresses" and veils of the local Italian women (*SM* 1:90; cf. 2:25): "before a bonnet the poet drops his pen, the sculptor his chisel, and the painter his brush."[31] While the old world was on the wane, Italy was not reaping the benefits of the new, and he doubted whether in its present state of "half slumber and half despair" it could throw off foreign controls and the weight of its past to join the ranks of modernity. "As we have no past, so Italy seems to have no future"; "poor in thought and action" (*SM* 2:317), it lacks "opportunity" (*SM* 2:452). As such, it is no permanent place for an American (except perhaps an American artist) so that a side benefit of Italian travel is to find "fresh cause of gratitude for having been born where he was."[32] A moderate sojourn (six months?) enlarges the mind and raises the spirits (and relaxes the American nerves), but "the image of Italy dwells in our hearts like that of a women whom we have loved" (*SM* 2:450).[33]

Like Hillard, Margaret Fuller was steeped in Italy's "great past"; unlike him, she believed in its "great future" (*L* 4:295). Hillard was an "old acquaintance" of Fuller's long before they met in Rome in April 1848, when she entrusted him with a small mosaic to take home to her mother (*L* 4:61, 68, 103). She had earned the soubriquet of the American Corinne by New Englanders for her superior culture, her feminism, and her linguistic ability, even before she went to Italy and became even more deeply identified with the Staëlian heroine. She did not live to write an Italian travel book, nor do we know how seriously she may have contemplated one. In October 1847, after six months of touring, she said, "I begin to know as well as to feel" about the country to the point where "a book would be too short" (*L* 4:305–6). Another time, praising Rome, she admits it is "useless to try and write of these things, volumes would hardly begin to tell my thoughts." Then she reverses herself, "the Italian sun has wakened a luxuriant growth that covers my mind"; "Oh how much I might write, if I had only force!" (*L* 5:100–101). Passing remarks on her desire to "gather the fruit of my travels" (*L* 4:301) or write the "narrative of my European experience" (*L* 5:73) may refer to her history of the Roman revolution, or autobiography, not travel writing per se, though some comments are tantalizing. While she cannot present "all the details" of her stay in Ravenna to *Tribune* readers, "I shall write them out some time . . . Padua, too."[34] Each day in Italy, she wrote in 1849, has been "so rich in joys and pains, actions and sufferings, to say nothing of themes of observation, I have never yet had time to know the sum total—to reflect" (*L* 5:283). Her travel sketches in the letters and newspaper dispatches would make a book longer than many travelogues.

If the idea of an Italian travel book crossed Fuller's mind, what form might it have taken? The genre was thoroughly congenial: she had published one such book, *Summer on the Lakes,* and, as Jeffrey Steele comments, "many of her succeeding texts— *Women in the Nineteenth Century,* her New York essays, and her Italian dispatches—were also shaped by the model of travel writing."[35] This plastic, open genre mixes empirical description, historical fact, fiction, commentary, argument, and autobiography; it can absorb almost anything into itself and include a wide range of authorial tones. Fuller, always in need of money, might have been wise to publish such a book because "no other genre of American literature enjoyed greater popularity or a more enduring prominence in the nineteenth century."[36]

Writing in 1845, the year before her traveling to Europe, Fuller theorized on the elements of the genre: a traveler should (1) be "in good health" lest "partial" or "exaggerated" comments arise from a "morbid state"; (2) have an alert, cultivated mind not "too much burthened with theories and opinions"; (3) have knowledge of both science and the fine arts to receive the "peculiar influences and the most expressive features of life in each land"; (4) have "poetic sensibility" and "sympathy" for what is "special and individual in both nations and men"; (5) balance intellectual power to generalize with well-reported particulars, lest "we have only an inference, when we want the facts also"; (6) know that it is the journey, not the arrival, that matters: "the traveler should have no special object in traveling, beyond the delight of new and various impressions, or, if he has one, it should only absorb enough of his time and attention to give earnestness and spring to the rest."[37] A seventh quality, unlisted but exemplified by Fuller herself, is humility: in Rome "you rise in the morning knowing there are a great number of objects worth knowing, which you may never have the chance to see again. You go every day, in all moods, under all circumstances; feeling, probably, in seeing them, the inadequacy of your preparation for understanding or duly receiving them" (*AHA* 258). Fuller singled out Goethe's *Italian Journey,* the supreme masterpiece of European travel writing, and Joseph

Forsyth's *Remarks on Antiquities, Arts and Letters during an Excursion in Italy, in the Years 1802 and 1803* as "two that could not fail to be of great use to the student who wishes really to see the Italy of Italy, and to take, not Italo-American, but Italian views of the garden of the world."[38] Elsewhere she recommends De Staël, William Beckford's *Italy*, John Bell's *Observations on Italy* (1825), and Luigi Antonio Lanzi's *History of Painting in Italy* (1828).[39]

"To speak with any truth of Italy . . . requires *genius*," Fuller writes; "*talent*, which is made to serve most purposes now, entirely fails here" (*L* 4:272). Fuller had the genius to write the truth, first, because of her preparation in Italy's language, history, and culture. She spoke Italian moderately well, enabling her to become close to the people — she would never have been entrusted with a hospital directorship during the revolution if she had not an ability to communicate quickly and accurately. Her method for learning the language is direct and uncompromising: "six months total abstinence from English" (*L* 5:172); "I have been quite off the beaten track of travel, have seen, thought, spoken, dreamed only what is Italian" (*L* 5:251).[40] Her Roman letters tell how she pored over books on the city and Italian history. Watching travelers waste large sums of money, she is disconsolate that she "cannot afford reference books, little journals, many things that would be of great use" (*L* 5:213), such as prints for teaching and lecturing. Ovid's birthplace, Sulmona, had to be passed up, for "the want of a few dollars" (*L* 5:103). When Fuller wanted to buy her sister a gift, she said that an engraving of Titian's *Assumption* is "one of those I should like most, if I had money" (it cost $4.50) (*L* 5:47).

In an essay published many years ago A. William Salomone focused upon Fuller as the "shining exception" among America's passionate pilgrims before 1860 to comprehend the fundamental ideological issues of the Risorgimento, the one who moved beyond what Norton called the "day of Cacciaguida" to embrace the "day of Farinata."[41] How did this come about? She lived in the cities and the countryside; she traveled alone and with friends; she had a balanced interest in the past and the present, and in pagan mythology and Catholic Rome. Her understanding of the present — what would be her special contribution — meant a more than passing acquaintance with Italians, "of all ranks, from the very highest to the lowest" (*L* 4:299), from Belgioioso and Arconati Visconti in Milan, to the central Apennines where "I see no one but Italian Contadines" (*L* 5:74). Her lack of funds, if it had a blessing, brought her nearer to common life: "foreigners cannot live [on a few cents a day], but I could" (*L* 5:149), implying she is no longer a traveler, but a resident.[42] This approach contrasts sharply with Hillard who condescended, "we can no where escape from the debasing associations of actual life" (*L* 1:291). That she was familiar with the extremes (and not only in her hospital work) is well illustrated by an offhand comment, made shortly before she embarked for America, and invoking the Italian topos of splendor vs. squalor: her ship is "laden with mar[ble] and rags, a very appropriate companionship for wares of Italy" (*L* 6:83).[43] One can only speculate whether the heavy cargo of marble contributed to the shipwreck of the *Elizabeth*, which hit a sandbar in a gale off Fire Island in July 1850; Fuller, her husband, and child were drowned.

Though she knew the larger cities, she was, like Hillard, fascinated by the smaller ones, "those true Italian towns, where the old charm is unbroken" (*L* 4:301). The charm is "unbroken" because of the enduring strength of social, cultural, and historical bonds between past and present. That deep organic connection to its past endured longer in Italy than it did in northern Europe and America, and still remains in some measure. In Fuller's terms, Italy will be one of the last places in Europe to break completely with its past. (George Eliot, whose novels explore these hidden links between past and present, similarly understood the Italians in *Romola*, *Middlemarch*, and *Daniel Deronda*.) Siena is "a real untouched Italian place" (*L* 5:43); Vicenza, "a truly Italian town, with much to see and study" (*L* 4:298); Bologna, "full of expression, of physiognomy" (*AHA* 232), "really an *Italian* city, one in which I should like to live, full of hidden things" (*L* 4:291); Perugia, "so much to see which excites generous and consoling feelings" (*L* 5: 265); "Brescia in fact almost all Italian towns" (*L* 5:274). Writing from Rieti where her son was born, Fuller expresses an ideal of happiness: "living peaceably in one beautiful provincial town after another" (*L* 5:254–55). These words, coming near the end of her sojourn, could only have been written by someone who knew Italy well.

The use of the "charm" (or "magic," "grace," "dream") to characterize Italy was common in nineteenth- and twentieth-century travel writing. It refers to the pleasing as opposed to the disturbing and was frequently connected to the feminine; the bourgeois wanted to enjoy themselves without disagreeable associations. This is exactly the kind of word that Santayana would put down as "genteel"; Mary McCarthy fulminates against this breed in *The Stones of Florence*.[44] Yet Fuller did not fall victim to the "tourist gaze," the imaginary of information, opinion, prejudice, and expectation with which the tourist confronts the Other.[45] If charm was all that some tourists felt, it formed only part of her complex response to what is strange, heathen, Catholic, dangerous, and unbidden—the "fearfully human." Stendhal said, "I feel a charm *(charme)* in this country which I can hardly define; it is like love"; and no one would accuse Stendhal of being a bourgeois gazer; far from it, he loved Italy because it was so antibourgeois.[46]

Like Goethe and Ruskin, Fuller stresses the need to see things slowly, "quietly *looking* one's fill" (her italics) (*L* 4:273): this kind of seeing completes a physical process and is the beginning of spiritual growth, "fill" being an image of plenitude.[47] A long list might easily be compiled of Fuller's references to the two kinds of seeing, outward and inward, often contrasted in the same passage: "I cannot look merely with a pictorial eye on the lounge of the Roman dandy, the bold, Juno gait of the Roman Contadina . . . the natural expression of these fine forms will animate them yet" (*AHA* 260). Staring (eyes wide open, fixed gaze, potential rudeness) gives way to "natural" or essentialist seeing. "I am . . . no longer a staring, sight-seeing stranger, riding about finely dressed in a coach to see the Muses and the Sibyls. I see these forms now in the natural manner" (*L* 4:310). While "staring" is a kind of unnatural seeing that does not penetrate the surface, "seeing" lessens the distance between subject and object: "it must be torture merely to *travel* to Italy and give a passing stare at the beautiful body without ever having time or peace to come in contact with its soul" (*L* 4:306). Titian's *Sacred and Profane Love*, then in the Palazzo Borghese, "has developed my powers of gazing to an extent unknown before" (*AHA* 223). The English stand out as the "most unseeing" of travelers (*AHA* 220). Fuller did not embrace New England Anglophilia, though there is no reason to suppose that the English were any more or less "unseeing" than the Americans or, for that matter, any other nationality.[48] "Now I saw the true Rome . . . I came to live in tranquil companionship, not in the restless impertinence of sight-seeing" (*L* 4:298): deliberateness over speed, seeing over sight-seeing, friendly relations over rudeness. Spurning a "coffee-house intelligence" (*L* 4:295), she writes that "I am really seeing Italy, differently from what mere travellers do" (*L* 4:304). To take in the whole of Italy is impossible, so Fuller resorts to synecdochic condensation by which "the great features of the part pursue and fill the eye" (*AHA* 220), another image of plenitude.

Fuller's Italian journey resembles a pilgrimage in which the religious feelings of her youth are secularized and subsumed. Her ideal traveler undergoes a loss of self through "intimacy of feeling" with, and an "abandonment" to, the "spirit of the place" (*AHA* 220). The moment captures the Coleridgean "coalescence of subject and object"; it is the transcendent intuition or "revelation," the "real knowledge, the recreative power induced by love," which is succeeded by the imaginative "assimilation" of "soul and substance" within an enlarged self (*AHA* 258). In December 1847 she wrote that the driving rhythms of the saltarello danced by humble folk (perhaps Trasteverini) beside the Colosseum "carried me quite beyond myself." Bored and "catching cold from the damp night-air," and probably fearful of Roman fever, her American companions wanted to leave and "remember it against me" for keeping them waiting (once again, the outsider). But Fuller would not be denied the "delight"; though she might have been just as cold, she was "heated by enthusiasm," and the dance was like "Italian wine," "Italian sun." Afterward, she kept returning to the scene to absorb its meaning: "I love to see and study it much" (*AHA* 267).[49] The episode is structured along the contrast between life and death: sun, light, heat, wine, health, artistry, ecstasy vs. night, cold, dampness, illness, boredom. Fuller experiences such heightened moments with the intensity of satisfying a natural instinct: "I thought and *drank in* the spirit of Rome" (my italics, *L* 5:40); the "spirit" of Rome "must be *inhaled wholly*, with the yielding of the *whole* heart. It is really something transcendent, both spirit and body" (my italics, *L* 4:290). In the "painful process of sight-seeing," "there is no quiet to let that beauty *breathe its life* into the soul" (my italics, *AHA* 258).[50] Again, as external to internal, sightseeing opposes the kind of seeing that informs both "heart" and "soul."

The Chapels of the Cemeteries on the slopes of the Janiculum provide the setting for one of Fuller's most memorable encounters.[51] She happened upon the scene on one of her solitary, undirected walks in early November 1847, following All Souls Day.[52] A Franciscan friar, a pregnant woman, beggars, and a few boys among others are kneeling in prayer before the Stations of the Cross; the boys chant a hymn. Longfellow in *Outre-Mer* had recoiled at the emotionalism of prostrate churchgoers in Genoa; tolerant and fastidious, Hillard warns against disrespect. Only Fuller overcame the cultural and religious distance ("as from pole to pole") to join the people in prayer:

> It was a beautiful moment, and despite the wax saint, the ill-favored
> friar, the professional mendicants, and my own removal, wide as pole
> from pole, from the position of mind indicated by these forms, their
> spirits touched me, and I prayed too; prayed for the distant, every way
> distant,—for those who seem to have forgotten me, and with me all we
> had in common; prayed for the dead in spirit, if not in body; prayed for
> myself, that I might never walk the earth "The tomb of my dead self";
> and prayed in general for all unspoiled and loving hearts,—no less for
> all who suffer and find yet no helper. (*AHA* 261)

Repeated four times, "prayed" emphasizes her desire to collapse the
distance between herself and others, and to dispel the loneliness of a
single woman in a foreign country. Lest she walk the earth as the "'tomb
of my dead self,'"[53] she prays in earnest for that spiritual rebirth that so
many of her fellow New Englanders associated with Italy. In love, and
to be a mother herself within a year, she may identify with the pregnant
women praying for the yet unborn child. Fuller then "took my road by
the Cross, which marks the brow of the hill" and in an *imitatio Christi*
climbed the Janiculum and is rewarded for her prayers: "Before me lay
Rome,—how exquisitely tranquil in the sunset! Never was an aspect
that for serene grandeur could vie with that of Rome at sunset" (*AHA*
262). As in the episode of the saltarello, the antithesis of death and rebirth, further supported by the liminal hour, helps structure the concrete details and the symbolism: cemetery at sunset and resurrection;
loneliness and community; low ground, depressed spirits, cordoned
view vs. hilltop panorama, the sublime, and serenity; turmoil and peace.

These examples of her travel writing—and they could easily be
multiplied—reveal that Fuller is neither abstract, nor labored, nor excessively concerned with the self. Like the finest travel writers, she
shares the palm with the object.

The intensification of her spiritual life through travel represents a
stage in the secularization of Protestant inwardness, within just a few
decades to take various directions in American life, from the therapeu-
tic, to the aesthetic, and the revivalist. With Fuller, however, the goal is
post-Romantic self-realization through an active interchange with the
universe: "a full communion with the spirit of Rome" (*L* 5:192), the
"much more full and true way" (*L* 5:283) of living that she found in Italy.
Perhaps here as elsewhere, she puns on her name, a mark of plenitude.
In one of her finest statements on traveling, she draws on religious metaphor: "All these things [the country, the people, the spectacles] are only

to me an illuminated margin on the text of my inward life" (*L* 4:271). Bearing the spiritual mystery of the inward life, the spiritual self as text is read like a sacred word, which the travels and commentaries in the "margin" help to interpret and "illuminate." As in her Puritan-Protestant background, the word is central, the image is *outside*. Fuller's hospital work during the siege of Rome brought her life in Italy— public and private, political and cultural—to its highest point in self-understanding and fullness of being. Her "rebirth" on a small scale participates in Italy's spiritual and political renewal on the grand scale.

With a knowledge of Italy and Italians deeper than that of most of her American contemporaries, Fuller could give the major topoi a more personal interpretation. Like the Romantics, she believed the child to be the "father of the man" and accepted the common notion of the Italian as having a childlike simplicity and naturalness. But she goes further and identifies with the child, for its imaginative wholeness and happiness. Within a few months of her arrival, Fuller writes, "Italy receives me as a long lost child" (*L* 4:293). Not long after she confides in her mother, "I have not been so well since I was a child, nor so happy ever" (*L* 4:312), implying Italy and Rome are mothers too: "Rome! oh my mother! How sadly tender I return into thy arms" (*L* 5:156). She speaks of her "passive child-like well being" (*L* 5:43) in Italy. Not least of the reasons for this metaphor, as Margaret Allen writes, Italy enabled her to "recapture some of [her] lost childhood."[54] Though Fuller recognizes the intellectual differences between her and her husband, she also admires what she finds wanting in herself: Ossoli possesses "unspoiled instincts" (*L* 5:270), a "simple child-like piety" (*L* 5:301), a "perfectly unconscious character" (*L* 6:46); he is "simple and uniform though not monotonous more than are the flowers of spring" (*L* 5:302; cf. 5:271). No one has loved her "as genuinely" "except little children or mother" (*L* 5: 300). Perhaps his innocence and sincerity, misunderstood by so many others as ignorance or doltishness, was part of what captivated her.

Connected to the theme of the child is that of "coming home" to one's true self. The metaphor recurs in letters from early in her sojourn. At first, she "could not yet find myself at home in Italy" but quickly became "absorbed in [Rome's] peculiar life" (*L* 4:290); within weeks, "I feel myself at home" (*L* 4:293), "really *in* Rome," but the "English and Americans are not at home here" (*L* 4:310). More readily than her fellow New Englanders, the Italians appear to have accepted her individuality and circumstances: they "sympathize with my character and understand my organization, as no other people ever did," and "highly prize my intelligent sympathy"; "they say, I am so *simpatica*" (*L* 4:299, 5: 86). In other words, there is mutual sympathy. She understands her Americanness through her separation from America: "Since I have experienced the different atmosphere of the European mind, and been allied with it, nay, mingled in the bonds of love, I suffer more than ever from that which is peculiarly American or English" (*L* 4:310). The more one sees and experiences, the more the lines of one's character become sharper: "The American in Europe, if a thinking mind, can only become more American" (*AHA* 250)—with which Lowell would agree. No phrase rings more commonly in the letters than a passage from Byron's *Childe Harold's Pilgrimage* (IV.LXXVIII): "Oh Rome! my country! city of the soul! / The orphans of the heart must turn to thee, / Lone mother" (*L* 5:68, 147, 156, 157, 240, 241, 274, 275). The images combine the themes of the child, exile, "home," and the "Lone mother." Fuller thought of herself as an "orphan," as when she wonders if she could ever return to Boston, "*I* have no 'home,' no peaceful roof to which I can return" (*L* 5:76–77). But later she writes, again citing Bryon, Rome is "*my* country" (her italics, *L* 5:147), "my *home*" (her italics, *L* 5:274), "oh Rome, *my* Country!" (her italics, *L* 5:275). During the revolution she regarded herself, in Robert N. Hudspeth's words, as "a Roman defending her home" (*L* 5:12). Exiled to Florence, she is "home-sick for Rome" (*L* 5:274). As with other members of the tradition, the recourse to the home metaphor also signals a desire to recover and make familiar the relation to the cultural past.

One speculates further on the travel book Fuller might have written. It is possible that she would have devoted more attention to politics, class, and the common people. She appreciates the "winning sweetness" of the poor, their "ready and discriminating love" of beauty, and their "delicacy in the sympathies," lack of which made her "sick" in America (*AHA* 425).[55] As in Hillard, the "unaffected" behavior of Italian women ("you can see what Heaven meant them to be" [*AHA* 262]) contrasts with the artificiality of foreigners. Her comments on the fine arts would likely have been developed—as they stand, they are within the boundaries of taste that Hillard inhabited. Michelangelo is "my demigod"; his *Moses* is "the only thing in Europe, so far, which has entirely outgone my hopes" (*AHA* 224). A great admirer of Titian, she finds Domenichino "very unequal" or uneven in his paintings, "but when he is grand and free, the energy of his genius perfectly satisfies" (*AHA* 223)—which is the modern judgment. Unlike Hillard, she recommends the Carracci, though her interest in Guercino wanes. The Certosa outside Pavia, which Ruskin detested, impresses her; but she does not mention the Romanesque S. Michele, which he admired. As for American artists, she prefers Hicks and Greenough. She comments less on architecture than on painting and sculpture.

Some of the memorable set pieces in the letters and dispatches could pass directly into a travel book: the Campagna when the Tiber had overflowed its banks and her coach seems to glide on moonlit water. Or, the Roman Carnival, during which the heavy downpours fail to dampen the spirits of the people. Or, the mountain chapels beyond Rieti (Hillard, unlike Ruskin, thought the Apennines dull compared with the Alps and almost dismisses them [*SM* 1:103]). William Vance speaks of "the People" as the true hero of Fuller's dispatches, and Brigitte Bailey argues that her view of Rome is "defined by citizens in motion, by political processions, funerals, troop movements, and religious festivals whose meaning is increasingly political"; the crowd "shapes itself into a political community."[56] At the same time, however, Fuller does not let the individuals in a crowd dissolve like drops in the ocean. When she could not walk from the Corso to St. Peter's owing to the "most vivacious, various, and good-humored crowd," "so I saw only themselves; but that was a great pleasure. There is so much individuality of character here, that it is a great entertainment to be in a crowd" (*AHA* 267). Also, if in Rome Fuller cast her lot with the future, she knew the cost: "we are enjoying the last hours of her old solemn greatness" (*L* 5:158).

Fuller's attitude toward Catholicism changed on living in Italy, or rather, opposing sides of her response matured. As a reviewer and reporter in New York she "spoke positively of Catholics in order to goad her readers," for example, praising the Catholic family ideal; in Italy, however, she "associated political and social progress with Protestant rather than Catholic versions of Christianity."[57] Yet she felt the tension between her skeptical Protestant view and the aesthetic attractions of Italian Catholicism, not unlike British women who traveled to Italy. For Dorothy Wordsworth, Mary Shelley, Hester Thrale Piozzi, and Charlotte Eaton, "Italian Catholicism provided two conflicting versions of the sublime," comments Jane Stabler, "one based on absolute political papal authority and one on the transcendent aesthetic possibilities of music, art and communal festive joy."[58] Though Fuller rejects doctrinal Catholicism and expresses extreme displeasure at the ceremony of the nun taking the veil, she is fascinated by papal Rome in its "united and poetic meaning" (*AHA* 259). Referring paradoxically to the rituals as a "gorgeous mummery," she admits to being "charmed" by their "poetry" and "picture" (*AHA* 243). Her relationship to Catholicism exemplifies her ability to balance opposite viewpoints, in this case, moral objection, emotional attachment, and aesthetic feeling. This capability, which expands the scope of her vision and colors her observations not only on religion but on other issues as well, "accounts for her constant effort to transcend the otherness of Italian culture" and assimilate it within her experience.[59] With her capacity to "see" trained to unconscious habit, Fuller observes the funeral procession of Councilor Silvani in the Corso: "the whole had that grand effect so easily given by this artist people, who seize instantly the natural poetry of an occasion, and with unanimous tact hasten to represent it" (*AHA* 268).

Almost defiantly, Fuller preferred Rome to Florence. Why, on the contrary, did Hillard and so many Anglo Americans prefer Florence to Rome? smaller, more manageable, tidily bourgeois? unbaroque, i.e., less overtly Catholic, less Counter-Reformation? Giuliana Artom Treves entitled a chapter of her book on the Anglo Florentines "The Boston of Italy." The Catholic Mary McCarthy who comments on the supposed likeness to Boston admires the "protestant," "iconoclastic image-breaking nature" of "four-square and direct" Florence, a "city of progress," "sobriety," "decorum," and Savonarola, a "puritan" town that is the very opposite of Rome with its "snaky" baroque Catholicism: the baroque is "a style utterly un-Florentine."[60] In one of the *Tribune* dispatches Fuller states flatly, "I do not like Florence as I do cities more purely Italian" because the "natural character is ironed out here, and done up in a French pattern" (*AHA* 231), that is, more organized, administered, "civilized" as Stendhal (who disliked Florence) would say. Florence is "more in its spirit like Boston, than like any Italian city," "a kind of Boston to me,—the same good and the same ill; I have had enough of both"; the Florentines are "busy and intellectual" (*L* 4:291; 5: 161; cf. 5:273–74). She likes Mrs. Greenough, "but not the Boston part of her" (*L* 6:77): provincial, inbred, emotionally inhibited, highly cerebrated: perhaps Mrs. Greenough reminded her of weaknesses that she had overcome in herself. Florence "will never charm me as have"—and she lists a string of Italian cities and towns (*L* 5:274). "Rome is not as cheap a place as Florence, but then I would not give a pin to live in Florence" (*L* 4:310; cf. 4:278); "it is a place to work and study in; simple life does not seem so great" (*L* 5:274), "great" (or sublime) as opposed to business- and work-oriented. In 1850, after six months in Florence, Rome "is worth ten million Florences" (*L* 6:69). Despite her association with bourgeois republicans (who stood in the forefront of the Risorgimento), her choice of sublime Rome over bourgeois Florence is another indication of the profound temperamental and intellectual divide separating her from so many American travelers. She was not one of them, and they resented it—most of them silently; some like Lowell, Hawthorne, and Joseph Mozier, openly.

They disliked her antibourgeois nature, expressed in her radicalism, politics, and sexual freedom, the more shocking in a woman. Unlike the New Englanders, for whom Boston was the hub of the universe, Fuller was, in Hudspeth's phrase, "the de facto citizen of a cosmopolitan world" (*L* 6:15), the international European culture of George Sand, Marchioness Arconati Visconti, Princess di Belgioioso, Mickiewicz, Princess Radziwill, Prince Poniatowski, and Mazzini, who recognized her as one of their own and who are, in her words, "exquisitely witty, original, and no less generous and kind" (*L* 6:78). Her disapproving brother Richard, however, is "amazed at [her] *worldliness*" (*L* 6:66); her wealthy uncle Abraham teased her in withholding money and, "far from aiding, wished to see me fall" (*L* 5:71); her "Aunt Mary" Rotch, aware of her plight, bequeathed a large fortune to her lawyer and another friend, when a small fraction of it would have made an enormous difference to Fuller. It is true that at times Fuller might have exaggerated her isolation. In the fall of 1848 Eliza Farrar raised money from among Fuller's friends to provide her with an annuity of $300 for life. Yet so used to being slighted had Fuller become that she might have overlooked those rare instances when she was met with generosity. There was always some slight for her to point to. For Hawthorne she was a "great humbug." When Lowell pilloried her in *A Fable for Critics*, William Wetmore Story came to her defense; even at that, he was more pleading and sentimental than principled and firm: "because fate has really been unkind to her, & because she depends on her pen for her bread & water (& that is nearly all she has to eat) & because she is her own worst enemy, and because through her disappointment & disease, which embitter every one, she has struggled most womanfully & stoutly, I could have wished you had let her pass scot free." Lowell spoke for a multitude in his cruel reply: the "general verdict was 'served her right'" (*L* 6:80n). After her death she was poorly edited by her friends and treated in a caddish way by Henry James, who referred to her "poverty of knowledge" and "magnificent egotism," calling her "a somewhat formidable bore"; she "left nothing behind her," except for the "unquestionably haunting Margaret-ghost."[61]

She was "odd and unpleasing" (*L* 6:59), to quote her on herself; "people rarely think one like me worth serving and saving" (*L* 5:104). Yet if she was spurned by many of her fellow countrymen, she found herself at home in Italy: "Who can ever be alone for a moment in Italy? Every stone has a voice" (*AHA* 229).[62] Drawing on the trope of death and rebirth she described a walk in Rome, passing the house "where Keats died where he lived," then by the houses of Raphael, Goethe, Poussin, and Claude Lorrain. "Ah, what human companionship here, how everything speaks" (*L* 5:181). She recalls that Hans Christian Andersen had set his *L'improvvisatore* in the apartment where she was living. Also, she knows her connection in people's minds with De Staël's Corinne, an *improvvisatrice*. The artists and writers are dead, yet live again and "speak" to her, while those back home are living but no company at all. Perhaps she knew that Keats had written a sonnet on this theme, "Great Spirits now on Earth are sojourning." Emma Keats, the poet's niece, had been a pupil of Fuller's in New England.

Reviewing Alfieri's autobiography, Fuller digressed to consider how various countries might instruct America, concluding: "But there is not on earth, and, we dare to say it, will not be again genius *like* that of Italy, or that can compare with it in its own way."[63] Italy had proven an inexhaustible source of intellectual and emotional pleasure, moral teaching, and spiritual rebirth. Like Alfieri, she made herself a part of the history of its struggle for unification.[64] Greatly to be lamented is the loss of Fuller's manuscript history on the Roman revolution. Yet one also laments the loss of the many other works, among which might have been an Italian travel book worthy to be placed beside Goethe, De Staël, and Stendhal.

Notes

1. Martin B. Duberman, *James Russell Lowell* (Boston: Houghton Mifflin, 1966), 127.

2. Nathalia Wright, *American Novelists in Italy: The Discoverers; Allston to James* (Philadelphia: Univ. of Pennsylvania Press, 1965), 17.

3. Prévost had not read deeply in Dante, Tasso, and Ariosto or he would otherwise have admired the "happy genius" of a language "which can express every thing with a simplicity, a grace, a force, in fine, that cannot be approached by any other living language." Anonymous reviewer, quoted in Angelina La Piana, *Dante's American Pilgrimage: A Historical Survey of Dante Studies in the United States, 1800–1944* (New Haven, Conn.: Yale Univ. Press, 1948), 30.

4. Jared Sparks, "The Augustan Age in Italian Literature," *North American Review* 4, no. 13 (1817): 315.

5. See John Paul Russo, "The Harvard Italophiles: Longfellow, Lowell, and Norton," in *L'esilio romantico: forme di un conflitto,* ed. Joseph Cheyne and Lilla Maria Crisafulli Jones (Bari: Adriatica, 1990), 303–24.

6. Still, Santayana and Brooks treated the Big Three as primary representatives of the genteel tradition. See *The Genteel Tradition: Nine Essays by George Santayana,* ed. Douglas L. Wilson (Cambridge, Mass.: Harvard Univ. Press, 1967), and Van Wyck Brooks, *America's Coming of Age* (New York: Huebsch, 1915).

7. *Letters of Charles Eliot Norton,* ed. Sara Norton and Mark A. DeWolfe Howe, 2 vols. (Boston: Houghton Mifflin, 1913), 2:207–8; "in the long run, in memory, the appeal to the imagination proves the stronger and the most abiding."

8. *Letters of Norton,* 1:404. The hope for rebirth comes at the end of a passage that refers significantly to the Italian people as having maintained the "spark" of life through death, together with a reference to "Renaissance": "I have been living mainly on Italian Chronicles and cinquecento biographies. How this people kept any spark of sweetness and charity and humanity alive through the burnings and massacres of the middle ages and through the wanton wickedness of the Renaissance, must always be a matter of wonder. And now, if one knows how to live with them, they are the sweetest people on earth." 1:404.

9. *Letters of Norton,* 1:406. "Italy is the country where the American, exile in his own land from the past record of his race, finds most of the most delightful part of that record." 1:349.

10. *Complete Writings of James Russell Lowell,* vol. 1, *Fireside Travels,* Elmwood Edition (Boston: Houghton Mifflin, 1904), 139, 149, 150, 152, 153, 166, 168, 225–26, 229, 242, 243; Horace E. Scudder, *James Russell Lowell: A Biography,* 2 vols. (Boston: Houghton Mifflin, 1901), 1:342.

11. Lowell, *Fireside Travels,* 3.

12. "Nowhere are such study and knowledge more needed than in America . . . ," writes Norton; "nowhere are the conditions of life more prosaic; nowhere is the poetic spirit less evident, and the love of beauty less diffused." *Letters of Norton,* 2:8.

13. Pauline Chase Harrell and Margaret Supplee Smith, eds., *Victorian Boston Today: Ten Walking Tours* (Boston: Victorian Society, 1975), 87.

14. Paul R. Baker, *The Fortunate Pilgrims: Americans in Italy, 1800–1860* (Cambridge, Mass.: Harvard Univ. Press, 1964), 29.

15. *The Correspondence of John Lothrop Motley*, ed. George William Curtis, 2 vols. (New York: Harper, 1889), 1:189.

16. Hillard, *Six Months in Italy*, 2 vols. (Boston: Ticknor, Reed, and Fields, 1853), 2:335 (hereafter cited in text and notes as *SM*).

17. Hillard alludes to Johnson: a tourist in the Vatican is "like the shepherd in the Rambler who asked to have the river Euphrates flow through his grounds, and was taken off his feet and borne away by the stream . . . but long before the great circuit is completed, his knees knock together with fatigue, and his worn brain refuses to receive any new impressions. But time and patience, which conquer all things, conquer the Vatican." *SM* 1:236–37.

18. Vance, *America's Rome*, vol. 1, *Classical Rome* (New Haven, Conn.: Yale Univ. Press, 1989), 87–88.

19. Like Emerson before him, and Sumner, Santayana, and Bernard Berenson after him, Hillard attended Boston Latin School (class of 1824).

20. Hawthorne expresses the thought of at-homeness most powerfully in the long, single-sentence first paragraph of chapter 36 of *The Marble Faun:* "When we have once known Rome, and left her where she lies, like a long decaying corpse, retaining a trace of the noble shape it was, but with accumulated dust and a fungous growth overspreading all its more admirable features;—left her in utter weariness . . . ; when we have left Rome in such a mood as this, we are astonished by the discovery, by-and-by, that our heart-strings have mysteriously attached themselves to the Eternal City, and are drawing us thitherward again, as if it were more familiar, more intimately our home, than even the spot where we were born!" In its climactic position, the word "born" is both an end and a beginning.

21. Ware, *Sketches of European Capitals* (Boston: Phillips, Sampson, 1851), 199; Scudder, *Lowell*, 1:342–43.

22. "The author of the 'Modern Painters' is a great writer on art, and when he is wrong, it is often only from pushing right principles to an extreme. His book is a golden book, steeped in the poetry and the religion of art, just in theory and exquisite in spirit . . . but the author will undoubtedly live to admit that all its vehement and impetuous judgments are not correct." *SM* 1:371–72.

23. In sculpture, the Vatican "not only surpasses any other collection, but all other collections put together." *SM* 1:234.

24. Heinrich Wölfflin, *Classic Art: An Introduction to the Italian Renaissance*, trans. Peter and Linda Murray (New York: Phaidon, 1953), 210, 216, 235, 239, 252, 254; Adrian Stokes, *The Stones of Rimini* (New York: Putnam, 1934), chap. 4.

25. Indicating his own preference, Wölfflin comments "with what a sense of relief the eye turns to Raphael's compositions, with their multitudes of

figures—I am speaking of his Roman works, for the *Entombment* is still lacking in this kind of [compositional] clarity." *Classic Art*, 267.

26. In William Wetmore Story's phrase, the "hideous *baldacchino*." *Roba di Roma*, 7th ed. (London, 1876), 250.

27. Camillo von Klenze, *The Interpretation of Italy during the Last Two Centuries* (Chicago: Univ. of Chicago Press, 1907), 10, 43. For Vance's critique of Hillard on the baroque, see *America's Rome*, vol. 2, *Catholic and Contemporary Rome*, 78–79.

28. Udo Kultermann, *The History of Art History* (New York: Abaris Books, 1993), 136–37.

29. Lowell, *Fireside Travels*, 179. Pius later reversed his decision.

30. *The Letters of Margaret Fuller*, ed. Robert N. Hudspeth, 6 vols. (Ithaca, N.Y.: Cornell Univ. Press, 1988), 4:273 (hereafter cited as *L* in text and notes). On the subject of work and time, Longfellow said the Italians were "poor—and lazy, and happy." *The Letters of Henry Wadsworth Longfellow*, ed. Andrew Hilen, 6 vols. (Cambridge, Mass.: Harvard Univ. Press, 1966–82), 1:279. Lowell on the other hand distinguished indolence from mere laziness: the Italian was not "lazy," only time was "of no account" in the "Eternal City." "When a Roman does nothing, he does it in the high Roman fashion"; he "spends from a purse of Fortunatus"; his "*piccolo quarto d'ora* is like his *grosso*, a huge piece of copper, big enough for a shield, which stands only for a half dime of our money." *Fireside Travels*, 156–57, 243.

31. Cf. *Letters of Norton*, 1:411: "dress has become uniform all over Europe, and not only the habit of the body but the apparel of the mind also has lost in variety, and character is, like coats, cut more and more upon one pattern."

32. "The traveller must leave all his notions of progress and reform at the gates, or else he will be kept in constant state of protest and rebellion; . . . He must try to forget such things as a representative government, town-meetings, public schools, railways, and steam-engines." *L* 1:204.

33. This was a common trope: "The Teutonic man, one may say, feels toward the spirit of his own race as toward a brother, but toward the Greek spirit as toward a mistress." Charles Horton Cooley, "Genius, Fame, and Race," *Annals of the American Academy of Political and Social Science* 9, no. 3 (May 1897): 28.

34. Margaret Fuller Ossoli, *At Home and Abroad, or, Things and Thoughts in America and Europe*, ed. Arthur B. Fuller (1856; repr., Port Washington, N.Y.: Kennikat Press, 1971), 233 (hereafter cited in text and notes as *AHA*).

35. *The Essential Margaret Fuller*, ed. Jeffrey Steele (New Brunswick, N.J.: Rutgers Univ. Press, 1992), xxii–xxiii.

36. Jeffrey Alan Melton, *Mark Twain, Travel Books, and Tourism: The Tide of a Great Popular Movement* (Tuscaloosa: Univ. of Alabama Press, 2002), 16.

37. "Books of Travel" (1845), in *Margaret Fuller, Critic: Writings from the New-York Tribune, 1844–1846*, ed. Judith Mattson Bean and Joel Myerson (New York: Columbia Univ. Press, 2000), 299–300.

38. Ibid., 301–2. On Goethe's *Italian Journey* she comments: "it is this patience, this depth, this serenity consequent on a great scope of vision, and clear discernment of the infrangible links between cause and effect, that are so opposed to our hasty, overemphatic, superficial mode of action" (302). Joseph Forsyth is praised for his "tone of high culture, refined taste and harmonious thought"; "one who wanted aid in forming taste, or to be stimulated to a higher point of view and more accuracy and delicacy in observation than contents the crowd will find a preceptor and a friend in Forsyth" (302). Forsyth's *Remarks* (1813) has been edited by Keith Crook (Newark and London: Univ. of Delaware Press, Associated Univ. Presses, 2001).

39. Beckford published *Italy*, a neglected masterpiece of travel writing, in 1783 under the title *Dreams, Waking Thoughts, and Incidents, in a Series of Letters, from Various Parts of Europe;* it was withdrawn by Beckford's family, which feared scandal. Though copies were known to have circulated, Fuller almost certainly read the edition that Beckford published fifty-one years later *(Italy, with Sketches of Spain and Portugal).*

40. A common theme in the letters: "the traveller passing along the beaten track, vetturinoed from inn to inn, ciceroned from gallery to gallery, thrown, through indolence, want of tact, or ignorance of the language, too much into the society of his compatriots, sees the least possible of the country"; it is "quite out of the question to know Italy . . . without long residence, and residence in the districts untouched by the scorch and dust of foreign invasion." *AHA* 220.

41. Salomone, "The Nineteenth-Century Discovery of Italy: An Essay in American Cultural History. Prolegomena to a Historiographical Problem," *American Historical Review* 73, no. 5 (1968): 1378; see also 1367–68, 1373–74; *Letters of Norton,* 1:399. Vance examines American forerunners of Fuller who went beyond stereotypical oppositions and approached Rome (and Italy) in an inductive spirit: Catharine Maria Sedgwick, William Mitchell Gillespie, Henry T. Tuckerman. *Catholic and Contemporary Rome,* 109ff.

42. "I have screwed my expenses down to the lowest possible peg; at least it seems so now, but I dont know;—that art seems to be capable of . . . indefinite perfection in Italy." *L* 5:158.

43. The topos appears in one of her dispatches: After a time one learns to distinguish ancient from "Anglicized Rome" and "to wash away all this dirt, and come at the marble yet." She does not mean the modern population, but only the touristic side of the modern city ("taverns, lodging-houses, cheating chambermaids, vilest *valets de place,* and fleas"). *AHA* 259.

44. McCarthy, *The Stones of Florence* (New York: Harcourt Brace Jovanovich, 1987), 10.

45. John Urry, *The Tourist Gaze: Leisure and Travel in Contemporary Societies* (London: Sage, 1990).

46. Stendhal, *Rome, Naples et Florence en 1817*, in *Voyage en Italie*, ed. Victor Del Litto (Paris: Gallimard, 1973), 98 (May 24, 1817); for other references to *charme*, see 11, 81, 151, 377. The particular city to which Stendhal refers is Pesaro, not Milan, as Matthew Josephson reports in *Stendhal; or, The Pursuit of Happiness* (Garden City, N.Y.: Doubleday, 1946), 198.

47. Goethe "is one of those whose office it is to stem the tide that hurries us on so fast." "Books of Travel," 302. If we want to see, said Ruskin, it is first necessary to *slow down:* "a turn of a country road, with a cottage beside it, which we have not seen before, is as much as we need for refreshment; if we hurry past it, and take two cottages at a time it is already too much"; "all travelling becomes dull in exact proportion to its rapidity. Going by railroad I do not consider as travelling at all; it is merely 'being sent' to a place and very little different from becoming a 'parcel.'" *The Works of John Ruskin*, ed. E. T. Cook and Alexander Wedderburn, 39 vols. (London: G. Allen, 1903–12), 5:370.

48. "I am sorry to say that a large portion of my countrymen here take the same slothful and prejudiced view as the English, and, after many year's sojourn, betray entire ignorance of Italian literature and Italian life." *AHA* 246. "Ah! how joyful to see once more *this* Rome, instead of the pitiful, peddling, Anglicized Rome, first viewed in unutterable dismay from the *coupé* of the vettura." *AHA* 259.

49. Leonardo Buonomo speaks of her "intense involvement," her "desire to participate"; unlike previous travelers, she was "willing to compromise, to endanger [her] privileged point of view." *Backward Glances: Exploring Italy, Reinterpreting America, 1831–1860* (Madison, N.J.: Associated Univ. Presses / Fairleigh Dickinson Univ. Press, 1996), 29.

50. "This consciousness [the sightseer's eagerness to see Rome] would be most valuable if one had time to think and study, being the natural way in which the mind is lured to cure itself of its defects; but you have no time; you are always wearied, body and mind, confused, dissipated, sad." *AHA* 258. Fuller could be caustic and judgmental, as if separating the quick and the dead: "No; Rome is not a nine-days wonder; and those who try to make it such lose the ideal Rome (if they ever had it), without gaining any notion of the real. To those who travel, as they do everything else, only because others do, I do not speak; they are nothing. Nobody counts in the estimate of the human race who has not a character." *AHA* 258.

51. The editors of Fuller's foreign dispatches place the Chapels of the Cemeteries "along the Via Giulia"; in fact, they were in the Cimitero di S. Spirito near the Porta S. Spirito, across the river on the Janiculum. The editors also claim that "at the end of the street [Via Giulia] is a good view of Rome." Yet the land at either end of the Via Giulia does not rise high enough for such a view. Fuller says, "I went to Santo Spirito. This Cemetery stands high"; from

that height on the slope of the Janiculum she walked higher, to the Cross, "which marks the brow of the hill," for her panoramic view of Rome at sunset. *"These Sad But Glorious Days": Dispatches from Europe, 1846–1850,* ed. Larry J. Reynolds and Susan Belasco Smith (New Haven, Conn.: Yale Univ. Press, 1991), 169–71. Mariano Armellini published an engraving of the Cimitero di S. Spirito, announcing it is to be demolished (1887); two chapels are described briefly: S. Maria del Rosario and Cappella del Crocifisso. *Le Chiese di Roma dal secolo IV al XIX* (1887, 1892: Rome: Edizioni R.O.R.E. di Nicola Russolo, 1942), 806–7.

52. "Each day I am out from eleven till five, exploring some new object of interest, often at a great distance." *L* 4:313. "I now really live in Rome, and I begin to see and feel the real Rome. She reveals herself day by day; she tells me some of her life. Now I never go out to see a sight, but I walk every day; and here I cannot miss of some object of consummate interest to end a walk." *AHA* 259.

53. I have been unable to identity the source of this quotation.

54. Allen, *The Achievement of Margaret Fuller* (University Park: Pennsylvania State Univ. Press, 1979), 155.

55. "Yes I shall like to go back and see our 'eighteen millions of bores,' with their rail-roads, electric telegraphs, mass movements and ridiculous dilettant [*sic*] phobias, but with ever successful rush and bang." *L* 6:64. The "eighteen millions of bores" is Thomas Carlyle's description of America.

56. Vance, *Catholic and Contemporary Rome,* 132–33; Bailey, "Fuller, Hawthorne, and Imagining Urban Spaces in Rome," in *Roman Holidays: American Writers and Artists in Nineteenth-Century Italy,* ed. Robert K. Martin and Leland S. Person (Iowa City: Univ. of Iowa Press, 2002), 180–81.

57. Kimberly VanEsveld Adams, *Our Lady of Victorian Feminism* (Athens: Ohio Univ. Press, 2001), 136–37.

58. Stabler, "Devotion and Diversion: Early Nineteenth-Century British Women Travellers in Italy and the Catholic Church," in *Unfolding the South: Nineteenth-Century British Women Writers and Artists in Italy,* ed. Alison Chapman and Jane Stabler (Manchester: Manchester Univ. Press, 2003), 17.

59. Buonomo, *Backward Glances,* 43.

60. Treves, *The Golden Ring: The Anglo-Florentines, 1847–62,* trans. Sylvia Sprigge (London: Longmans, Green, 1956), 160–75; McCarthy, *Stones of Florence,* 4, 14, 33, 36, 40, 55, 60, 61, 63, 87, 88, 93. Buying into the myth of the two Italies without really questioning it, McCarthy goes so far as to make Florence almost a northern European city, complete with Irish Jansenist Catholicism. Stendhal found the Florentines a "race of holy-minded *castrati*. All passion is extinct within their souls." *Rome, Naples and Florence,* trans. Richard N. Coe (London: John Calder, 1959), 123; cf. 311, 324. See also Paul Giles, *American Catholic Arts and Fictions: Culture, Ideology, Aesthetics* (Cambridge: Cambridge Univ. Press, 1992), 459.

61. Hawthorne, *The French and Italian Notebooks*, ed. Thomas Woodson, 156; James, *Hawthorne* (New York: Harper and Bros., 1880), 68–69, 76; James, *William Wetmore Story and His Friends* (Boston: Houghton Mifflin, 1903), 127–28.

62. "Every grain of dust seems instinct with spirit from the Past, every step recalls some line, some legend of long-neglected lore." *AHA* 229.

63. "Italy [Alfieri]" (1845), in Bean and Myerson, *Margaret Fuller, Critic*, 255. Fuller admired Alfieri's patriotism, his courage, his moral grandeur, and his loyalty and devotion to the Countess of Albany. "Many geniuses have spoken worthily of women in their works, but he speaks of women as she wishes to be spoken of and declares that he met the desire of his soul realized in life. This, almost alone, is an instance where a great nature was permanently satisfied, and the claims of man and women equally met, where one of the parties had the impatient fire of genius" (257). The passage happily characterizes her own marriage to Ossoli.

64. A tablet in Fuller's honor was raised in the Piazza Barberini (she lived at no. 60), by the corner of the Via Sistina, the day following the conference at which this paper was given, "Margaret Fuller: tra Europa e Stati Uniti d'America," November 20–22, 2000, American Academy, Rome.

7

Realism, Idealism, and Passion in Margaret Fuller's Response to Italy

FRANCESCO GUIDA

Drawing upon Margaret Fuller's private letters as well as her dispatches written for the *New-York Daily Tribune,* this essay critically examines her observations and judgments during her 1847–49 travels in Europe, with particular attention to the revolution in Italy. As she recorded her reactions to people and events, Fuller also explored ideas, offered political solutions, and proffered advice to her fellow Americans. While often penetrating, her observations were sometimes idealized and sometimes wholly foreign to the actual Italian situation.

Many scholars have viewed Fuller's writings in these years as direct, unmediated responses to events in Europe and especially in the Italian states. In fact, she brought with her a panoply of sophisticated attitudes and ideological preoccupations formed by years of study, writing, and cultural participation. She was also an experienced journalist, having edited the American Transcendentalists' magazine, the *Dial,* and collaborated for several years on Horace Greeley's *New-York Daily Tribune,* for which she would serve as European correspondent. Greeley, an ardent admirer of the French utopian socialist Charles Fourier, but not a "radical," viewed the *Tribune* as a vehicle for elevating mass culture.[1]

Fuller shared this goal, but she took the *Tribune* position for practical as well as intellectual reasons. Her essays and reviews provided a needed income and, in 1847–49, enabled her to remain in Italy.

Although her work was a necessity, she did not take it lightly. "Newspaper writing is next door to conversation and should be conducted on the same principles," she wrote, but as a journalist she crafted prose that was anything but careless.[2] Indeed, during her European and Italian years, her attention to style intensified, distancing her from those Transcendentalist writers who prized spontaneity and were suspicious of literary forms. Possessing what Roland Barthes has called "the pleasure of the text," Fuller loved to write, and she appreciated a well-composed work.

Her journalism also had a strong pedagogical dimension. Her dispatches to the *Tribune* were full of exhortations to her fellow Americans that were quite independent of the tumultuous events she was witnessing. Her well-known observation that "the American in Europe, if a thinking mind, can only become more American" is central to understanding her writings from abroad.[3] To Fuller, becoming "more American" meant reconnecting with an ideal of citizenship derived from the spirit of 1776. She faulted the United States for forgetting its founding principles when initiating a war of expansion against Mexico. She criticized it for failing to resolve such fundamental problems as slavery; the exploitation of workers; and the subordination of women, including domestic abuse by violent men.

Her European vantage point gave her a clearer grasp of problems in her native country, and she expressed regret at not having been as active as she should have been in addressing them. While still keeping her distance from the abolitionist movement, she declared in a dispatch that only in Italy had she come to appreciate the movement's importance and virtues. By grasping the meaning of the Italian Revolution, she believed, Americans could better live up to their own ideals.

Fuller divided Americans traveling in Europe into three types. First, the contemptuous (and contemptible) unthinking man, slavishly seeking status. Second, the presumptuous person who denigrates European culture and art, and instead praises only what is produced by Americans. Finally, those gifted with a critical sense and ready to put to use the best that Europe has to offer. (Artists she set apart in a separate category.) While disdaining the first category, Fuller held out hope for those in the second because of the honesty of their response, however clumsy and mistaken in expression. Her full sympathies lay with the third category. (These classifications seem valid not only for mid-nineteenth-century travelers from an insecure but ambitious America, but for visitors from more mature nations in other eras as well. How many tourists of the first and second categories does each of us know?)

Fuller herself, of course, was a tourist of the spirit and of the ideal, committed to "a profound and sympathetic engagement" with the cultures and peoples she encountered.[4] To be sure, her literary reputation and talents gave her access to experiences that were not possible for everyone. In England and France she met not only icons like William Wordsworth but other writers and intellectuals who made a significant impression on her, including Thomas Carlyle, Giuseppe Mazzini, George Sand, and the Polish poet and patriot Adam Mickiewicz.

But her facility for engaging people from all classes and backgrounds served her well in approaching the common people of Rome and elsewhere, many of whom she came to know well. She took a keen interest in the lives and welfare of the servants she hired, and was drawn to stories of persons of humble origins who overcame adversity to make something of themselves, such as the orphan boy (Germano) so well cared for and educated by friends of his deceased parents that he became an apprentice in the studio of the sculptor Giovanni Maria Benzoni (L 5:80; SG 185). Her growing democratic proclivities stand in contrast to the development of her spiritual father, Ralph Waldo Emerson, from whom she had for some years been distancing herself. Emerson, too, visited England in 1847, where he displayed increasing appreciation for the mental habits of its ruling classes. Fuller, meanwhile, exhibited a growing hostility precisely to these classes.[5]

Fuller's capacity for human sympathy had a strong feminist component. In an October 1847 poem she sent to the London editor William James Linton, a passionate supporter of Mazzini and the revolutionary cause, she suggested that Rome would rise again through the efforts of new vestal virgins, the temple priestesses of ancient Rome. She professed great admiration for twenty-one-year-old Colomba Antonietti from Foligno, killed on June 13, 1849, beside her officer husband, on the ramparts around Rome as French troops shelled the city. She similarly wrote admiringly of the woman who grabbed and extinguished one of the first bombs the French hurled at Rome later that month. Careful to underscore the female presence in the revolution, she even responded as a feminist on visiting a church where "there was no good place for women to sit" even though "as many female saints and martyrs are venerated as male."[6]

All these traits shaped her response to events in Italy. She urged the progressive spirits among her countrymen to express their sympathy for the infant Roman Republic through concrete action.[7] It would please her much, she wrote, to see a cannon "bought by the contributions of Americans" and bearing the names of Washington or Cabot. Inspired by Mazzini, she urged the U.S. government to take a decisive stance in support of the republic. She even ventured so far as to describe the ideal diplomat who should be nominated as ambassador: a citizen of integrity, attuned to the problems of Italy, and fluent in French if not Italian (which Fuller spoke well, but wrote quite imprecisely). "Another century, and I might ask to be made Ambassador myself," she mused in December 1848, "but woman's day has not come yet."[8]

Fuller's aspiration to see the United States well represented in Rome was satisfied by the appointment of Jacob Martin as chargé d'affaires to the Papal States in April 1848, but he died of malaria that August, less than two weeks after presenting his credentials. Next came Lewis Cass Jr., a Democrat from Michigan. Initially unsympathetic to revolutionary ideologies, and instructed by the administration in Washington to be cautious in his political dealings, Cass demonstrated growing support for the republican cause. After the fall of the Roman Republic in 1849, he procured U.S. passports for Mazzini, Giuseppe Avezzana (another revolutionary leader), and Giovanni Angelo Ossoli.[9]

In the interval between Jacob Martin's death and Lewis Cass's arrival, the U.S. government was represented in Italy by two consuls, Nicholas Brown in Rome and James E. Freeman in Ancona on the Adriatic. These two diplomats were among the few foreign representatives to attend the opening of the Roman Constituent Assembly in the Piazza del Campidoglio, seat of the ancient Roman Republic, on February 5, 1849. Indeed, Brown was recalled by Washington for his too explicit support for the Roman Republic, including an incident in July 1849 when he fought off French soldiers attempting to enter his official residence on the pretext of conducting a search for hidden persons (*SG* 282, 307–8).

Fuller had good reason for her preoccupation with securing U.S. recognition of the short-lived Roman Republic. From where could come support for the fragile republican experiment if not from the premier republic in the world? Another republic, France, worked actively to overthrow the Roman Republic, while another liberal power, Great

Britain, fearful of inciting social revolution, provided no support for those who had ended the theocracy (papal rule) in Rome.

To be sure, important differences existed between the United States and the Roman Republic. The Roman constitution, for example, had not the slightest similarity to the federal model of the United States.[10] Yet the larger democratic affinities between the two nations were strong, and Washington's failure to extend recognition had important consequences. In a recent essay, Giuseppe Monsagrati argues that America's lack of recognition seriously undermined the new government's chances of survival.[11] Yet, as always, Fuller's concern was with America as well as with Italy. From her perspective, support for the Roman Republic represented a golden opportunity for America to pursue a course that would be faithful to its origins. Instead, the United States took a Realpolitik approach not unlike that of the imperialistic powers of the Old World.

This very unusual journalist, on one hand, entered fully into the Roman events of 1847–49, while, on the other—it should not seem paradoxical—remained somewhat extraneous to them. No evidence suggests that her relationship with Giovanni Ossoli significantly enlarged her political contacts, but given her intelligence and initiative, she did become sufficiently familiar with the political scene, both before and after the proclamation of the republic by the Constituent Assembly in February 1849, to evaluate the situation critically. She observed the pope's behavior, followed the operations of different governments, read newspapers of differing political views, and gauged the effects of the various political options on the common people and on public opinion.

She also knew the deeper culture of the Roman people. A separate chapter could be written on her frequent visits to Roman churches. (Sant'Agnese and San Luigi dei Francesi were her favorites.) And she made definite political choices, as is clear from her rejection of the politics of the conservative press, and her understanding of the nuances among them. "I am perfectly disgusted with this *Epoca*, it has become a reactionary paper," she wrote Ossoli on April 4, 1849. In March, she had told Ossoli of her preference for *La Pallade* over the moderately liberal *La Speranza Italiana* (*L* 5:219, 222).

Her assessments of political leaders were equally decisive, as one sees in her comments on Terenzio Mamiani, the writer and politician who in 1848 served briefly as prime minister under Pope Pius IX. In dispatches to the *Tribune*, Fuller dismissed Mamiani as "a man of rhetoric, merely" who was "unequal to such a position" and "untried as yet as a leader or statesman." In a May 1848 letter to her friend and confidante the Marchioness Costanza Arconati Visconti, she had echoed the latter's negative judgment of Mamiani and of another prominent politician, Francesco Orioli, dismissing them as "self-trumpeted celebrities, self-constituted rulers of the Roman state." Despite these unfavorable assessments, Fuller nevertheless concluded that no other politician was suited to govern in view of Pius IX's increasing hostility to the republican cause and his opposition to the war to free Italy of Austrian control. It must be added, however, that in her comments on Mamiani she failed to understand the complexity of the situation or the role played by *Don Pirlone*, the satirical journal that she loved, like everyone else, and considered the *Punch* of Rome. Behind *Don Pirlone* were friends of Mamiani like Michelangelo Pinto (not coincidentally the founder of *Epoca*) and Leopoldo Spini.[12]

Elsewhere Fuller found leaders with whom she wholeheartedly sympathized. In Milan, the young members of the provisional government struck her as more open minded than the moderate Tuscans, Romans, or Neapolitans. As part of her dispatches to the *Tribune* she included the written appeals that the Milanese provisional government sent to the German-speaking peoples as well as to the Italians under Austrian rule.[13]

Of all those she admired, none outshone Giuseppe Mazzini. In the early phase of the revolution, Mazzini the confirmed republican seemed to her the exemplary, unheeded Cassandra, free of some Italian patriots' unfounded enthusiasm for the idea of a monarchy. Although there are no known letters between her and Mazzini during 1848, the impression he had made on her in London remained strong. As Larry J. Reynolds, among others, has observed, Fuller was becoming increasingly radical, espousing a republicanism with socialist elements. Others have cited this shared vision as the basis of her unshakable faith in Mazzini. However, the similarity that has been proposed between Fuller's opinion of Italian republicans and Antonio Gramsci's later judgment on the Italian Risorgimento is a bit overstated, if for no other reasons than the difference in time periods and in the quite different points of view from which their respective ideas derived.[14]

Among Fuller's closest Italian friends and confidants were two women with whom she often visited, the Marchioness Costanza Arconati Visconti and Cristina Trivulzio, the Princess Belgioioso. Although Arconati Visconti supported the monarchy, she gave Fuller economic support and opened her way to many contacts and acquaintances, though more elsewhere than in Rome. In the crucial period of early 1849 when the Roman Republic was first proclaimed and then squelched, the letters between the two trailed off to almost nothing, only to begin again when the revolutionary adventure ended, despite their ideological differences.

Belgioioso, a free-spirited Milanese noblewoman of strong patriotic sympathies, in 1848 led two hundred volunteers from Naples to Milan to help free that city from Austrian rule. In April 1849, she was appointed by the revolutionary government to a committee to administer Rome's military hospitals as the city came under siege from French forces. Fuller worked as a volunteer with Belgioioso at the central field hospital, Trinità dei Pellegrini; helped set up a hospital in Rome's Quirinale district, near the papal residence; and directed a field hospital called Fatebenefratelli. Fuller's letters to Belgioioso, and her comments to others, testify to their strong friendship marked by mutual esteem. Writing to her brother Richard in February 1848 (before their shared work as volunteer nurses) Fuller said of Belgioioso: "She is a woman of gallantry which [George] Sand is not, though she also has had several lovers no doubt." Since Sand had previously constituted a source of great attraction for Fuller as "her own androgynous ideal," this comparative assessment is most significant.[15]

Fuller clearly would have liked to emulate Belgioioso, but as she fully conceded, she remained primarily a witness and supporter, rather than a heroine, of the revolution. Nevertheless, hers was an important role. As Reynolds has observed: "The history she told to America as she witnessed it imposed form and meaning upon a failed revolution and upon her life as well."[16]

In Fuller's comments on the Roman people, one can detect realism, skepticism, idealism, and idealization. Once the republican struggle was underway, she conceded the people's ignorance of events, but nevertheless attributed to them "an instinct to recognize measures that are good for it." This understanding was proven, she thought, by the turnout of (male) voters for the January 1849 elections of the Constituent Assembly in the Papal States. In fact, she judged that a higher proportion of voters went to the polls than in the United States.[17] While admitting that had Pius IX not fled Rome in November 1848 the citizens would have remained loyal to him, she believed that the Italian Revolution, "like all genuine ones, has been instinctive" and resulted from a true moral reform of the people. She illustrated this by composing a hypothetical speech by a citizen commenting skeptically on the high moral claims of the Church: "Yes, it ought to be so. Priests ought to be better and wiser than other men; if they were they would not need pomp and temporal power to command respect. Yes it is true, we ought not to lie; we ought not try to impose upon one another. We should rather our children would work honestly for their bread than get it by cheating; begging[;] or the prostitution of their mothers. It would be better to act worthily and kindly, [and this] probably would please God more than the kissing of reliques. We have long darkly felt that these things were so; *now* we know it" (*SG* 250).

Following the April 1849 attack on the Roman Republic by French troops, aided by Neapolitan and Spanish forces, the popular mentality changed profoundly. While noting that the first to wear the "liberty cap" were the poorest and most vulgar citizens (even as they invoked supernatural aid with such sentiments as "Madonna protects us against the bombs; she wills not for Rome to be destroyed"), Fuller later affirmed that "the noblest sentiments are heard from every lip" (*SG* 256).

But as the French occupation continued, it seemed to Fuller that the Roman people lost the extraordinary qualities that the revolutionary events had impressed upon them. When the revolution started, she wrote on July 10, 1849, "The men of Rome had begun, filled with new hopes, to develop unknown energy—they walked quick[ly], their eyes sparkled, they delighted in duty, in responsibility; in a year of such life their effeminacy would have been vanquished." But then she drew a contrast with the present reality: "Now, dejectedly, unemployed, they lounge along the streets feeling that all the implements of labor, all the ensigns of hope, have been snatched from them." An anonymous proclamation of July 4 calling upon the people of Rome (even the courtesans) to rediscover a love of country and display a spirit of passive but disdainful resistance toward the occupiers had little effect, she noted (*SG* 308–10).

Ultimately, perhaps, Fuller had a more intense physical and aesthetic response to Rome in its totality than to its inhabitants as individuals. She described the hopeful Carnival parties of 1847, still under the papal regime, and of 1849, under the republic. Farmers played *morra*. Mendicants, ragged children, and prostitutes filled the streets. In the narrow streets of the Trastevere district, across the Tiber, residents were always ready with a knife. Rome was also, of course, a city of the nobility with their carriages and servants in livery, but, significantly, this class was largely absent from Fuller's writings. She focused rather on the Roman who "still plays amid his serious affairs." "The Roman legions went out singing and dancing to fight in Lombardy," she wrote, "and they fought no less bravely for that." In love with the Eternal City, she delighted in describing its atmosphere and color and the impressions it aroused in her. The destruction of trees, gardens, monuments, and houses by bombs or by preventive security measures during the siege were so many wounds inflicted on her sensitive spirit.[18] Yet one wonders whether Fuller was wholly aware of the minimal contribution Rome could make to the national war, or of the city's own unpreparedness for attack. In her inspection rounds during the French occupation, she conceded that she had realized only too late that the leaders of the city's defense had failed to understand the tactical and technical organization of the French assault (*SG* 310).

Fuller's analysis of political developments in Rome was largely dependent upon her individual informants and on newspapers. The latter, while mostly liberal and democratic, were often at odds, providing her with a certain breadth of observations. Nevertheless, in January 1849 she confessed to her friend Emelyn Story (wife of the expatriate American sculptor William Wetmore Story) that her circle was shrinking to just Ossoli and Pietro Maestri, a leader of the republican party. A friend since Fuller's stay in Milan, Maestri, when he had time, was a rich source of information. She did attempt to enlarge her political relationships, for example, by trying to facilitate the request of Domenico Masi, editor of the *Contemporaneo*, "the organ of the new movement in [the] Papal States" to exchange copies with a few U.S. newspapers (*L* 5:52, 5:169, 6:371).

As her caustic assessment of Mamiani suggests, Fuller held strongly negative opinions of many of the political protagonists of the revolution. She called the Catholic philosopher and politician Vincenzo Gioberti a "pompous verbose charlatan." Briefly president of the council in 1848–49, Gioberti advocated a "League of Princes" confederating the four Italian states of Piedmont-Sardinia, Tuscany, the Pontifical State, and the Kingdom of the Two Sicilies (Sicily and Naples). In promoting this wholly impractical scheme, Fuller believed, Gioberti may have become the pawn of Piedmont's king Charles Albert. The latter she considered a man of physical courage but devoid of mental courage and, in the final analysis, a betrayer of the national cause. Arconati Visconti disagreed with this assessment but, despite their friendship, failed to persuade Fuller to change her view.[19]

Fuller also bitterly criticized the Tuscan Duke Leopold II and even the Florentine people who, after a brief flirtation with revolution, had reached an agreement with the Austrians. And while she had only praise for the Tuscan politician Giuseppe Montanelli, she failed to grasp the fundamental differences between his views and those of Mazzini. Montanelli favored a constituent assembly and a federation of states; Mazzini a united Italian republic (*SG* 245, 255, 258, 261).

Not surprisingly, Fuller leveled her harshest accusations against the aggressor and gravedigger of the republic, the French General Nicolas Oudinot, a "cowardly man" whose defects and deceptions she frequently pointed out. By contrast, the "boyish and foolish" French *envoyé* Ferdinand de Lesseps, sent to Rome to negotiate with the leaders of the republic, seemed to her simply ineffectual and naive (*SG* 298).

Of the tragic figure Pellegrino Rossi, the president of the papal government assassinated in November 1848, Fuller generally echoed the judgment of Italy's democratic party that he was a politician determined either to stop the reforms or empty them of meaning. Writing to her mother, Fuller drew a striking comparison between Rossi and Mazzini. Both had been granted Roman citizenship after returning from abroad. Mazzini had never renounced his Italian origins; Rossi, on the other hand, had become a Peer of France, renouncing his own roots and origins. Twenty-four hours after receiving the Roman citizenship, he was cut down by the knife of Luigi Brunetti, son of the wine carter and populist leader Angelo Brunetti, known by the nickname Ciceruacchio. As for the assassination itself, she judged it an act of violence that nevertheless expressed popular justice and was also full of grandeur.[20]

Fuller's estimates of important secondary figures largely followed the democratic line, although often with nuance. She had kind words for Carlo Emmanuele Muzzarelli, the last president of the council who, although nominated by Pius IX, participated in the transition toward the republic. Fuller admired him for his dignity and courage, and for the way he presented himself on the political scene as a layman and not a monsignor of the Church, which he was. By contrast, she was caustic toward the powerful Torlonia family, known for its charitable donations. When Carlo Torlonia died, some attributed it to heartbreak over the accusations that had been leveled against his brother, Alessandro, a great property owner and speculator. Fuller, with enlightened insight, quoted the popular judgment: "All [Alessandro] gives to Rome is taken from Rome" (*SG* 200, 259–60).

Fuller's opinion of Pius IX changed over the course of months, as did much of Roman and Italian public opinion. Being close to the democratic position she was far from enchanted by him, acknowledging his personal kindness but finding his mind unexceptional. Even between 1847 and the early part of 1848, during the pope's more liberal phase, she wrote of him with caution. By May 1848 she was accusing him of blindness toward the Jesuits, whom he defended as if they were being attacked for their religious vocation and not, as was the case, for their political activity. Of the Jesuit controversy she concluded: "the end was in half measures, always the worst possible. He [the pope] would not entirely yield, and the People would not at all. The Order was ostensibly dissolved, but [a] great part of the Jesuits really remain here in disguise, a constant source of irritation and mischief."[21]

Fuller's absence from Rome from the spring of 1848 until the end of the year, during her pregnancy, interrupted her dispatches to the *Tribune,* making it impossible to follow the evolution of her opinions of the pope and of the governments of Eduardo Fabbri and Pellegrino Rossi, which he installed.[22] She resumed reporting in early December, when the political situation had become very hot and the pope had abandoned all plans of reform and taken refuge in Gaeta where, as Fuller reported, the satirical publication *Don Pirlone* depicted him in a bird cage, ready to sing whatever tune the king of Naples wanted. In general, Fuller's comments in this period were not excessively heavy-handed, attributing to the pope more weakness than malice. In the absence of anyone with comparable authority, she wrote, "the loss of Pius IX is for the moment a great one," implying that it would have been easier to develop a reform program with him on the scene than in his absence. With Pius's speech against liberalism on April 29, 1849, however, she wrote that "the last lingering illusion" had fallen and "the last frail link is broken that bound to him the people of Rome." Were he to return to Rome, she predicted, his reign would be characterized by despotism.[23]

In the gallery of figures populating Fuller's pages, both before and after the birth of the republic, Mazzini, as we have seen, occupies a unique place as the true hero, a man of faith and principles, firm as a rock even in the most difficult moments, and incapable of any cowardly gesture. Such men, she wrote, "conquer always—conquer in defeat."[24] Garibaldi appears less often, but of him, as well, her judgment was positive, with idealizing nuances. For example, she often describes his appearance as youthful, reflecting his spiritual energy. Rebutting well-meaning critics, including Americans, she even painted Garibaldi's retinue in positive colors. The men in red tunics were brigands, she acknowledged, but so were Jesus, Moses, and Aeneas. "To me," she wrote, "men who can throw so slightly aside the ease of wealth, the joys of affection, for the sake of what they deem honor, in whatsoever form, are the 'respectable.'" But she did not deny that Garibaldi's forces included adventurers and desperate men, and in letters of March and July 1849 she expressed fears of abuses of power, or unwarranted violence, by barbaric elements.[25]

Fuller's vision of the European political scene and, more deeply, of the Italian scene, did not go much beyond the observations of the Italian democratic press at the time. She paid close attention to events, however, and her judgments were sharp. She understood that the polls for the French Legislative Assembly on May 13, 1849, which would be decisive for Rome's fate, offered little to rely on. And she emphasized the English ruling class's aversion to the revolution, which she considered greater even than that of the Russian czar. Symptomatic, she believed, was the way many members of Rome's English community turned against the city's English-language newspaper, the *Roman Advertiser*, failing to renew their subscriptions when the paper under a new owner adopted a progressive and pro-republican editorial policy (*SG* 279, 294).

The recurring suspicion of plots and provocations in her dispatches and correspondence sometimes becomes obsessive. In every incident, actual or possible, from Naples to Milan, Rome to Florence, she saw an attempt by reactionaries determined to throw a negative light on the forces of progress or to induce the populace to rise up against the revolution. Strangely, too, Fuller did not inform her readers of the social reforms enacted by the republic, including abolition of the tax on wheat, employment for textile workers and unemployed artisans, confiscation and distribution of church properties, and the allocation to the poor of the rooms that had housed the Holy Office.[26]

Fuller's judgment in some cases was clearly shaped by her own privileged background. For instance, she wrote that in French-occupied Rome, Louis Bonaparte's soldiers and the Roman Republic volunteers were as different as "that of a body compared with spirit." In retrospect, one can see that she held impossibly high standards for troops lacking intellectual refinement and performing an ugly, unpleasant job. Yet her assertion that "in two days of French 'order' more acts of violence have been committed than in two months under the Triumvirate" (the government of the Roman Republic) was not far from the truth (*SG* 306, 307–8).

Fuller's emotional engagement with the Italian Revolution was profound. She collected funds from supporters in America to help the republic, as others had done earlier for Greece and Poland, and from that intense involvement came many pages of genuine literary and historical merit. As Larry J. Reynolds has written, her journalistic dispatches from Italy represent her best and most lasting work. Above all, she placed these events in a universal context. The struggle between the forces of democracy and of reaction could last half a century, she wrote, "but the result is sure. All Europe . . . is to be under Republican Government in the next century."[27]

Given all this, one can only regret the loss of her history of the Roman Republic in the shipwreck that took her life, along with those of Giovanni Ossoli and their son. At least some of her contemporaries held the same opinion. In the days following the disaster, Henry David Thoreau searched in vain for Fuller's manuscript among the papers that floated ashore on the beach of Fire Island.[28]

The destruction of the Roman Republic did not end Margaret Fuller's hopes for a better future. "The memory will console amid the spectacles of meanness, selfishness and faithlessness which life may yet have in store for the pilgrim," she wrote on June 21, 1849, as French bombs fell on Rome. "Go where I may," she added a few days later, "a large part of my heart will ever remain in Italy." Earlier, in April 1848, she had written: "Should my hopes be dashed to the ground, it will not change my faith, but the struggle for its manifestation is to me of vital interest."[29] For this reason she had chosen to stay in Rome, despite pleas to return home. A century and a half later, one can recognize how profoundly her letters and dispatches from Italy document her belief in the progress of human thought and human society. Indeed, the years after her death saw the realization of many of the dreams of this passionate "American pilgrim."

Notes

1. Bell Gale Chevigny, *The Woman and the Myth: Margaret Fuller's Life and Writings*, rev. ed. (Boston: Northeastern Univ. Press, 1994), 288.

2. Larry J. Reynolds, *European Revolutions and the American Literary Renaissance* (New Haven, Conn.: Yale Univ. Press, 1988), 78. See also Christina Zwarg, *Feminist Conversations: Fuller, Emerson, and the Play of Reading* (Ithaca, N.Y.: Cornell Univ. Press, 1995).

3. *"These Sad But Glorious Days": Dispatches from Europe, 1846–1850*, ed. Larry J. Reynolds and Susan Belasco Smith (New Haven, Conn.: Yale Univ. Press, 1991), 161 (hereafter cited in text and notes as *SG*).

4. *The Essential Margaret Fuller*, ed. Jeffrey Steele (New Brunswick, N.J.: Rutgers Univ. Press, 1995), xlii. Steele here is specifically writing about her Italian experience. Note also Fuller's September 1847 comment: "Italy receives me as a long lost child and I feel myself at home here." *The Letters of Margaret Fuller*, ed. Robert N. Hudspeth, 6 vols. (Ithaca, N.Y.: Cornell Univ. Press, 1983–94), 4:293 (hereafter cited in text and notes as *L*).

5. Zwarg finds a key to Fuller's development "as a feminist and as a theorist" in her relationship with Emerson. *Feminist Conversations*, 2. Chevigny notes "the modern radical analysis toward which she was moving when her life ended." *Woman and the Myth*, 369.

6. The letters to Linton and to Elizabeth Hoar, June 17, 1849, referring to Colomba Antonietti, are in *L* 4:241; the quote from Fuller and her allusion to an anonymous woman's heroism are in *SG* 205.

7. *SG* 259, 310–11. Only one U.S. citizen, Thomas Crawford, joined the Roman Civil Guard. Other Americans in Rome, Fuller wrote, dismissed the Italians and the Romans as "not like our people." Fuller, *At Home and Abroad, or, Things and Thoughts in America and in Europe*, ed. Arthur B. Fuller (1856; Port Washington, N.Y.: Kennikat Press, 1971), 346–48.

8. *SG* 161, 245. Fuller's reference to Cabot doubtless alluded to the Italian-born John Cabot who, under a patent issued by England's King Henry VII, explored North America's Atlantic coast in 1497–98.

9. *SG* 276–77, 282, 308. On October 5, 1849, Cass wrote to Fuller in Florence that he had provided three passports (without specifying the names of their holders). Emma Detti, *Margaret Fuller Ossoli e i suoi corrispondenti* (Florence: Le Monnier, 1942), 333–34. The day before, Fuller had written to Cass that Ossoli was being harassed by the police despite the fact that he held a U.S. passport. *L* 5:267.

10. Emilia Morelli, "La Costituzione americana e i democratici italiani dell'Ottocento," *Rassegna storica del Risorgimento* 76, no. 4 (1989): 428.

11. Monsagrati, "Alle prese con la democrazia. Gran Bretagna e U.S.A. di fronte alla Repubblica Romana," *Rassegna storica del Risorgimento* 86, no. 4 (1999): 287–306.

12. *L* 5:69; Detti, *Fuller Ossoli*, 299–300; *SG* 229, 232 (Fuller's comments on Mamiani in the *Tribune*). On Pinto, see Francesco Guida, *Michelangelo Pinto, un letterato e patriota romano tra Italia e Russia* (Rome: Archivio Guido Izzi, 1998).

13. *SG* 217–19. The Milanese provisional government included sixteen ministers, with Gabrio Casati as the president and Cesare Correnti as the general secretary.

14. Joseph Rossi, in *The Image of America in Mazzini's Writings* (Madison: Univ. of Wisconsin Press, 1954), 61, affirms that with Fuller's death, Mazzini lost a key propagandist at a time when American public opinion was swinging toward the more conservative and authoritarian policies of the Italian statesman Count Camillo Benso di Cavour. On Fuller's own evolving political views, Reynolds writes that in these years she "acquired the socialism that became such a firm and intense part of her thought." *European Revolutions*, 60. Zwarg goes further. Noting that Karl Marx became a contributor to the *New-York Daily Tribune* two years after Fuller's death, Zwarg writes: "One could argue that she prepared a space for Marx." *Feminist Conversations*, 198. That Fuller was on the verge of embracing Marxist socialism, and that the manuscript that disappeared in the shipwreck in which she lost her life was dedicated not only to Italian events but also to the 1848 Paris uprising, is an interesting hypothesis, but supported by only a few clues. See Chevigny, *Woman and the Myth*, 382–83, 395, 399n22. On the alleged similarities between Fuller and Gramsci, see Zwarg, *Feminist Conversations*, 196.

15. *L* 5:53; Chevigny, *Woman and the Myth*, 300. On Fuller's hospital service see Donato Tamblé's "Documents in the State Archive of Rome" in this volume.

16. Reynolds, *European Revolutions*, 78.

17. *SG* 255 (quoted passage), 282. As Paula Blanchard has noted, Fuller neglected to emphasize that the so-called universal suffrage was limited to men. Blanchard, *Margaret Fuller: From Transcendentalism to Revolution* (New York: Delacorte Press, 1978), 300.

18. *SG* 249 (quoted passages), 276, 284, 293. Fuller described her dismay at the effects of the French attack on Rome in a disconsolate letter to Ralph Waldo Emerson. See Blanchard, *Fuller*, 309.

19. *SG* 210, 225, 234–35, 247–48, 254–55. For Costanza Arconati Visconti's high opinion of Gioberti, see Detti, *Fuller Ossoli*, 299. Fuller's negative opinion may have been conditioned by Gioberti's status as a Catholic priest.

20. Howard R. Marraro, *American Opinion on the Unification of Italy* (New York: Columbia Univ. Press, 1932), 51; Marraro, in turn, cites William Ellery Channing et al., eds., *Memoirs of Margaret Fuller Ossoli*, 2 vols. (Boston: Phillips, Sampson, 1852; Boston: Roberts Brothers, 1881), and *At Home and Abroad*, the collection of Fuller letters published by her brother Arthur B. Fuller. Jeffrey Steele, discussing Fuller's description of the Rossi assassination, comments: "It is difficult to believe that she was not present." *Essential Fuller*, xlii. On her comparison of Rossi and Mazzini, see also the *Tribune* dispatches quoted in *SG* 260, 262.

21. *SG* 227. Chevigny, in noting Fuller's "slowly evolving portrait of the Pope and the people of Rome," suggests that in the early phase of Pius IX's pontificate, Fuller, whose father had died when she was twenty-five, saw the pope as a strong father figure. *Woman and the Myth*, 378.

22. Giovanni Ossoli was with Fuller briefly around the time of her delivery (September 5, 1848), but then returned to Rome to serve in the Civic Guard in which he had been enrolled since November 15, 1847 (and for which service he received a promotion). Chevigny (*Woman and the Myth*, 374) and Nicole Tonkovich (*Domesticity with a Difference: The Nonfiction of Catharine Beecher, Sarah J. Hale, and Margaret Fuller* [Jackson: Univ. of Mississippi Press, 1997], 187) assert that the couple's separation at this time related to Ossoli's military duties, not to the necessity of hiding their relationship.

23. *SG* 229, 247, 295; Marraro, *American Opinion*, 51–53.

24. *SG* 224–25, 262–64 (quoted passage, 264). Fuller did cite one limitation in Mazzini: "He sees not, perhaps would deny, the bearing of some events, which even now begin to work their way. . . . I allude to that of which the cry of Communism, the systems of Fourier, &c, are but forerunners." *SG* 225. See also Fuller, *At Home and Abroad*, 320.

25. *SG* 305; *L* 5:207, 245. Earlier, she had offered food and drink to some followers of Garibaldi she met on the way back to Rome after visiting her child in Rieti. Blanchard, *Fuller*, 305.

26. Chevigny, *Woman and the Myth*, 386.

27. *SG* 278; Reynolds, *European Revolutions*, 57.

28. *Margaret Fuller. Un' Americana a Roma, Lettere 1847–1849*, ed. Rosella Mamoli Zorzi (Pordenone: Studio Tesi, 1986), xxx.

29. *SG* 230, 300–301, 310; see also 320. Cf. Blanchard's observation that Mazzini, even though he recognized that the defense of Rome was hopeless, knew that "even a useless defense could be an inspiration to Italians in the years ahead. It was not a remarkable view for a man who, even to look at him, seemed made for martyrdom. What was remarkable was that the whole city shared it." *Fuller*, 308.

8

Righteous Violence

The Roman Republic and
Margaret Fuller's Revolutionary Example

LARRY J. REYNOLDS

In her dispatches from Italy during 1848 and 1849, Margaret Fuller spoke as an American on behalf of what she called "my Italy" and celebrated the romantic heroism of the defenders of the Roman Republic. "The voice of this age," she wrote after the republic fell, "shall yet proclaim the names of some of these Patriots whose inspiring soul was JOSEPH MAZZINI—men as nobly true to their convictions as any that have ever yet redeemed poor, stained Humanity."[1] After she, her husband, Ossoli, and their son, Angelino, fled Rome for Florence, she remained a defiant supporter of the Risorgimento. Uncertain of the future yet retaining a sense of divine mission, she assumed the role of a seeress in her dispatches and created a vision of righteous violence and destruction that echoes Isaiah and the coming era of Emmanuel. In her last dispatch, on January 6, 1850, she fiercely declares,

> The seeds for a vast harvest of hatreds and contempts are sown over every inch of Roman ground, nor can that malignant growth be extirpated, till the wishes of Heaven shall waft a fire that will burn down all, root and branch, and prepare the earth for an entirely new culture. The next revolution, here and elsewhere, will be radical. . . . Sons cannot be

long employed in the conscious enslavement of their sires, fathers of their children. That advent called EMMANUEL begins to be understood, and shall no more so foully be blasphemed. . . . Do you laugh, Roman Cardinal, as you shut the prison-door on woman weeping for her son martyred in the cause of his country? Do you laugh, Austrian officer, as you drill the Hungarian and Lombard youth to tremble at your baton? Soon you, all of you, shall "*believe* and tremble." (*SG* 321–22)

As I have argued elsewhere, of all American authors, Fuller alone "had the opportunity, the inclination, and ultimately the resolve to align herself wholeheartedly with European democratic liberalism." This alignment, moreover, sharpened rather than clouded her vision, and her dispatches remain one of the most stirring accounts of the people and events involved in the Italian revolutions of 1848–49. As Barbara Packer has pointed out, they are also "one of the most absorbing, brilliant, and far-ranging of all texts written by the Transcendentalists."[2] My goal in this essay is to trace their more remarkable effects on American thought and writing in the period from their appearance to the Civil War. Her example, I will suggest, may have indirectly inspired that war. Her support of political violence in Europe prefigured a major change in antislavery thinking in the United States and influenced the pro-war attitudes of some of its most important northern intellectual advocates.

Although Fuller in her dispatches celebrates the heroism of Mazzini, Garibaldi, and the Roman republicans who fought unsuccessfully against the French army that restored Pope Pius IX to power, her own sustained commitment to the revolution struck many in America as heroic, especially after her tragic death at sea in 1850. In his 1852 introduction to a reprinting of Fuller's *Papers on Literature and Art,* Horace Greeley refers to "Italy's last struggle for liberty and light" and credits Fuller with having been "a portion of its incitement, its animation, its informing soul. She bore more than a woman's part in its conflicts and its perils; and the bombs of that ruthless army which a false and traitorous government impelled against the ramparts of Republican Rome, could have stilled no voice more eloquent in its exposures, no heart more lofty in its defiance, of the villany [*sic*] which so wantonly drowned in blood the hopes, while crushing the dearest rights, of a people, than those of Margaret Fuller."[3] Fuller's brother Arthur, who would distinguish himself as a fighting chaplain in the Civil War, similarly credited Fuller's *At Home and Abroad* (1856) (the first reprinting of her *Tribune* dispatches) with the potential to "inspire its readers with an increased love of republican

institutions, and an earnest purpose to seek the removal of every national wrong which hinders our beloved country from being a perfect
example and hearty helper of other nations in their struggles for liberty."[4] The main "wrong" he alludes to, of course, is slavery, or "this
horrible cancer of Slavery," as his sister called it in her December 1847
dispatch from Europe (*SG* 165).

Although Greeley and Arthur can be suspected of bias because of
their attachment to Fuller, her defiant voice and heart indeed inspired
many Americans in the decade following her death, especially those in
New England who turned to political violence as a means to rid the
country of slavery. In the early 1840s, Fuller had kept her distance from
the abolitionists, considering them too fanatical in their activities. In
1845, however, she published seven pieces in the *Tribune* against slavery,
and in Europe, perhaps due to the influence of her traveling companions, the abolitionist Quakers Rebecca and Marcus Spring, she had a
change of heart. "How it pleases me here to think of the Abolitionists!"
she wrote from Italy in late 1847. "I could never endure to be with them
at home, they were so tedious, often so narrow, always so rabid and exaggerated in their tone. But, after all, they had a high motive, something
eternal in their desire and life; and, if it was not the only thing worth
thinking of it was really something worth living and dying for to free a
great nation from such a terrible blot, such a threatening plague. God
strengthen them and make them wise to achieve their purpose!"[5]

As John Demos has pointed out, the European revolutions of 1848–
49 persuaded a number of abolitionists to accept the need for violent
resistance to tyranny and oppression. Thus Theodore Parker asserted,
"All the great charters of humanity have been *writ in blood*, and must
continue to be so for some centuries." While William Lloyd Garrison
and his followers continued to argue for nonresistance, others such as
Angelina Grimké Weld, Samuel May, Wendell Phillips, Henry Wright,
and Parker Pilsbury all abandoned their "peace principles" in the 1850s
and argued for armed resistance. Pilsbury even told the Massachusetts
Anti-Slavery Society that "he longed to see the time come when Boston
should run with blood from Beacon Hill to the foot of Broad Street."
Parker, Franklin Sanborn, and Thomas Wentworth Higginson—
Transcendentalists all—went beyond rhetoric by conspiring with John
Brown, as part of his "Secret Six," and provided him with the money
and arms he used in "Bleeding Kansas" and Harpers Ferry. Meanwhile, Fuller friends Alcott, Thoreau, and Emerson sanctified Brown

after his capture and beat the drums of war. In a journal entry of 1843 Emerson called Fuller "an inspirer of courage, the secret friend of all nobleness" and added, "she rose before me at times into heroical & godlike regions."[6] After her death, and the sensational newspapers accounts devoted to it, she became even more heroic in his eyes and in those of her other readers.

When Fuller's *Tribune* dispatches first appeared in America, they evoked massive public sympathy for the defenders of Rome and antipathy for Pope Pius IX and the French army that came to his aid. Throughout June and July of 1849, Fuller's reports inspired sympathy meetings in New York City, New Orleans, and elsewhere. (Southern defenders of slavery and conservative New England Whigs condemned the European revolutions privately.)[7] Crowds of supporters adopted numerous resolutions calling for the United States to support the republican struggle "by every means possible." And a number of American writers, including James Russell Lowell and John Greenleaf Whittier, joined Fuller in her commitment to the Roman republicans. In his poem "Freedom," Lowell alludes to the issue of American slavery as he depicts Italy as a beautiful pearl lying before the swine of Austria and declares, "Welcome to me whatever breaks a chain, / That surely is of God and all divine." Whittier's "To Pius IX," written after the fall of the republic, depicts the pope as a cowardly tyrant and extends the following sarcastic challenge: "Stand where Rome's blood was freest shed, / Mock Heaven with impious thanks and call / Its curses on the patriot dead, / Its blessing on the Gaul!" Walt Whitman, too, inspired by Fuller's dispatches, wrote in "Resurgemus," which became the first poem of *Leaves of Grass:* "Not a grave of those slaughtered ones, / But is growing its seed of freedom, / In its turn to bear seed, / Which the winds shall carry afar and resow, / And the rain nourish."[8] The "grass" of *Leaves of Grass* thus has one of its origins in Italy, though transformed into a symbol of American democracy by an aspiring national bard.

Though the leading intellectuals and writers and American people, who were predominantly Protestant, sympathized with the Italian revolutionaries, Catholics in America strongly opposed them for obvious reasons and resented Fuller's criticism of the pope. Bishop Hughes of New York in a widely reprinted letter to the New York *Courier and Inquirer* denounced the "revolutionists in Rome" and asserted that they had established "a reign of terror over the Roman people." Hughes pointed out that no ambassador had recognized the Roman Republic, "except it be the female plenipotentiary who furnishes the *Tribune* with diplomatic correspondence."9 (The U.S. government had instructed the new chargé d'affaires in Rome, Lewis Cass Jr., to delay recognition of the Roman Republic until it showed it could sustain itself, a reticence Fuller found especially galling.) Fuller responded to Hughes's denigration of the Roman republicans by declaring the city safe, and asserting "I, a woman, walk everywhere alone, and all the little children do the same, with their nurses."10

The limited opposition in America to the Roman Republic was fueled by columns reprinted from the ultraconservative London *Times*. During the siege of Rome, the reporter for the *Times*, who traveled with the French army, claimed the city was defended by "the degenerate remnant of the Roman people" and by "a nest of adventurers, from every part not only of Italy but of Europe."11 The *Times* thus became another target of Fuller's hostility. "There exists not in Europe a paper more violently opposed to the cause of freedom than the *Times*," she informed her readers, "and neither its leaders nor its foreign correspondence [*sic*] are to be depended upon" (*SG* 294). The American poet Henry Wadsworth Longfellow agreed that the *Times* "falsified and adulterated the generous wine of Truth," and he marveled "that it should be sent over here, as the genuine article, and that the good people here should smack their lips over it, and twirl it round in their little hearts, as in small glasses, and say 'How delightful!'" The New York *Herald*, a rival of the *Tribune*, drew most heavily from the *Times* for its coverage, and ironically it was Fuller's good friend Emerson who most enthusiastically promoted the *Times*, calling it in 1848 "the best newspaper of the world."12

Throughout 1849, after he had returned from his trip abroad, Emerson prepared lectures based on his stay in England that would form chapters of his book *English Traits*. He devotes an entire chapter to the *Times*, calling it "a living index of the colossal British power. Its existence honors the people who dare to print all they know, dare to know all the facts."13 It was not just the ultraconservative coverage of this English paper, though, that made Emerson skeptical of the European revolutions of 1848–49. His faith in individualism also shaped his attitude, which most often took the form of sarcasm and condescension. At the very moment Fuller was ardently asking for American support of the revolutionary effort in Rome, Emerson was entering comments such as the following in his journal: "There will be no revolution 'till we see new men"; "All spiritual or real power makes its own place. Revolutions of violence, then, are scrambles merely"; "Hungary, it seems, must take the yoke again, & Austria, & Italy, & Prussia, & France. Only the English race can be trusted with Freedom."[14]

The wide gulf separating Emerson's fatalism and Fuller's activism in the late 1840s had developed over the course of the decade, and it grew out of a small difference in the transcendental idealism they once shared. Both authors during the early 1840s subscribed to the central concept of the Romantic movement—organicism—and they believed that the singular soul, like the human race itself, was involved in an ongoing process of perfection whereby the seed of the divine at the center of the self and humanity was being impelled toward a perfect form; however, for Emerson the self was primary, social institutions secondary, for he believed that as one perfected the self the world would change for the better. As he explained, "Spirit alters, moulds, makes" the world we live in. "As soon as you conform your life to the pure idea in your mind, that will unfold its great proportions. A correspondent revolution in things will attend the influx of the spirit. So fast will disagreeable appearances, swine, spiders, snakes, pests, madhouses, prisons, enemies, vanish; they are temporary and shall be no more seen."[15] Fuller, however, came to believe that social conditions could thwart the spiritual growth of the individual, and thus one needed to strive to perfect society to allow for the more important perfection of the self. She develops this thesis in *Woman in the Nineteenth Century*, using Goethe to make her point. As she puts it, "Goethe thinks, As the man, so the institutions! . . . A man can grow in any place, if he will. Ay!, but Goethe, bad institutions are prison walls and impure air that make him stupid, so that he does not will."[16] So, while Emerson in the midst of the European revolutions declares "we are authorized to say much on the destinies of one, nothing on those of many" (*JMN* 10:310), Fuller insists upon "the necessity of some practical application of the precepts of Christ" (*SG* 119).

After Fuller's death, Emerson, as one of the three editors of her *Memoirs*, struggled to come to terms with her life, as it was revealed to him through the journals, letters, and other materials that came into his hands from various sources, and her memory informed his own growing political engagement. Passage of the Fugitive Slave Law, the Kansas Nebraska Act, the trial and remission of Anthony Burns, the beating of Charles Sumner on the floor of the United States Senate, and, in 1859, John Brown's raid on Harpers Ferry all drew Emerson away from detached idealism and into the political fray, as a body of recent criticism has shown.[17] Moreover, to read through the collection *Emerson's Anti-slavery Writings* (1995), edited by Len Gougeon and Joel Myerson, is to be impressed by the extent and fervor of this participation, even knowing that Emerson's journals periodically disdain his efforts.

In his essay "Fate," published in *The Conduct of Life* (1860), Emerson discloses the shift in his attitude regarding the limitations one must confront to attain freedom, as he declares, "We must see that the world is rough and surly, and will not mind drowning a man or a woman, but swallows your ship like a grain of dust." His reference to shipwreck and drowning suggests he may have been thinking of Fuller, and he not only arrives at Fuller's position on political oppression by declaring "every spirit makes its house; but afterwards the house confines the spirit," he also, as Cristina Zwarg has shown, uses Fuller as the undisclosed heroine of his essay, as he lauds the power of the exceptional person to overcome fate.[18] In his journal Emerson cites Fuller by name, writing, "A personal influence towers up in memory the only worthy force when we would gladly forget numbers or money or climate, gravitation & the rest of Fate. Margaret, wherever she came, fused people into society, & a glowing company was the result. When I think how few persons can do that feat for the intellectual class, I feel our squalid poverty" (*JMN* 11:449).

In "Fate," Fuller's name is removed, and her gender altered, as she becomes Emerson's "hero": "Society is servile from want of will, and therefore the world wants saviours and religions. One way is right to go; the hero sees it, and moves on that aim, and has the world under him for root and support. He is to others as the world. His approbation is honor; his dissent, infamy. . . . A personal influence towers up in memory only worthy, and we gladly forget numbers, money, climate, gravitation, and the rest of Fate." Emerson's need to turn heroism into a masculine quality, though informed by Fuller's example, responds to the dominant assumptions of the day, of course, and almost all of his contemporaries, including women, shared this assumption. Louisa May Alcott, in her novel *Moods*, for example, paid tribute to Fuller, her role model, by having two of her male protagonists go to Italy to fight alongside Garibaldi on behalf of the Roman Republic. Her female heroine stays at home.[19]

Despite his inability to go beyond his gendering of political power,[20] Emerson revealed in a lecture in 1855 that his thinking about collective effort had changed: "Whilst I insist on the doctrine of the independence and the inspiration of the individual, I do not cripple but exalt the social action." He added, "It is so delicious to act with great masses to great aims."[21] Ten years previously, such a sentiment would not have escaped his lips, given his commitment to self-reliant individualism. During the late 1850s, Emerson also altered his views on violent means, becoming more and more outraged at southern intransigence and aggression. In 1859, he quoted with approval what John Brown said to him privately about the Golden Rule and the Declaration of Independence: "Better that a whole generation of men, women and children should pass away by a violent death than that one word of either should be violated in this country."[22] By the time the Civil War began, Emerson had become "merciless as a steel bayonet,"[23] according to Hawthorne, and this was not an overstatement. "Ah! Sometimes gunpowder smells good" Emerson declared while visiting the Charlestown Navy Yard, and in an address at Tufts College, he asserted, "The brute noise of cannon has a most poetic echo in these days, as instrument of the primal sentiments of humanity."[24]

Years before her friend Emerson turned radical, Fuller in her dispatches revealed a fierceness about achieving the utopian ends she sought, and she defended violence as a means to resist oppression and bring about justice. She had met Mazzini in England before journeying to Italy, and her willingness to accept violence partly flowed from her support of his radical position with the Risorgimento. Mazzini had plotted a number of insurrections against Italian rulers throughout the 1820s and 1830s, and he was living in exile under sentence of death. His revolutionary nationalism, calling for a unitary Italian republic, stood in sharp contrast to the conservative federalism of the Neo-Guelph movement, which sought a federation of Italian states under papal leadership, and to the moderate constitutionalism of northern Italian progressives who sought a free and united Italy under a constitutional monarch.[25] Fuller disparaged both the so-called Moderate Party and the Neo-Guelph movement as she defended Mazzini's revolutionary politics, and she went beyond her abstract republican principles while doing so. The most dramatic and central example of this was her approval of the assassination of Count Pellegrino Rossi. On November 16, 1848, Rossi, the new prime minister of the Papal States, was stabbed in the throat as he entered the Chamber of Deputies. In the *Tribune* Fuller reported that afterward soldiers and citizens joined in singing "Blessed the hand that rids the earth of a tyrant," and, she added, "'Certainly, the manner *was* grandiose'" (*SG* 240). This was her private sentiment as well, and she told her mother, "For me, I never thought to have heard of a violent death with satisfaction, but this act affected me as one of terrible justice."[26] To some Americans, such as her friends the Springs, Fuller had gone too far, but she defended her position in a letter to them:

> What you say is deeply true about the peace way being the best. If any one see clearly how to work in that way, let him in God's name. . . . Meanwhile I am not sure that I can keep my hands free from blood. I doubt I have not the strength. . . . You, Marcus, could you let a Croat insult Rebecca, carry off Eddie to be an Austrian serf; and leave little Marcus bleeding in the dust? . . . If so, you are a Christian; you know I never pretended to be except in dabs and sparkles here and there." (*L* 5:295–96)

Fuller's religion was eclectic, and the New Testament was but one of many books that shaped her self-image and sociopolitical thought.

A primary reason she responded as she did to Rossi's murder, and became an advocate of righteous violence, was that she viewed it through the lens of her reading in classic literature, which dominated her youth. Her first publication, an article written when she was twenty-four, was a defense of the character of Brutus, which drew heavily upon Plutarch's *Lives*,[27] and in Rome she assumed that task again. Like Plutarch and like Shakespeare in *Julius Caesar*, she imagined Brutus as the ideal patriot, motivated by a sense of duty and honor. In her Boston Conversations, Fuller and her students discussed whether a woman could ever perform Brutus's "great action" and show his moral courage and sense of duty, a "higher law," as the Transcendentalists would call it. As Elizabeth Peabody put it in her transcription, "A great deal of talk arose here—and Margaret repelled the sentimentalism that took away woman's moral power of performing stern duty." In her Roman diary, in an entry for February 1849, Fuller returned to the murder of Rossi, agreeing with a "young Frenchman" that "the act would have been heroic, if the murderer had stood firm and avowed it. It would indeed then have been the act of Brutus."[28] Of course, there are a number of other distinctions Fuller elides (Rossi was no powerful tyrant), but my point is that this literary and historical treatment determined her perspective.

For some conservatives in the United States, though, the lens through which they viewed such an event was not the defense of the

Roman Republic from Caesar's tyranny in 44 BC, but rather, the French Revolution of 1789. In antebellum American society the nearness in time to the revolution's 1794 Reign of Terror gave terms such as "jacobinical," "bloody," and "revolutionary" such powerful associations, now lost to us by the passage of time. Sensational reports about the horrors of the Santo Domingo slave revolts between 1791 and 1804 also provided terrifying images for those like Hawthorne who pondered the relation between abolitionist exhortation and slave violence.[29] It was because of this alternative lens that Hawthorne, for one, saw Fuller as a threatening figure. James Russell Lowell in his "Ode to France" had described the two Liberties familiar to the public, one "a maiden mild and undefiled / Like her who bore the world's redeeming child," the other "Vengeance, axe in hand, that stood / Holding a tyrant's head up by the clotted hair." In her dispatches, Fuller assumed both personae. At times she became Liberty leading the people; at others, the Virgin Mary, especially the Mater Dolorosa, an image that had fascinated Fuller for years.[30]

Despite Fuller's attempts in Italy to keep her actual motherhood secret, rumors of her liaison with Ossoli and the existence of a love child circulated in the United States and affected responses to her dispatches. Moreover, by committing herself so wholeheartedly to the European revolutionary scene, by creating a fierce public female persona speaking on behalf of the Italian people, by supporting the violent overthrow of the most powerful politico-religious leader in the world, she inspired both admiration and anxiety. Nathaniel Hawthorne's response seems to have contained a mixture of the two. In *The Scarlet Letter* (1850), he allows his heroine, Hester Prynne, to assume the role of Divine Maternity in the opening tableau of his novel, as she stands with the illegitimate Pearl on the scaffold, subjected to public humiliation, and he then presents her as the Mater Dolorosa in the final tableau, as she holds her lover, the dying Arthur Dimmesdale, in her arms. In the interval between these scenes, Hawthorne emphasizes the turmoil and wickedness Hester stirs up in her role as a revolutionary. Without the influence of Pearl, he writes, "she might, and not improbably would, have suffered death from the stern tribunals of the period, for attempting to undermine the foundations of the Puritan establishment."[31]

Throughout the summer of 1849, Hawthorne, like Pope Pius IX, sought a political restoration, writing letters to friends, to be published in the newspapers, and later telling readers of "The Custom House" that he had been victimized by the bloodthirsty Whigs, who acting out of a "fierce and bitter spirit of malice and revenge" (*SL* 32) had struck off his head with the political guillotine and ignominiously kicked it about. Hawthorne's association of Fuller with political assassination and revolutionary violence informed not only *The Scarlet Letter* but later works as well, as Thomas R. Mitchell points out in his excellent book *Hawthorne's Fuller Mystery*. In the *Blithedale Romance* (1852), for example, we learn that Zenobia, obviously based on Fuller, has the look of a woman about to plunge a dagger into her rival, an act of passion more likely "in Italy, instead of New England."[32] Some eight years later, in *The Marble Faun*, Hawthorne draws upon his knowledge of Fuller's sexual and political activities in Rome to create Miriam's relationships with the villainous unnamed model and with her childlike friend Donatello, who murders the model at her bidding. As Mitchell points out, "In a parallel to Fuller's efforts to articulate an ideological justification for the republican insurrection in Rome by linking it to democratic revolutions of the past, Miriam directs Donatello to Pompey's forum immediately after the murder and 'treading loftily past,' proclaims: 'For there was a great deed done here! . . . a deed of blood, like ours! Who knows, but we may meet the high and ever-sad fraternity of Caesar's murderers, and exchange a salutation?'"[33]

Obviously Hawthorne understood Fuller's perspective on the revolutionary events of 1848–49, but by using the term "murderer" to denote Brutus and his co-conspirators, Hawthorne revealed his rejection of it. The notorious "defective and evil nature" Hawthorne attributed to Fuller in his Italian notebooks may thus stem from repressed political, as well as sexual, anxieties. In one of his last unfinished romances, "Septimius Felton," Hawthorne declared, "In times of Revolution and public disturbance, all absurdities are more unrestrained; the measure of calm sense, the habits, the orderly decency, are in a measure lost. More people become insane, I should suppose; offenses against public morality, female license, are more numerous; suicides, murders, all ungovernable outbreaks of men's thoughts, embodying themselves in wild acts, take place more frequently, and with less horror to the lookers-on."[34] This is Hawthorne's nightmare world, and one has to believe that the ghost of Margaret Fuller haunts it.

At the opposite end of the political spectrum from Hawthorne, a number of ardent abolitionists responded with admiration to Fuller's revolutionary example and became active advocates of violent resistance to slavery in the United States. Samuel Gridley Howe, one of John Brown's Secret Six, was married to the popular poet Julia Ward Howe, who idolized John Brown and Fuller both. She had been a student of Fuller's in Boston and took her as her role model. After Fuller's death, Howe went to Rome and socialized with Fuller's friends there and even took a lover, as Fuller had done. In her poem "From Newport to Rome, 1848" (published in 1854), Howe pays tribute to Fuller's revolutionary example by imagining herself witnessing the defeat of the Roman Republic:

> I hear the battle-thunder boom,
> Cannon to cannon answering loud;
> I hear the whizzing shots that fling
> Their handful to the stricken crowd.
> I see the bastions bravely manned,
> The patriots gathered in the breach;
> . . . The walls are stormed, the fort is ta'en,
> The city's heart with fainter throb
> Receives its death-stroke—all is lost,
> And matrons curse, and children sob.

Howe concludes the poem hopefully, however, punning on Fuller's name:

> With fuller power, let each avow
> The kinship of his human blood;
> With fuller pulse, let every heart
> Swell to high pangs of brotherhood.
> With fuller light, let women's eyes
> Earnest, beneath the Christ-like brow,
> Strike this deep question home to men,
> "Thy brothers perish—idlest thou?"[35]

During the Civil War, when Howe penned the most famous lyrics of her career, "The Battle Hymn of the Republic," she not only recalled Fuller's power, pulse, and light, but also assumed her apocalyptic discourse, creating a vision of righteous violence and destruction that echoes Isaiah and the coming era of Emmanuel. The words are no doubt familiar.

> Mine eyes have seen the glory of the coming of the Lord:
> He is trampling out the vintage where the grapes of wrath are stored;
> He hath loosed the fateful lightning of His terrible swift sword:
> His truth is marching on.

Notice that Howe barely alludes to events of the Civil War itself, but in the role of a female seeress envisions regeneration through violence, inflicted upon the sinful. A later verse goes,

> In the beauty of the lilies Christ was born across the sea,
> With a glory in his bosom that transfigures you and me:
> As he died to make men holy, let us die to make men free,
> While God is marching on.[36]

As Edmund Wilson has pointed out, "Note that Christ is situated 'across the sea'; he is not present on the battlefield with His Father, yet, intent on our grisly work, we somehow still share in His 'glory.'"[37] The transatlantic connection Howe imagines, then, between God the angry father and Christ the glorious son, expresses the antebellum sense of the struggle for liberty as an international, rather than strictly national, project. Howe, like Emerson, wrote a biography of Margaret Fuller, and in her conclusion she suggested that the secret of Fuller's life was heroic nobility: "When all that could be known of Margaret was known, it became evident that there was nothing of her which was not heroic in intention." She was, Howe added, "an example of one who, gifted with great powers, aspired only to their noblest use."[38]

Perhaps the most heroically inclined of the radical abolitionists Howe and her husband knew was Thomas Wentworth Higginson, another member of John Brown's Secret Six. Like Julia Ward Howe, Higginson regarded Fuller as his role model and became one of her early biographers. As a boy, he knew Fuller as a fascinating friend of his older sister, and, as Barbara Miller Solomon has pointed out, he "drew strength from Fuller's call for an American hero. He identified his own striving with hers."[39] After graduating from Harvard at age seventeen, Higginson became a Unitarian minister, radical abolitionist, journalist, woman's rights advocate, and colonel of the first Union regiment of former slaves during the Civil War. At a women's rights meeting in 1853, he criticized the editors of Fuller's *Memoirs* for failing to appreciate the obstacles she had faced in her career as a woman of "genius." In his biography of Fuller, published in 1884, he acknowledged her influence during his formative years. "Margaret Fuller," he declared, "had upon me, through her writings, a more immediate intellectual influence than any one except Emerson, and possibly Parker." Trying to correct the emphasis on self-culture that he felt the editors of the *Memoirs* had made, he stated that the goal of *his* biography was to keep before his readers "the fact that the best part of intellect is action, and that this was always her especial creed." In the final pages of the biography he compares her to Emerson and praises her for emphasizing action over thought. "In later years she had the fulfillment of her dreams. . . . She showed in great deeds. She was the counselor of great men, she had a husband who was a lover and she had a child."[40] Such a plotting of Fuller's life effectively transformed tragedy into triumph.

In the decade after Fuller's death, Higginson himself sought to participate in "great deeds," with some success. In 1854, furious at the government's enforcement of the Fugitive Slave Law, he led an attack on the Boston courthouse in a failed attempt to free the remitted runaway slave Anthony Burns. In the melee a guard was murdered and Higginson received a saber cut to his chin.[41] Soon afterward he delivered a sermon in which he defended himself by adopting the persona of a European revolutionary: "I am glad of the discovery . . . that I live under a despotism . . . For myself, existence looks worthless under such circumstances; and I can only make life worth living for, by becoming a revolutionist. . . . I see now, that while Slavery is national, law and order must constantly be on the wrong side. I see that the case stands for me precisely as it stands for Kossuth and Mazzini, and I must take the consequences."[42] In 1856, like Fuller, he became a correspondent for Greeley's *Tribune*, traveling to "Bleeding Kansas" where he wrote dispatches describing events in revolutionary terms, casting antislavery settlers as fighting for freedom against oppressive proslavery forces backed by a tyrannical U.S. government: "As Hungary, having successfully resisted her natural enemy, Austria, yielded at length to the added strength of Russia; so the Kossuths of Kansas, just as they had cleared her borders of Missourians are subdued by the troops of the United States."[43] The solution to slavery for Higginson was guerrilla warfare and slave insurrection. Even Fuller's gentle friend William Henry Channing agreed, writing Higginson, "the next thing to do is *guerrilla war* at every chance. They shall not sleep whether they pull down their caps or not." Higginson met John Brown in Kansas and became his loyal backer. In fact, as Jeffery Rossbach has said, he "played a vital role, perhaps the key role, in coaxing the Secret Committee of Six to support John Brown's raid, and he provides the only example of unambivalent behavior for the entire group."[44]

Although the raid failed and Brown was hanged for treason, he "began the war that ended American slavery and made this a free

Republic," as Frederick Douglass pointed out. "Until this blow was struck, the prospect of freedom was dim, shadowy and uncertain. The irrepressible conflict was one of words, votes and compromises. When John Brown stretched forth his arm the sky was cleared. The time for compromises was gone . . . and the clash of arms was at hand."[45] Brown acting on his own would not have had such an effect, of course. It was evidence of the conspiracy that alarmed the South by confirming its worst fears about the terrorist methods of northern abolitionists. As the historian James McPherson has pointed out, "Those Yankee fanatics would soon cause southern opinion to evolve into a third phase of unreasoning fury," making disunion seem inevitable. "Thousands joined military companies; state legislatures appropriated funds for the purchase of arms," and the attack on Fort Sumter soon followed.[46] John Brown's Secret Six, encouraged by Higginson's resolve and Fuller's example, thus had an impact far exceeding that suggested by their small number.

Throughout the twentieth century, American literary histories ignored the connection between the European revolutionary scene and the American Civil War, emphasizing American exceptionalism instead; however, many of Fuller's contemporaries, including Harriet Beecher Stowe, saw the connection and articulated it. At the conclusion of *Uncle Tom's Cabin* (1852), Stowe observes, "This is an age of the world when nations are trembling and convulsed," and she warns of a war that will take place on American soil. "And is America safe? Every nation that carries in its bosom great and unredressed injustice has in it the elements of this last convulsion."[47] Whereas Stowe urged emancipation and colonization to avoid such a convulsion, Fuller showed its heroic appeal. The violence of a Frederick Douglass, not the pacifism of an Uncle Tom, best represented her idea of how to respond to oppression. During the antebellum period, figures such as Cromwell, Washington, Lamartine, Kossuth, Mazzini, and Garibaldi provided the most popular models of male heroism to the American public, yet Fuller's secret female example, linked to the relatively unpopular struggles for women's rights and the abolition of slavery, had perhaps a more profound and far-reaching effect on her country's future. If nothing else, she advanced the powerful idea, adopted by her fellow Transcendentalists, that oppression, when resistant to words and moral suasion, must be met with righteous violence. Even after the loss of 620,000 lives in the Civil War, this idea has retained its purchase on the thinking of political activists throughout the world.

Notes

1. *"These Sad But Glorious Days": Dispatches from Europe, 1846–1850*, ed. Larry J. Reynolds and Susan Belasco Smith (New Haven, Conn.: Yale Univ. Press, 1991), 315 (hereafter cited in text and notes as *SG*).

2. Reynolds, *European Revolutions and the American Literary Renaissance* (New Haven, Conn.: Yale Univ. Press, 1988), 171. For extended discussion of Fuller's achievement in the dispatches, see introduction, *SG* 1–35; Packer, "The Transcendentalists," in *Prose Writing, 1820–1865*, vol. 2 of *The Cambridge History of American Literature*, ed. Sacvan Bercovitch (Cambridge: Cambridge Univ. Press, 1995), 544.

3. Quoted in Margaret Fuller Ossoli, *At Home and Abroad, or, Things and Thoughts in America and Europe*, ed. Arthur B. Fuller (1856; repr., Port Washington, N.Y.: Kennikat Press, 1971), vii.

4. Ibid., x.

5. *SG* 166. After revolutions broke out all over Europe in the spring of 1848, Fuller imagined the spirit of liberty being more alive there than in the United States. "My country is at present spoiled by prosperity, stupid with the lust of gain, soiled by crime in its willing perpetuation of Slavery, shamed by an unjust war." Thus she argues that America, which "is not dead, but in my time she sleepeth," must heed Europe's example. "I hear earnest words of pure faith and love. I see deeds of brotherhood. This is what makes *my* America." *SG* 230.

6. Demos, "The Antislavery Movement and the Problem of Violent 'Means,'" *New England Quarterly* 37 (December 1964): 501–26; Parker quoted in ibid., 519; Pilsbury quoted in ibid., 523; *The Journals and Miscellaneous Notebooks of Ralph Waldo Emerson, Volume 8, 1841–1843*, ed. William H. Gilman and J. E. Parsons (Cambridge, Mass.: Belknap Press, 1970), 368–69. Hereafter the sixteen-volume Belknap edition of Emerson's *Journals and Miscellaneous Notebooks* (1960–82, edited by Gilman and others) will be cited in text and notes as *JMN*.

7. See Reynolds, *European Revolutions*, 16–19.

8. Lowell, perhaps, was trying to make amends for his hurtful satire of Fuller in his *Fable for Critics*. See Joan von Mehren, *Minerva and the Muse: A Life of Margaret Fuller* (Amherst: Univ. of Massachusetts Press, 1994), 311; "Freedom" quoted in Roy M. Peterson, "Echoes of the Italian Risorgimento in Contemporaneous American Writers," *PMLA* 47 (1932): 228; "To Pius X" quoted in ibid., 228; for Fuller's influence on Whitman, see Reynolds, *European Revolutions*, 137–39.

9. See Howard R. Marraro, *American Opinion on the Unification of Italy, 1846–1861* (New York: Columbia Univ. Press, 1932), 68–69; Hughes letter in *Boston Post*, June 29, 1849, 1.

10. *SG* 294. What she omitted, though, was that indeed priests had been murdered. According to the twentieth-century historian George Macaulay

Trevelyan, one of the Roman republicans, Callimaco Zambianchi, in early
May 1849, massacred "six persons in holy orders, whom he declared to have
been preaching sedition and conspiring against the Republic." *Garibaldi's Defense of the Roman Republic, 1848–49* (London: Longmans, Green, 1941), 149–50.

    11. *Times,* May 11, 1849, 4.

    12. Andrew Hilen, ed., *The Letters of Henry Wadsworth Longfellow,* vol. 3, *1844–
1856* (Cambridge, Mass.: Harvard Univ. Press, Belknap Press, 1972), 208;
Ralph L. Rusk, ed., *The Letters of Ralph Waldo Emerson,* vol. 4, *1848–1855* (New
York: Columbia Univ. Press, 1939), 39.

    13. Edward Waldo Emerson, ed., *The Complete Works of Ralph Waldo Emer-
son,* vol. 5, *English Traits* (1903–4; repr., New York: AMS Press, 1968), 271.

    14. *JMN* 11:94, 98, 148. Emerson often revealed a streak of social Darwin-
ism in his thinking and even his antislavery commitment is tainted by it. In 1844
he asserted, "If the black man is feeble & not important to the existing races,
not on a par with the best race, the black man must serve & be sold & extermi-
nated." *JMN* 9:125. Nine years later, he entered in his journal the following
quotation from Karl Marx: "The classes & races too weak to master the new
conditions of life must give way." *JMN* 13:127. As he did in his poem "Ode, Inscribed to W. H. Channing," Emerson often asserted that might was wedded to
right, and that the god "who exterminates / Races by stronger races, / Black
by white faces,—Knows to bring honey / Out of the lion." *Collected Poems and
Translations* (New York: Library of America, 1994), 64.

    15. "Nature," in *Ralph Waldo Emerson: A Critical Edition of the Major Works,* ed.
Richard Poirier (New York: Oxford Univ. Press, 1990), 36.

    16. *Woman in the Nineteenth Century,* ed. Larry J. Reynolds (New York:
Norton, 1998), 74. Julie Ellison has pointed out that in Europe, Rome became
feminized for Fuller and her advocacy for women's rights thus transformed
into advocacy for Rome. The city became "at once a fascinating woman of
electromagnetic appeal, seducing Fuller, and a maternal sanctuary of "repose."
Delicate Subjects: Romanticism, Gender, and the Ethics of Understanding (Ithaca, N.Y.:
Cornell Univ. Press, 1990), 290.

    17. See Packer, "The Transcendentalists," 329–604; Len Gougeon, *Virtue's
Hero: Emerson, Antislavery, and Reform* (Athens: Univ. of Georgia Press, 1990);
Albert J. von Frank, *The Trials of Anthony Burns: Freedom and Slavery in Emerson's
Boston* (Cambridge, Mass.: Harvard Univ. Press, 1998), and "Mrs. Brackett's
Verdict: Magic and Means in Transcendental Antislavery Work," in *Transient
and Permanent: The Transcendentalist Movement and Its Contexts,* ed. Charles Capper
and Conrad Edick Wright (Boston: Massachusetts Historical Society, 1999),
385–407; T. Gregory Garvey, ed., *The Emerson Dilemma: Essays on Emerson and So-
cial Reform* (Athens: Univ. of Georgia Press, 2001), especially the essays by Linck
C. Johnson, Michael Strysick, Len Gougeon, Harold K. Bush, and David M.
Robinson.

18. Quotes from "Fate" in Poirier, *Emerson*, 347, 348; see Zwarg, *Feminist Conversations: Fuller, Emerson and the Play of Reading* (Ithaca, N.Y.: Cornell Univ. Press), 293–94. Zwarg speculates on how many of Emerson's readers would have caught his reference and concludes, "I suspect that there were more knowing readers than one might initially assume, particularly given Emerson's confession in the *Memoirs* that her 'personal influence' was the strongest he had ever experienced." 294n35.

19. Quote from "Fate" in Poirier, *Emerson*, 357; Alcott's two male protagonists, Adam Warwick and Geoffrey Moor, are modeled on Thoreau and Emerson. See "Explanatory Notes" in Louisa May Alcott, *Moods*, ed. Sarah Elbert (1864; repr., New Brunswick, N.J.: Rutgers Univ. Press, 1991), 284. In a small town outside Rome, Warwick joins a group of red-shirted Garibaldians, saves the town from marauding Croats through his brave cannoneering, and after taking a bullet in the chest is honored by Garibaldi, who places his famous gray cloak over the wounded American. On their way back to the United States, Warwick and Moor suffer a shipwreck just off the American coast, and Warwick drowns while saving Moor by tying him to a spar.

20. For a useful discussion of this topic and its relevance to the Emerson-Fuller relationship, see Jeffrey Steele, "The Limits of Political Sympathy: Emerson, Margaret Fuller, and Woman's Rights," in Garvey, *Emerson Dilemma*, 115–35.

21. "Lecture on Slavery: 25 January 1855," in *Emerson's Antislavery Writings*, ed. Len Gougeon and Joel Myerson (New Haven, Conn.: Yale Univ. Press, 1995), 103, 105.

22. "Remarks at a Meeting for the Relief of the Family of John Brown," in E. Emerson, *Complete Works*, vol. 11, *Miscellanies*, 268.

23. *The Centenary Edition of the Works of Nathaniel Hawthorne*, vol. 18, *The Letters, 1857–1864*, ed. Thomas Woodson et al. (Columbus: Ohio State Univ. Press, 1987), 544.

24. Quoted in E. Emerson, "Notes," in *Miscellanies*, 579.

25. See Charles Breunig, *The Age of Revolution and Reaction: 1789–1850* (New York: Norton, 1970), 227–29.

26. *The Letters of Margaret Fuller*, ed. Robert N. Hudspeth, 6 vols. (Ithaca, N.Y.: Cornell Univ. Press, 1988), 5:147 (hereafter cited in the text as *L*).

27. See Charles Capper, *Margaret Fuller: An American Romantic Life*, vol. 1, *The Private Years* (New York: Oxford Univ. Press, 1992), 144–45.

28. Peabody quoted in *Woman in the Nineteenth Century*, 177; Leona Rostenberg, "Margaret Fuller's Roman Diary," *Journal of Modern History* 12 (June 1940): 217–18.

29. In a speech before the Nashville Convention in 1851, General Felix Huston of Mississippi declared that the San Domingo insurrection "having occurred so near to us, and being within the recollection of many persons living,

who heard the exaggerated accounts of the day, has fastened itself on the public imagination, until it has become a subject of frequent reference." Quoted in John Weiss, "The Horrors of San Domingo," *Atlantic Monthly* 11 (June 1863): 773.

30. As Jeffrey Steele has pointed out, Fuller's finest poem, "Raphael's Deposition from the Cross" (1844), concerns itself with this image, perhaps inspired by a copy of the Raphael painting now known as *The Entombment.* "'Freeing the Prisoned Queen': The Development of Margaret Fuller's Poetry," in *Studies in the American Renaissance 1992*, ed. Joel Myerson (Charlottesville: Univ. Press of Virginia, 1992), 137–75, 169. The poem begins "Virgin Mother, Mary Mild! / It was thine to see the child, / Gift of the Messiah dove, / Pure blossom of ideal love, / Break, upon the 'guilty cross' / The seeming promise of his life." In Rome her identification with the Virgin Mother recurs as she describes her activities in the hospital on Tiber Island, tending the wounded young men. "I was the Mater Dolorosa," she writes her sister Ellen, "and I remembered that the midwife who helped Angelino into the world came from the sign of the Mater Dolorosa." *L* 5:293. The irony here, of course, is that Fuller had left Angelino in the countryside with a wet nurse for weeks at a time while she joined Ossoli in Rome during the fall, winter, and spring of 1848–49. In Rome, the childlike Ossoli, as well as the wounded young republicans, may have taken the place of Angelino for Fuller, evoking and fulfilling her maternal instincts. She had engaged in the same kind of imaginative act earlier in her life, in her relations with Samuel Ward. As John Gatta has pointed out, with Ward, who put an end to their romantic relationship, she enacted a "rather bizarre self-portrayal as Mary waiting by the sepulchre." *American Madonna: Images of the Divine Woman in Literary Culture* (New York: Oxford Univ. Press, 1997), 157n25. "You have given me the sacred name of Mother," Fuller wrote Ward, "and I will be so indulgent, as tender, as delicate (if possible) in my vigilance, as if I had borne you beneath my heart instead of in it. But Oh, it is waiting like the Mother beside the sepulchre for the resurrection, for all I loved in you is at present dead and buried, only a light from the tomb shines now and then in your eyes." *L* 2:91.

31. Hawthorne, *The Scarlet Letter*, ed. Seymour Gross (New York: Norton, 1988), 113 (hereafter cited in the text as *SL*).

32. Hawthorne, *The Blithedale Romance*, ed. Seymour Gross and Rosalie Murphy (New York: Norton, 1978), 73.

33. Mitchell, *Hawthorne's Fuller Mystery* (Amherst: Univ. of Massachusetts Press, 1998), 235.

34. *The Centenary Edition of the Works of Nathaniel Hawthorne*, vol. 13, *The Elixir of Life Manuscripts*, ed. Edward H. Davidson, Claude M. Simpson, and L. Neal Smith (Columbus: Ohio State Univ. Press, 1977), 67.

35. Julia Ward Howe, *Passion-Flowers* (Boston: Tichnor, Reed, Fields, 1854), 61–63.

36. "Battle Hymn of the Republic," *Atlantic Monthly* 9 (February 1862): 145.

37. Wilson, *Patriotic Gore: Studies in the Literature of the American Civil War* (New York: Farrar, Straus and Giroux, 1962), 96.

38. Howe, *Margaret Fuller* (Boston: Roberts Brothers, 1883), 278. For an excellent discussion of Fuller's influence on Howe, see Gary Williams, *Hungry Heart: The Literary Emergence of Julia Ward Howe* (Amherst: Univ. of Massachusetts Press, 1999), 108–14, 165–66, 210–12.

39. Solomon introduction to *Margaret Fuller Ossoli*, by Thomas Wentworth Higginson (1898; repr., New York: Confucian Press, 1980), xiii.

40. Ibid., xiv, 2, 6, 314. In his novel *Malbone: An Oldport Romance*, which appeared serially in the *Atlantic Monthly* in 1869, Higginson draws upon Fuller in fashioning his two heroines: Hope the virginal, Sibyl-like American; and Emilia, her foreign half-sister, passionate and reckless, who steals Hope's fiancé Malbone and drowns trying to join her Swiss lover, Antoine, during a storm at sea.

41. One reason Higginson failed in his charge on the courthouse was that no one followed his lead after the initial repulsion, except for another Transcendentalist admirer of Fuller's, Bronson Alcott. As Higginson later narrated, "In the silent pause that ensued there came quietly forth from the crowd the well-known form of Mr. Amos Bronson Alcott, the Transcendental philosopher. Ascending the lighted steps alone, he said tranquilly, turning to me and pointing forward, 'Why are we not within?' 'Because,' was the rather impatient answer, 'these people will not stand by us.' He said not a word, but calmly walked up the steps,—he and his familiar cane. He paused again at the top, the centre of all eyes, within and without; a revolver sounded from within, but hit nobody; and finding himself wholly unsupported, he turned and retreated, but without hastening a step." Higginson, *Cheerful Yesterdays* (1898; repr., New York: Arno Press, 1968), 158. Thoreau called the entire episode at the courthouse "bloody & disinterestedly heroic," and thus expressed his admiration of his Transcendentalist friends, even the otherworldly Alcott, who had become willing to take action against an oppressive government. See *Writings of Henry David Thoreau: Journal, Volume 8; 1854*, ed. Sandra Harbert Petrulionis (Princeton, N.J.: Princeton Univ. Press, 2002), 175.

42. "Massachusetts in mourning! A SERMON," *National Anti-Slavery Standard*, June 24, 1854, 20.

43. *Tribune*, October 10, 1856, quoted in Tilden G. Edelstein, *Strange Enthusiasm: A Life of Thomas Wentworth Higginson* (New Haven, Conn.: Yale Univ. Press, 1968), 188.

44. Channing to Higginson, July 4, 1855, Higginson-Burns Collection, Boston Public Library, quoted in Jeffery Rossbach, *Ambivalent Conspirators: John Brown, the Secret Six, and a Theory of Slave Violence* (Philadelphia: Univ. of Pennsylvania Press, 1982), 44; Rossbach, *Ambivalent Conspirators*, 274.

45. Douglass, "John Brown: An Address at the Fourteenth Anniversary of Storer College" (1881; repr. in *Allies for Freedom: Blacks on John Brown,* ed. Benjamin Quarles (n.p.: Da Capo, 2001), 66.

46. McPherson, *Battle Cry of Freedom: The Civil War Era* (New York: Oxford Univ. Press, 1988), 208, 213.

47. Stowe, *Uncle Tom's Cabin, or, Life among the Lowly* (1852; repr. New York: Collier Macmillan, 1962), 510.

III

European/American Others

9

A Humbug, a Bounder, and a Dabbler

Margaret Fuller, Cristina di Belgioioso, and Christina Casamassima

CRISTINA GIORCELLI

Even before leaving for Europe Margaret Fuller had already acquired a reputation as a woman and an intellectual with the potential to disturb the entire group of New England scholars and artists who knew her— Henry James Sr., Ralph Waldo Emerson, Nathaniel Hawthorne, and James Russell Lowell, among others. What she turned out to be while in Italy, however, upset every American whose opinion mattered during the rest of the nineteenth and most of the twentieth century.[1] A prime example is Henry James Jr., who could not have known her personally, but who inherited, unchallenged, the views of his masters—and with a vengeance.

It is my thesis in this essay that the last stain on a reputation already *maimed*—due to Fuller's intelligence, culture, feminist stance, wit, personal choices, and, occasionally, also her arrogance and egotism—came from her association with Princess Cristina di Belgioioso.

These two women, similar in age (Belgioioso was born in 1808, Fuller in 1810), met in Rome in late January 1848.[2] They may have known each other through Mary Clarke, or Giuseppe Mazzini, or one of the radical intellectuals Fuller had encountered in Milan, or, possibly, through a very good Italian friend of Fuller's, Marchioness Costanza Arconati Visconti, although the very pious Visconti did not particularly like "la belle joyeuse"—as Belgioioso had been snidely rebaptized in France—on account of her too audacious behavior.[3] Whatever the circumstances of their encounter, Cristina di Belgioioso was sufficiently impressed by Fuller either to remember her or to agree with Mazzini's perhaps suggesting her, more than a year later, at the end of April 1849, when Belgioioso needed capable women to direct the Roman hospitals during the siege of the city.[4] For over a month Belgioioso and Fuller saw each other frequently. When duties ended at the Fatebenefratelli Hospital on the Tiberina Island, Fuller would join Belgioioso either at the nearby Hospital della Trinità dei Pellegrini, where the princess held her headquarters, or at the Quirinale, where they both went to assist the wounded.

Numerous similarities connect these two, seemingly different, women.[5] Indeed, on account of their many similarities, one would not be surprised if, sometime before she had revealed the existence of her secret family in Italy to her friends and relatives back home, Fuller had confided in Belgioioso.

Cristina di Belgioioso was an extremely intelligent and learned woman; and thus, in the very traditional Italian world of her time, she was perhaps even more of an exception than was Fuller in hers. Coming from a noble, wealthy, and politically radical family, the Trivulzios of Milan, she had been well educated and knew Latin and French to perfection; Fuller also knew these two languages well. And while Belgioioso also acquired English, Fuller learned German and was fairly fluent in Italian.[6] Belgioioso was well versed in history, philosophy (she had translated Vico's *Scienza Nuova* into French), theology, and politics as, in her own way, was Fuller, who had translated works by and about Goethe and had applied Romantic philosophy to gender and literary questions. Belgioioso was proficient in music and painting, while Fuller was knowledgeable about both. Unlike Fuller, however, Belgioioso possessed some understanding of economics, medicine, and agronomy.

While she was in France, the philosopher Victor Cousin had defined Cristina di Belgioioso as "foemina sexu, ingenio vir." Similarly, Fuller believed that "there is no wholly masculine man, no purely feminine woman" and upheld and chose as a model the sagacious, belligerent, and androgynous Minerva from among the Latin goddesses.[7] Fuller had absorbed transcendentalism, whose principles she invoked in attempting to reform American society; Belgioioso knew Fourier's theories, along the lines of which she organized her large estate at Locate in Lombardy. Well in advance of her time, she instituted a kindergarten and schools for the farmers' children. She also established laboratories to help talented peasants improve their economic and social status; in the wintertime she even provided large, heated rooms where peasants could gather, take a meal, and warm up. Besides learning, therefore, Belgioioso and Fuller also shared a profound concern for the welfare of people and the amelioration of society.

Both Fuller and Belgioioso had fragile physical constitutions. Fuller suffered from migraines and nightmares all her life, and Belgioioso had terrible spells of epilepsy from childhood—the rumor that she was an opium addict (much publicized by Camillo Benso di Cavour himself) could have been caused by the medicines she had to take when experiencing an attack.

Both women had unhappy private lives. Until she met the Marquis Giovanni Ossoli, Fuller had a capacity to fall in love with people who did not love her, such as Samuel Gray Ward, James Nathan, and, in a complexly sublimated way, Emerson. For her part, Marchioness Cristina Trivulzio was married at the age of sixteen to the *beau* Prince Emilio di Belgioioso, a gambler and a womanizer, who infected her with syphilis. Four years after their marriage she unofficially separated from him. After two more years, during which she traveled in both Italy—she was in Genoa, her much loved Florence, and Rome—and Switzerland, she settled in Paris, where she became the envied hostess of a prestigious salon. Young, intelligent, rich, and beautiful—her diaphanous skin was so famous that when a habitué of her salon was asked whether he considered her beautiful, he answered, "She must have been very beautiful when she was alive!"—Cristina di Belgioioso was also very free.[8]

In the world's most splendid and pleasure-seeking capital, there were rumors of Belgioioso's taking many lovers: from Balzac, to Heine, to Mignet, to Liszt, to de Musset, to Thierry, even to George Sand. In 1838 she bore a child, Maria, legitimized as Belgioioso only in 1860, two years after Emilio's death, but who may instead have been the daughter of François Mignet.[9] If Belgioioso had a questionable reputation, the fact of having been, at times, ostracized, regardless of her generosity and ideals, taught her to rely on people who were also socially rejected. During the siege of Rome, for instance, in great need of nurses for the wounded, she sought the help of prostitutes, who proved to be capable and devoted. As she commented, "Those women and girls of the Roman streets had no moral sense, and in time of peace led a disorderly and selfish life, but in those circumstances they showed redeeming qualities."[10] Fuller was too much the offspring of her middle-class American background to be as sexually free as Belgioioso. In 1847 the revolutionary Polish expatriate poet Adam Mickiewicz went as far as to suggest that she lead a life not based only on books. And yet she, too, may have conceived a child out of wedlock.[11]

In the Risorgimento, both Fuller and Belgioioso found a heroic cause to which to devote their lives. Having pledged in 1841 a fierce agenda for herself ("I must die if I do not burst forth in genius or heroism"), Fuller was entirely devoted to Mazzini's republican project. The princess, although commanding Mazzini's esteem and friendship, still thought monarchy the more appropriate form of government for the Italians of the time.[12] This reservation notwithstanding, in the year before the Roman siege, Belgioioso had recruited a group of men in Naples, sailed with them to Genoa (as the only woman aboard), and then entered Milan with them waving the tricolor. Both Fuller and Belgioioso were also good friends of Mickiewicz, whom each had met in Paris (Fuller in the fall of 1846).

Independent and courageous women, Fuller and Belgioioso would never hesitate to challenge the opinions of their contemporaries and certainly would not be diverted from their purposes for fear of the consequences. As Raffaello Barbiera, the author of Belgioioso's first and best known biography, concluded, "This woman of temperament and of strong, domineering will . . . who wore austere turbans like a Domenichino sybil . . . sometimes irritates like a riddle. . . . In her, extravagances, braveries, mistakes; never meanness!"[13] In carrying out their respective rebellions, the aristocratic and rich Belgioioso, whose class and money gave her a certain immunity from social censure, probably needed less courage than her poor and democratic American friend.

While it is clear that neither Belgioioso nor Fuller conformed to the prevailing and pervasive model for women of the "angel in the house," there is more to the comparison.

Ideologically both were well in advance of their time: as with Fuller's *Woman in the Nineteenth Century* (1845), Belgioioso's essay "On the Present Conditions of Women and their Future" showed great sensitivity to the plight and cause of women. Belgioioso also wrote books on several historical topics such as: a history of Lombardy, a history of the House of

Savoy, the contemporary state of Italy and its future, and modern international politics. For her part, Fuller was the literary, artistic, and social critic of the *New-York Daily Tribune* for two years before being appointed its foreign correspondent in 1846. She became the first American woman to hold such a position. Through her dispatches she not only informed the American public of what was happening in Rome and in Italy, but also enthusiastically espoused the Italian republican unitary program, consistently trying to persuade her country of its duty to come to the aid of a budding sister democracy. During her last two years in Italy, she devoted much of her spare time to researching and writing a history of the Roman Republic and the Italian revolutionary movements, which was apparently almost completed when she died.[14]

Both Belgioioso and Fuller understood the tremendous impact of the press as an opinion maker. In Paris, Belgioioso often contributed to the *Revue des Deux Mondes* and founded several journals: *Rivista italiana*, *l'Ausonio*, *Il Crociato*, *l'Italie*, and *Gazzetta italiana*, one of the first Italian political magazines, which Terenzio Mamiani, the philosopher and politician, refused to codirect with her because she was a woman. Through these papers she aimed to disseminate information about the Italian situation and stimulate consensus regarding the country's right to independence. From 1840 to 1842, Fuller edited the transcendental journal *Dial*, to which she also contributed.

Finally, Belgioioso and Fuller shared a taste for the exotic. After her flight from Rome with her daughter in 1849, Belgioioso went to live in Turkey for six years—the first Western woman to go to the East unchaperoned—where she wrote Oriental narratives. Fuller, who had been considered physically and intellectually exotic by Emerson and W. H. Channing, lived for three years in Italy, a southern European country quite *foreign* in the eyes and minds of many New Englanders. In addition, she took a Mediterranean-looking lover and wrote "A Tale of Mizraim," set in Egypt and dealing with an "oriental" (Hebrew) subject.[15]

The lives of these two women seem, therefore, to have followed parallel tracks. As Deiss has written, Belgioioso "was, in a sense, a sophisticated, aristocratic, strangely beautiful, European Margaret Fuller. Or, alternatively, she was the fantasy Margaret Fuller of the real Margaret Fuller."[16]

Yet they obviously differed in many respects. Belgioioso was attractive and slender, with big dark eyes and shining black hair, while Fuller was plain, although she, too, possessed a magnetic and fascinating personality. Belgioioso was extremely elegant, with a gift for theatrical effects in clothing as well as in interior decoration. She dressed in white with only one accessory, a necklace of black coral, because white and black would dramatically accentuate the color of her skin, hair, and eyes. The same two colors pervaded her Parisian home. The walls and the upholstery of her apartment were covered with black velvet jotted with silver stars, while the furniture was made of ebony. Her bedroom, in contrast, was entirely white, ornamented with sumptuous silver objects.[17] Nothing similar characterized Fuller, whose financial means had always been too meager and who had had too many family obligations to be able even to think of such extravagances.

If Belgioioso broke many hearts (according to rumors, even those of women), she ended up living a life of solitude, with only the love of her daughter, and later her granddaughters. In Fuller's case, it was her heart (albeit without the sexual implications) that was broken several times by friends and/or potential lovers of both sexes.[18] And when she finally found love with Ossoli, it lasted, with misgivings and apprehensions, for only three years because of their untimely deaths. Also, while Fuller was plagued by a constant lack of money, Belgioioso was wealthy. However, because of her political ideas, her belongings were confiscated by the Austrian government on three occasions, and, for some periods of time, she too had to survive on scarce financial resources.

Their temperamental characteristics, daring demeanor, and participation in spectacular events may explain why both women were much criticized in their respective worlds, although both had many devoted friends. As far as Fuller is concerned, the question is: why were sensitive and intelligent writers, like Henry James and, before him, his mentor Nathaniel Hawthorne, so hostile to her? Moreover, why, despite their dislike of her, does her presence keep recurring in their work?[19]

In 1858 Hawthorne had seriously disparaged Fuller in a passage of his Italian notebooks that were edited and published by his son, Julian, in 1884 as *Nathaniel Hawthorne and His Wife*. In the passage the novelist gave responsibility for his recorded judgments to a sculptor who knew Fuller, Joseph Mozier.[20] After denigrating Ossoli ("entirely ignorant even of his own language, scarcely able to read at all, destitute of manners; in short, half an idiot") and criticizing the Ossoli family, Hawthorne reports that Fuller "had a strong and coarse nature . . . She was a great humbug" (*FI* 155–56). Then, he shifts to the first person pronoun, although significantly an instability of voices characterizes these pages, in which there is an almost obsessive insistence on Fuller's "nature," described as "strong, heavy, unpliable, and, in many respects, defective and evil." With a certain gusto Hawthorne seems to record such iniquitous verdicts: was it because he felt that a personality like hers was a dangerous paradigm for American women of the time or was he only— as was later claimed—jotting down the profile of a female character on whom he might have worked in future, artistic creations? We will probably never know, but it is an intriguing question. As if these contumelies were not enough, finally Hawthorne disparages her professional career, recording Mozier's opinion that she "had quite lost all power of literary production, before she left Rome, though occasionally the charm and power of her conversation would re-appear." In sum, "there appears to have been a total collapse in *poor* Margaret, morally and intellectually" (*FI* 156; my emphasis). Nothing more patronizing and derogatory could be expressed on her account given both the conventional sexual codes of antebellum America and her record of moral support to the Roman revolution.[21] At the end of this vicious report Hawthorne scarcely hides his satisfaction when he writes that because of her death "she proved herself a very woman, after all, and fell as the weakest of her sisters might" (*FI* 157). For him (and Mozier), Fuller's defiance, her public success, and her association with such a man as Ossoli showed that she was destined to be a "fallen" woman. Yet Fuller (whom he regards as "a riddle," *FI* 156) is likely to have been the model for several of his most important heroines: Beatrice, Hester, Zenobia, and Miriam.[22]

Mozier's/Hawthorne's negative opinion of her carried significant weight with Henry James. In his works he openly commented on Fuller on three occasions: in his critical biography *Hawthorne* (1879); in *William Wetmore Story and His Friends* (1903), where he also expanded on Belgioioso; and, more parenthetically, in *A Small Boy and Others* (1913).[23]

John Carlos Rowe has argued that Fuller exposed James's "masculine fear of nineteenth-century women's bid for economic, legal, and political powers." In truth, James had little liking for strong *and* especially literary women. (We have but to remember how he treated both Constance Fenimore Woolson, who was deeply attached to him, and Edith Wharton, who respected him immensely and whose coveted guest he frequently was both in Europe and in the United States.)[24] For this reason he did not care for Fuller and certainly would not care for Belgioioso. In addition, his socially conservative frame of mind could not but condemn their "irregular" and, figuratively speaking, overexposed lives.

Since James's biography *Hawthorne* came out five years before Hawthorne's Italian notebooks edited by his son, it shows how James's opinion was influenced by what he had heard or read about Fuller from other sources—perhaps from Emerson and from James Russell Lowell, Fuller's bitter enemy.[25] In *Hawthorne* James points out Fuller's negative traits: "This lady was the apostle of culture, of intellectual curiosity," but she was also characterized by "poverty of knowledge" (*H* 70). In other words, her eagerness for culture did not lead her to acquire it. Moreover, "She had a magnificent . . . egotism" (*H* 78). While Fuller's human qualities were, in his mind, abnormally defective, this "egotism" needs to be seen in relation to Emerson's "self-reliance," in which James did not much believe. The same year, in fact, he had shown the limitations of this principle in his characterization of Daisy Miller, the charming, but victimized protagonist of the novel by the same title, who incarnates it. In some respects, "self-reliance" entails for James a naive and self-defeating arrogance. By criticizing Fuller, who had worked so closely with Emerson, James may be also criticizing the apostle of the American belief in the individual's worth, regardless of the social context in which he/she moves.

In *Hawthorne* James also belittles Fuller's gifts by reducing them to one: "she was a talker; she was *the* talker; she was the genius of talk," contrasting, as it were, mere "talking" with serious thinking and writing. And yet he contradicts himself: after firmly maintaining that she "left behind her nothing but the memory of a memory" (*H* 78), he admits that "[s]ome of her writing has extreme beauty, almost all of it has a real interest, but her value, her activity, her sway . . . were personal and practical" (*H* 79). What he seems to be wanting to convey is that Fuller cannot aspire to great praise because, being "personal and practical," her published work (is he referring to her writing for a newspaper?) is ephemeral. When reading what James has to say about Fuller, his various reviews and critical essays (no fewer than nine) on another woman writer, George Sand, come to mind. In these he singles out the French novelist as both "a riddle" and as an exemplar of the un-self-conscious artist who writes from her own life instinctually, effortlessly.[26] For this reason, according to James, Sand cannot claim to be a *real* artist (like Fuller, Sand, too, is thus "personal and practical"). He concludes his ambiguous remarks on Fuller by summarizing that "she has left the same sort of reputation as a great actress" (*H* 79).

James was surely aware that this was what some of Fuller's friends had said of her. After extolling her powers of mimicry, Horace Greeley, the editor of the *New-York Herald Tribune*, had concluded that she might have been the United States' finest actress had she so chosen, and Emerson, Clarke, and Channing had linked her with de Stael's Corinne in her abilities as an "improvisatrice."[27]

Twenty-four years later, in the third chapter of *William Wetmore Story and His Friends*,[28] James summarizes previous definitions of Fuller, including Hawthorne's and his own, by arguing that "[her] identity was that of the talker, the moral *improvisatrice*" (*W* 128). But he has to concede that, after all she went through, many facts regarding Fuller "were not talk, but life" (*W* 130). As Ann Douglas has pointed out, James probably meant that, contrary to most of the Transcendentalists, she not only extolled experience, but also lived it.[29] And yet, if "life" is better than "talk," in his mind neither is better than the palace of art and the role of observer he had chosen for himself. Hence this comment is not the prelude to a revised opinion of Fuller.

After reporting verbatim the slandering judgments Lowell passed on Fuller in his letters to Story, James debates whether, had he met her, he would have judged her "a somewhat formidable bore" or "a really attaching, a possibly picturesque New England Corinne" (*W* 128)— neither alternative too flattering to Fuller.[30] But then—again revealing his contradictions on this subject—how could she be such a bore, if she was such a great talker? And how could she be so attaching, if he cannot help belittling her as merely "picturesque"? As he had already done in *Hawthorne*, he again (like Hawthorne) negates her literary production, "she left nothing behind her, her written utterance being naught" (*W* 127–28). In the longest reference to her in the book—a reference that closely follows Hawthorne's lead—Fuller is mentioned on the same page as both the incestuous and murderous Beatrice Cenci (who embodies a "strange riddle" for her gazers) and the allegedly adulterous and deceptive Beatrice di Tenda: while the Storys had gone to see (as one goes to a show) Beatrice Cenci's portrait by Guido Reni, later that day they and Fuller attended Bellini's *Beatrice di Tenda* at the Teatro Argentina in the spring of 1849.[31]

Clearly, James wishes to frame Fuller between two historical, strong, dangerous, Italian women (by the Anglo Saxon cliché, vehement and treacherous, who, besides, bear the same misleading name) and in a theatrical context.[32] In the next pages, after referring to Fuller as the "unquestionably haunting Margaret-*ghost*" (*W* 127; my italics) and before calling her, stretching Emerson's definition, the "angular Boston sybil" (*W* 130), James explicitly uses a theatrical metaphor to describe her: "Mme. Ossoli's circle represented, after all, a small stage" (*W* 129). Very interestingly, three pages later James brings together Fuller and "the great" Adelaide Ristori (*W* 132–34), the Italian actress who, during the Roman Republic, was at the rise of a formidable career that would make her internationally famous.[33]

What I would like to emphasize is that because of the way James chooses to cast Fuller in *Hawthorne* but even more so in *William Wetmore Story*, he subtly suggests that both the theatrical world, in general, and the roles of awesome, plotting theatrical heroines, in particular, became her (according to Hawthorne, had she not been "a great humbug"?). In the Roman theaters, against the background of the Roman siege, in a vertigo of seeing and being seen, Fuller was thus for James both spectator and character, and the fact that he conceived her as narcissistic and self-centered may have encouraged him in this outlook. Hawthorne's report that in Rome Fuller suffered "a total collapse . . . morally and intellectually" and James's statement that her "marriage" with Ossoli was "incongruous" (*W* 98) help combine political subversiveness and illicit sex, as they were often associated in the nineteenth century.

Not by chance in this revealing chapter James introduces Belgioioso (*W* 134). While the French troops, arrived at Civitavecchia, were menacing Rome, he informs that in the Piazza del Popolo the Storys and Fuller met the princess, "[b]ut," James adds, "it all winds up again, for the evening, with Ristori in another play by Scribe."[34] Belgioioso is an integral part of this theatrical context in which real and dramatic events overlap.

No doubt this mixture of exceptional facts and playful enjoyment—of protagonists in the historical drama and protagonists on the theatrical stage—is meant to underline James's thesis that the Storys—but also other Americans, like Fuller, as well as aristocratic Italians, like Belgioioso, in search of a *cause* to give their life meaning—did not genuinely participate in the Roman events. They were simply bystanders or observers, who *pretended* to feel deeply for the Italian Risorgimento, but, in effect, were much more taken up by the effervescent atmosphere that surrounded them and by the opportunity thus given them to shine. With this reductive view firmly rooted in his mind, it is not difficult for

James to imply that the exalted Fuller became involved in the Roman hospitals, and with a younger, titled, but "much *decaduto*" (*W* 130) and ignorant ("clownish," in Hawthorne's words) companion like Ossoli, for excitement and role playing (*FI* 156). This same attitude *must*, in his opinion, have also taken hold of Belgioioso.

In his long presentation of Belgioioso, James first defines her as "one of the figures intrinsically the most interesting and most marked we are likely to meet" (*W* 161). The adverb "intrinsically" is somewhat redundant, unless he wishes to signal that he will not stop at appearances, at exterior facts, but will probe her personality. Then, he writes: "Her striking, strange name (which, in connection with her title, seemed, always, of old, to scintillate, exotically, orientally, for eye and ear) was in the air . . . and with the note of the *grande dame* added, for mystification, to that of the belligerent" (*W* 161). Not only is Belgioioso contradictory for him because she is both a refined hostess and a rebel, but she also carries the note of "mystification," of deception (no wonder her surname seems "exotic" and "oriental"). After mentioning—and footnoting in full—the biography that Raffaello Barbiera had written on Belgioioso just the year before, James adds that the portrait the Italian writer had drawn "leaves us in depths of doubt—which are yet also not without their interest—as to the relation, in her character, of the element of sincerity and the element . . . of *cabotinage* . . . was she not . . . at once a sincere, a passionate crusader and 'a bounder,' as we elegantly say, of the real bounding temperament? Nothing is more curious . . . than the apparent mixture in her of the love of the thing in itself and the love of all the attitudes and aspects, the eccentricities and superfluities of the thing" (*W* 161–62). Since Barbiera had presented a eulogistic—if also somewhat moralistic—characterization of the princess, it is evident that James wants to distance himself from that view. Without denying Belgioioso's "sincere" and "passionate" participation in her crusades, James introduces the element of "*cabotinage*," that is, of poor acting and affected showing off. Being a "crusader" and a *cabotine*, Belgioioso is both hot-headed—if not superficial, certainly wayward ("eccentric")—and redundant—if not in bad faith, certainly excessive ("superfluous"). Here again, we may detect James's criticism of Emerson's principle of "self-reliance," since, to be sure, Belgioioso always lived according to the dictates of her own nature and ideals. But it is the definition he gives to Belgioioso as "a bounder" that is amazingly close to the one his predecessor Hawthorne had used for Fuller: "a great humbug."

James's malevolent satire, however, goes on. By writing that Belgioioso possessed a "strange, pale, penetrating beauty, without bloom, health, substance, that was yet the mask of an astounding masculine energy" (*W* 162), he arrives at the core of the matter: the princess's pitiful, physical fragility (so *ghostly* in its lack of "substance") hid a "masculine" force that is threatening, or, to use the words that in another context he had used for Fuller, "not altogether reassuring."[35] That the two women are close in his mind may be shown by the fact that they are both discussed at length in this chapter. In addition, a few pages later he reports a letter Story wrote to Lowell, in which Story defended Fuller from Lowell's attack with these words and arguments: "because fate has really been unkind to her, and because she depends on her pen for her bread-and-water . . . and because she is her own worst enemy, and because through her disappointment and disease, which (things) embitter every one, she has struggled most stoutly and *manfully*" (*W* 171; my italics). Like James, Story had both expressed a patronizing judgment ("she is her own worst enemy") and hinted at her threatening, "manly" power—a trait that associates her with the characteristics James had singled out for Belgioioso.

In his concluding comments on the Italian princess, James mentions explicitly her second alarming threat, which, again, connects her to Fuller: she is a writer. Her "'social position' [was] so oddly allied with her perpetual immersion in printer's ink, with the perpetual founding, conducting, supporting, replenishing, from her own inspiration, of French and Italian propagandist newspapers . . . the great political or social agitator is most often a bird of curious plumage."[36] The succession of the four present participles (culminating with the oddly employed "replenishing," as if with food and drink: woman's *true* task and vocation!) shows his deep irritation. Indeed, despite her apparent physical feebleness, Belgioioso was "masculine" *and* a writer and, as such, a competitor and a challenger, like Fuller. Moreover—and here I agree with Douglas again—besides being writers, both Fuller and Belgioioso focused on current and past events.[37] Consequently they were in some ways writers of history, the domain in which, after rescuing his novels from the sentimental province of so many successful women writers, James was painstakingly trying to have them included, as accurate, realistic histories of consciousness rather than having them subsumed under the domain of fantasy, of *fiction*.

At this point, James ends the chapter by reporting in Italian a sentence from Barbiera's biography of Belgioioso, where Barbiera had praised Fuller for the hospital service she performed during the Roman siege: "Glory to you, true friend of our beloved Italy! Glory to you, very strong woman!"[38] By now we know, however, that from James's point of view Barbiera and his high praise of Fuller must be read critically.

I have elsewhere contended that in James's fiction Italians are basically seen as actors. In his judgment, as he wrote of Adelaide Ristori, Italians are a people "in whom the feeling of the picturesque is a common instinct, and the gift of personal expression so ample" because they come of "a pre-eminently expressive and demonstrative race."[39] Story, too, thought that Italians "are the most naturally powerful of all actors" (*W* 301). Like actors, however, Italians are seen by these Americans— who, paradoxically, loved the theater precisely for its power to reveal *through* dissimulation—as intrinsically false. James also claims that, because of their "prompt theatric sense of the monstrous actual," Italians tend "to clap upon the stage, with abounding facility and . . . 'awful' effect, the leading crimes of the hour" (*W* 118). Seen as false, Italians are also judged as being naturally prone to sensationalism.

One has but to think of the theatrical manners and clothing of a minor character like the Italian butler, Eugenio, who accompanies James across twenty-three years. In *Daisy Miller* (1879) and in *The Wings of the Dove* (1902) the sinister Eugenio presides over the deaths of the protagonists: two rich and innocent American girls. Also, the full-fledged Italian protagonist of *The Golden Bowl* (1904), Prince Amerigo, is a later and more developed incarnation of the melodramatic and primitive count in "The Last of the Valerii"; like him, Amerigo is superstitious, and, like everybody else in this novel, both hypocritical and manipulative.[40]

There is a female character, however, who keeps returning in James's fiction as a dangerous paradigm of womanhood: Christina Light, married Casamassima. Of illegitimate American and Italian origins, Christina significantly had a maternal English grandmother who was an actress. Christina Light first appears in *Roderick Hudson* (1875) and then in *The Princess Casamassima* (1886). She is a femme fatale, par excellence. In both novels she is said to be, above all, extraordinarily beautiful, but also terribly selfish and capricious.

Roderick Hudson was published four years after Belgioioso's death on July 5, 1871, and, therefore, after Italian political circles and the press had inevitably, if quietly, mentioned her (without, however, assessing her contribution to the Italian cause as she deserved). James may have still heard echoes of these comments when, with his sister Alice and Aunt Kate, he traveled in northern Italy a year later, in the late summer of 1872.[41] In *Roderick Hudson* Christina Light (who, by her first name's etymology is "anointed" and by her surname's semantics is luminous and superficial) exposes the young sculptor protagonist's inner weaknesses that will finally drive him to (probably) commit suicide. In *The Princess Casamassima* Christina's irresponsibility is the last stroke that induces the naturally gentle Hyacinth Robinson, a bookbinder of exquisite talent, to kill himself. In both novels Christina thus has devastating effects on those who fall in love with her. Yet Christina Light Casamassima's role in both novels is more complex than at first it seems.

In the earlier one she is "a riddle," as Fuller had been for Hawthorne and Sand for James.[42] She is also the ideal beauty: when Roderick first sees her, he exclaims, "I don't believe she's living—she's a phantasm, a vapour, an illusion!" (*R* 95). One cannot help associating Roderick's calling Christina a "phantasm" to James's later definition of Margaret Fuller as a "ghost."[43] But in this novel there may be more precise, if indirect, references to Fuller and to Belgioioso, as indeed, in many ways, their personalities seem to merge in its author's mind.

Christina Light is said to have received the education of a "princess" because "she speaks three or four languages and has read several hundred French novels." After describing her as "a mixture of better and worse, of good passions and bad—always of passions, however," her chaperone, Madame Grandoni, maintains that she "has plenty of wit—also plenty of will" and adds, "whatever she is, she's neither stupid nor mean" (*R* 164). With this definition, James seems to anticipate by twenty-seven years Barbiera's concluding remark in his biography of Belgioioso, thus explaining why James quotes him verbatim in *William Wetmore Story and His Friends*.[44]

Rowland Mallet, the novel's central consciousness, sums up Christina Light's personality by stating, "She's intelligent and bold and free, and so awfully on the lookout for sensations" (*R* 297), like the two historical women—according to James's opinion of them. Christina is, thus, seemingly another self-reliant character, another version of Emerson's principle. Furthermore, like Fuller, who looked upon herself as "a living statue," Roderick Hudson dedicates a bust to Christina Light.[45] Moreover, after Roderick calls Christina "a creature of moods" (*R* 187), she herself says: "I'm frightfully egotistical" (*R* 208), "I'm a miserable medley of vanity and folly . . . I'm affected, I'm false" (*R* 260), "I should like to be a grandee . . . I would play my part well" (*R* 407), and even exclaims, "It seems to me I've posed enough" (*R* 157)—where "to pose" has more than one acceptation. It is finally Madame Grandoni who defines her twice as "an actress."[46] It is not by chance, then, that her dog is called Stenterello, like the Florentine mask in the Commedia dell'Arte. Accordingly, Christina "likes drama, likes theatricals . . . histrionics, for their own sweet sake" (*R* 369). Yet she is also a tragic heroine, since in the end she will be compelled by her parents, who have carried on an illicit, secret liaison throughout their life, to marry Prince Casamassima against her will.

Like Fuller and Belgioioso, Christina Light is intelligent, cultivated, willful, selfish, and melodramatic. She marries into the nobility like Fuller and is beautiful like Belgioioso. If she does not bear a child out of wedlock (possibly or formally, as in their respective cases), she herself was secretly born out of wedlock. The great difference from Fuller and Belgioioso is that in this novel she is not involved in politics. But, in the later novel that carries her name in its title, this interest develops.

In *The Princess Casamassima*, Christina Light, now Casamassima (a compound surname like Belgioioso) lives separately from her husband (like Belgioioso).[47] Out of eccentricity ("she must try everything; at present she's trying democracy, she's going all lengths in radicalism"), egotism, excitement, and role-playing ("To do something for others was not only so much more human—it was so much more amusing!"), she turns into an anarchist in this novel.[48] In the Preface, published in 1908 in the New York edition of his works, James confesses that this character had for long been "in the vague limbo of those *ghosts* we have conjured but not exorcised" and that he had taken the "chance to study the obscure law under which certain of a novelist's characters . . . revive for him . . . like *haunting ghosts*" (*P* 1:xviii; my italics). Christina is, thus, a *ghost*—precisely as Fuller had been in *William Wetmore Story* (published five years before). As in *Roderick Hudson*, Christina Casamassima is, like Belgioioso, very beautiful: "Her beauty had an air of perfection; it astonished and lifted one up, the sight of it seemed a privilege, a reward" (*P* 1:207). Furthermore, thanks to her social and economic position, the fictional princess can enjoy the "perfection of her indifference to public opinion" (*P* 2:80), that is, the aristocratic defiance that Belgioioso relished throughout her life.

Since Hyacinth judges Christina as gifted with "a radiance of grace and eminence and success" (*P* 1:207), on one occasion he waits for her as one would wait for "the entrance of a celebrated actress" (*P* 1:285) and on another he thinks that her "performance of the part she had undertaken to play was certainly complete."[49] In Paris "he saw of course a great many women and noticed almost all of them, especially the actresses; inwardly confronting their movement, their speech, their manner of dressing, with that of his extraordinary friend [Christina Casamassima]" (*P* 2:126–27). Her characterization as an actress is consciously sustained by James throughout the novel: the first time Hyacinth sees her she is framed in a theater box; afterward, she is said both to be performing on the "*mise-en-scène* of life" (*P* 1:268) and to be marked by "her power . . . of light mimetic, dramatic evocation" (*P* 2:273). At the end, she speaks "in a tone which would have made the fortune of an actress if an actress could have caught it" (*P* 2:411). She even says, "You think me affected of course and my behaviour a fearful *pose;* but I'm only trying to be natural" (*P* 2:245). Although this last statement may seem oxymoronic, interpreting and, in a sense, creating *naturalness* is the actor's task. As has been observed, "a pervasive theatricality runs through the novel."[50]

Both Lionel Trilling and John Carlos Rowe have underlined the inauthenticity of this character, who, in being so self-centered and coquettish, is also fully conventional.[51] In fact, while she represents "a perverse version of Emersonian self-reliance," she is the paradigm of what women of the higher classes were supposed to be.[52] Her bourgeois complacency with regard to extravagance is summed up by her words: "Every one here thinks me exceedingly odd" (*P* 1:298). Not only is she conventional, but, notwithstanding her anarchic pretenses, she may even be a spy for the government and, therefore, treacherous.[53] Not by chance, Mr. Vetch asks Hyacinth whether she is not "a dabbler in plots and treasons."[54] As such, she would be like—given their unsuccessful intrigues—Beatrice Cenci, Beatrice di Tenda, and, as far as political conspiracies go, like Belgioioso, who, after all her endeavours, saw the pitiful end of the Roman Republic. But also, because of the similarity James saw between Fuller and Belgioioso, like Fuller.

Princess Casamassima is thus a dabbler, Belgioioso is a bounder, and Fuller is a humbug. Though different, these derogatory definitions share the element of superficiality and fraud by which both the two real women and their fictional sister are, in James's and Hawthorne's opinion, lambasted.

Because Fuller and Belgioioso never drew strict lines between genders, and often played roles not commonly assigned to or acted by women, this element of androgyny was so present to James's mind that he gives Christina a (better) double: Hyacinth Robinson who, for his part, is in search of a proper gender identity.[55] While Hyacinth sees Christina as "his standard of comparison, his authority, his measure, his perpetual reference" (*P* 2:126), she wishes to carry out Hyacinth's pledge to the anarchists, "I should like to do it in his place'" (*P* 2:229). And if, according to traditional gender roles, she is *masculine* in her intrepid attitude toward society, he is *feminine* in his passivity, even gullibility.[56] In addition, Hyacinth, too, would like to be an actor and muses that he "was to go through life in a mask, in a borrowed mantle; he was to be every day and every hour an actor" (*P* 1:86). As James notes in the preface, "he has undertaken to *play a part*" (*P* 1:xviii; italics mine). His sense of living in a theatrical way is so acute that at one point he sees his situation as "a play within the play" (*P* 1:208).

Furthermore, like the princess, he is both illegitimate and born of different nationalities. And if she is a princess by marriage, he is a duke by (unrecognized) blood. Actually, they are both "class 'passers'":[57] Christina is an (acquired) aristocrat (although allegedly willing to subvert the social order), while the anarchist Hyacinth is undone by his aesthetic sense that, like art, is inevitably associated with those ruling classes he initially wishes to destroy (*LI* 70). Finally, he too is a "dabbler," since James writes that he is "[d]abbling deeply in revolutionary politics of a hole-and-corner sort" (*P* 1:xviii).

Let us bear in mind that, because Hyacinth is a (book)binder, the name of his craft is homophonic with "bounder"—James's definition of Belgioioso.[58] Besides, like Christina Casamassima (and like Belgioioso, who also contributed to it), Hyacinth reads the *Revue des Deux Mondes* (*P* 1:163; 2:16). We should also mention that his poor French mother (who had been given a life sentence for killing her seducer, an English duke) was called Florentine Vivier: improbable as Florentine is as a name (and her surname is also curious), it recalls Florence, the city that Belgioioso loved and in which Fuller spent the last year of her life with Ossoli and their child.[59]

The one trait that significantly distinguishes Hyacinth from Christina is his lack of opportunism. She is never as honest as he is. From this point of view it is relevant that in both novels she insists on being judged "honest," that is, she insists on people taking her by her word, as one, at the theater, takes actors. But she is affected by a "false seriousness" (*LI* 92). Oxymoronic as this definition inherently is, suggesting her incapacity to even know herself, it points to the sterile and exploitative pretentiousness of the society of which she partakes.[60]

In this novel, Fuller's and Belgioioso's hunger for fame is evoked when Christina's double, Hyacinth, confides that "he was haunted with the dream of literary distinction" (*P* 1:91).

Revealingly, when Hyacinth goes to see Christina to give her the book of poetry he has beautifully bound, he cannot find her, but he keeps the book as "a virtual proof and gage — as if a ghost in vanishing from sight had left a palpable relic" (*P* 1:300). "Ghost" foreshadows James's specific definition of Fuller in *William Wetmore Story*. Furthermore, the act he has pledged himself to commit is judged by Christina a "silly *humbug* in a novel" (*P* 2:274; my italics), a possible reminder of Mozier's/Hawthorne's definition of Fuller in the Italian notebooks published only two years earlier.

Although similar traits inform Fuller, Belgioioso, and Christina, one should not forget what James wrote, when alluding to Fuller as the model for Zenobia in Hawthorne's *The Blithedale Romance:* "There is no strictness in the representation by novelists of persons who have struck them in life . . . The original gives hints, but the writer does what he likes with them, and imports new elements into the picture" (*H* 134–35). Certainly, James introduced "new elements" in portraying Christina Light Casamassima, but Fuller's and Belgioioso's imprints may be found in the female protagonist of his two novels written temporally far apart.

With her complex identity, in which intelligence and force, creativity and daring, passion and weakness were interwoven, Fuller never ceased haunting him.

Notes

1. See Cristina Giorcelli, "La Repubblica romana di Margaret Fuller: tra visione politica e impegno etico," in *Gli Americani e la Repubblica Romana del 1849,* ed. Sara Antonelli, Daniele Fiorentino, and Giuseppe Monsagrati (Rome: Gangemi, 2000), 53–88. In the late 1920s, Vernon L. Parrington was virtually alone in declaring — albeit with qualification — that Fuller deserved to be remembered better than and over many other women of her times. "[N]o other

woman of her generation in America is so well worth recalling," he wrote. *Main Currents in American Thought*, 3 vols. (New York: Harcourt, Brace, 1930), 2:426. Parrington, however, appreciated her personality more than her writings.

2. *The Letters of Margaret Fuller*, ed. Robert N. Hudspeth, 6 vols. (Ithaca, N.Y.: Cornell Univ. Press, 1983–1994), 6:373 (Fuller to Marcus Spring, Rome, February 1, 1848).

3. Joseph Jay Deiss, *The Roman Years of Margaret Fuller* (New York: Thomas Y. Crowell, 1969), 111; Bell Gale Chevigny, *The Woman and the Myth: Margaret Fuller's Life and Writings* (1976; repr., Boston: Northeastern Univ. Press, 1994), 388. In the summer of 1847, through Costanza Arconati Visconti, Fuller had met Alessandro Manzoni.

4. Belgioioso appointed Fuller "regolatrice" of the Fatebenefratelli Hospital with a note written on April 30, 1849. Emma Detti, *Margaret Fuller Ossoli e i suoi corrispondenti* (Florence: Le Monnier, 1942), 352.

5. By this time, Fuller had, perhaps, acquired her title of nobility—even if, with one exception, the world would not know about her liaison with Marquis Giovanni Ossoli and about their child until late June 1849. The exception was Caroline Sturgis Tappan. *Letters of Fuller*, 5:208 (Fuller to Tappan, n.p., March 16, 1849). Lewis Cass, the American chargé d'affaires, Emelyn Wetmore Story, and Costanza Arconati Visconti were among the few to whom Fuller confided her secret. Only at the end of August did she muster the courage to let her mother know about her personal situation.

6. Fuller may have spoken well but her written Italian was mediocre. Belgioioso's writings in theology included *Essai sur la formation du dogme catholique*, 4 vols. (Paris: Jules Renouard et Cie, 1842–43).

7. Luigi Severgnini, *La Principessa di Belgioioso* (Milan: Virgilio, 1972), 10; Fuller, *Woman in the Nineteenth Century* (New York: Norton, 1971), 116; see Joan von Mehren, *Minerva and the Muse: A Life of Margaret Fuller* (Amherst: Univ. of Massachusetts Press, 1994).

8. Quoted in Beth Archer Brombert, *Cristina: Portraits of a Princess* (New York: Knopf, 1977), 76.

9. This is Archer Brombert's thesis.

10. "Quelle donne e ragazze delle strade romane non avevano senso morale e in tempo di pace conducevano una vita disordinata ed egoista, ma in quel momento si manifestarono in loro doti redentrici." Charles Neilson Gattey, *Cristina di Belgiojoso* (Florence: Vallecchi, 1974), 164 (my translation).

11. "The relationships which suit you are those which develop and free your spirit, responding to the legitimate needs of your organism." Leopold Wellisz, *The Friendship of Margaret Fuller D'Ossoli and Adam Mickiewicz* (New York: Polish Book Importing, 1947), 24. No documented evidence of her wedding has yet been found, but Charles Capper convincingly argues that after Fuller became pregnant she did marry Ossoli, probably in the spring or fall of 1848. See

Margaret Fuller: An American Romantic Life, vol. 2, *The Public Years* (New York: Oxford Univ. Press, 2007).

12. *Memoirs of Margaret Fuller Ossoli,* ed. R. W. Emerson, W. H. Channing, and J. F. Clarke, 2 vols. (Boston: Phillips, Sampson, 1852), 2:58. Mazzini wrote that Belgioioso was "[u]na donna che per zelo patriottico, doni di intelligenza, sincerità delle proprie opinioni, e tolleranza di quelle altrui, merita, anche quando è in disaccordo con noi, molta stima e molto affetto da parte nostra" (A woman who for patriotic zeal, gifts of intelligence, sincerity of her own opinions, and tolerance of others, deserves, even when she disagrees with us, much esteem and much affection from us). Archer Brombert, *Cristina,* 194.

13. "Questa donna [Belgioioso] d'istinto e di ferrea volontà dominatrice . . . dai severi turbanti come una sibilla del Domenichino . . . irrita talvolta come un enigma . . . In lei, stranezze, audacie, errori; mai la piccolezza!" Barbiera, *La Principessa Belgiojoso. I suoi amici e nemici. Il suo tempo* (Milan: Treves, 1902), 426–27 (my translation).

14. Fuller's *Woman in the Nineteenth Century* was first published as "The Great Lawsuit," *Dial* (1843). Belgioioso's essay, "Della condizione attuale delle donne e del loro avvenire," appeared in *Nuova Antologia* in 1866; her books included *Essai sur la formation du dogme catholique* (1842), *Etude sur l'histoire de la Lombardie* (1846), *Histoire de la Maison de Savoie* (1860), *Osservazioni sullo stato attuale dell'Italia e sul suo avvenire* (1868), and *Sulla moderna politica internazionale* (1869). Fuller's dispatches for the *Tribune* are collected in *"These Sad But Glorious Days": Dispatches from Europe, 1846–1850,* ed. Larry J. Reynolds and Susan Belasco Smith (New Haven, Conn.: Yale Univ. Press, 1991). Elizabeth Barrett Browning, who met Fuller in Florence in 1849, was put off by her fiery participation in the Italian Risorgimento cause. An advertisement for Fuller's forthcoming history of events in Italy appeared in the *New-York Weekly Tribune* of January 23, 1850: "S. Margaret Fuller . . . has nearly completed . . . an elaborate History of the late Revolutionary Movements in Italy." *"Sad But Glorious Days,"* 3.

15. Cristina di Belgiojoso, *Scènes de la vie turque,* Paris, 1858. While in Turkey she barely escaped death when she was stabbed five times by an Italian servant who held her responsible for his being rejected by her daughter's teacher. Comments about Fuller's appearance are in *Memoirs of Fuller:* Emerson wrote that he "felt her to be a foreigner . . . a cultivated Spaniard or Turk," 1:227; Channing saw in her attitude and look "the soft languor of southern races . . . Here was one . . . eager . . . for . . . passionate excitement," 2:36. If Hawthorne has Fuller in mind when portraying Hester Prynne, let us recall how he describes her: "She had in her nature a rich, voluptuous, Oriental characteristic." *The Scarlet Letter,* ed. Sculley Bradley, Richmond C. Beatty, and E. Hudson Long (New York: W.W. Norton, 1962), 63. Jeffrey Steele discusses Fuller's story in "'A Tale of Mizraim': A Forgotten Story by Margaret Fuller," *New England Quarterly* 62, no.1 (March 1989): 82–104.

16. Deiss, *Roman Years*, 120.

17. Gattey, *Cristina di Belgiojoso*, 53–4.

18. See Charles Capper, *Margaret Fuller. An American Romantic Life*, vol. 1, *The Private Years* (New York: Oxford Univ. Press, 1992), 100–102, 110–12, 246–47, 275–87, 329–30.

19. Not by chance James singles her out as "this ardent New Englander, this impassionate Yankee, who occupied so large a place in the thoughts, the lives . . . of an intelligent . . . society." *Hawthorne* (London: MacMillan, 1879), 78 (hereafter cited in text and notes as *H*).

20. Nathaniel Hawthorne, *The French and Italian Notebooks*, ed. Thomas Woodson (Columbus: Ohio State Univ. Press, 1980) (hereafter cited in text and notes as *FI*). In 1871 Sophia Hawthorne had edited her husband's notes in *Passages from the French and Italian Notebooks*, from which, however, she had suppressed the malignant gossip about Fuller. Instead, the judgments passed on Fuller in Hawthorne's son's 1884 edition of the notebooks created a big scandal among her friends. In the heat of the controversy, in trying to justify Nathaniel Hawthorne's attitude toward Fuller, James Freeman Clarke in a conciliatory tone described the notebooks as "all sorts of hints, and suggestions, as they occurred to him [Hawthorne], as the grounds for future imaginative characters," and therefore as "the last thing he himself would ever have thought of printing." *FI* 768. According to Thomas R. Mitchell, Julian heavily *revised* his father's entry on Fuller in order to "legitimize his own antifeminism" since "[b]y discrediting Fuller, [he] sought to discredit the aspirations of Fuller's descendant, the New American Woman." In Mitchell's opinion, "Hawthorne probably accepted Mozier's account with considerably more skepticism than Julian would have his readers feel." Mitchell, *Hawthorne's Fuller Mystery* (Amherst: Univ. of Massachusetts Press, 1998), 21, 11, 23. In fact, Hawthorne defines Mozier's judgments as "very curious" (*FI* 155), but this ambivalent qualification is omitted in *Hawthorne and His Wife*, which James might have read by the time he wrote *William Wetmore Story and His Friends*.

21. In the notebooks Hawthorne goes as far as to report that Fuller's relationship with Ossoli could only be "purely sensual." *FI* 155. This opinion was omitted by Julian Hawthorne in *Hawthorne and His Wife*, seemingly in order to protect his father "from charges of an ungentlemanly, indeed gratuitously profane and somewhat prurient, interest in Fuller's sexuality." Mitchell, *Hawthorne's Fuller Mystery*, 23.

22. See especially Mitchell, *Hawthorne's Fuller Mystery*. After maintaining that in the second half of *The Princess Casamassima* James "resuscitates *Blithedale [Romance]*'s plot," Richard H. Brodhead claims that "the Princess comes to resemble Hawthorne's Zenobia," as both characters show "the inevitable self-deception and self-indulgence involved in a willed descent of social status . . . it is their plight that even as they revolt against th[e existing social] order they

continue to derive from it, both temperamentally and financially." *The School of Hawthorne* (New York: Oxford Univ. Press, 1986), 160, 161.

23. In his autobiography James reports that as a child he heard of Fuller's death—while on a steamboat that would take him to Fort Hamilton—from Washington Irving speaking to his father and that at an exhibition he saw a painting of Fuller that was judged unfair to her by those who knew her. *Autobiography*, ed. Frederick W. Dupee (London: W. H. Allen, 1956), 37. In both cases James underlines the pathetic side of Fuller's life and circumstances.

24. Rowe, "Swept Away: Henry James, Margaret Fuller, and 'The Last of the Valerii,'" in *Readers in History: Nineteenth-Century American Literature and the Contexts of Response*, ed. James L. Machor (Baltimore: Johns Hopkins Univ. Press, 1993), 47. In the James short story "The Last of the Valerii" (1874), set in Rome, the protagonist's wife, an American named Martha, solves the problem caused by her Italian noble husband's falling in love with a statue of Juno unearthed in his villa when she resolutely buries the statue again. Concurrently, by turning into an "angel in the house" and picking up embroidery (one of the feminine skills presided over by Minerva), she conforms to the socially accepted— unassuming and docile—female-model. Rowe sees Martha as one of James's possible literary incarnations of Fuller, who, in the final year, kept house with her lover/spouse and son. For James's treatment of Woolson, see Lyndall Gordon, *A Private Life of James: Two Women and His Art* (New York: W. W. Norton, 1999). As for Wharton, in his short story "The Velvet Glove," James indirectly makes fun of her. See Adeline R. Tintner, "James's Mock Epic: 'The Velvet Glove,' Edith Wharton, and Other Late Tales," *Modern Fiction Studies* 17 (1971–72): 483–99; J. Frantz Blackall, "Henry and Edith: 'The Velvet Glove' as an 'In' Joke," *Henry James Review* 7, no.1 (1985): 21–25.

25. James became a friend of Lowell (1819–91) in Paris in 1872. In a letter (to his father, Paris, November 1872) he writes, "I have struck up a furious intimacy with James Lowell"; in another (to his brother William, Paris, December 1, 1872) he seems to have made up his mind about Lowell: "He is very friendly, entertaining and full of knowledge; but his weak point will always be his *opinions*." Henry James, *Letters, 1843–1875*, vol. 1, ed. Leon Edel (Cambridge, Mass.: Harvard Univ. Press 1974), 308, 313. James and Lowell spent time together also in Florence in 1874. Their friendship lasted till Lowell's death.

26. Henry James, *Literary Criticism: French Writers; Other European Writers; The Prefaces to the New York Edition*, 2 vols. (New York: Library of America, 1984), 773, 705, 717. Both Madame de Mauves (in the short novel written in 1874) and Daisy Miller, for instance, are a "riddle" to their male observers. "Riddle" seems the designation that they apply to women who do not conform to the generally accepted, "male-male" rules. Sand is the woman writer on whom James most often wrote. He published reviews and essays on her work in 1868, twice in 1876, twice in 1877, in 1897, in 1902, and twice in 1914.

27. *Memoirs of Fuller*, 1:95 and 311–13; 2:34. Some decades later, in her biography of Fuller, Julia Ward Howe too would judge her "grandiloquent." *Margaret Fuller* (Boston: Roberts, 1883), 85. As Ann Douglas put it, "Necessarily and helplessly histrionic, she [Fuller] strove desperately to inhabit and authenticate the postures she assumed for survival." "Margaret Fuller and the Search for History: A Biographical Study," *Women's Studies* 4, no. 1 (1976): 42.

28. James, "The Siege of Rome," chap. 3 in *William Wetmore Story and His Friends*, 2 vols. (Boston: Houghton, Mifflin, 1903), 1:93–163 (all quotations are from vol. 1, hereafter cited in text and notes as *W*).

29. Douglas, "Fuller and the Search for History," 42.

30. By 1849, however, Lowell had softened his opinion, as shown in the article he published in *National Antislavery Standard:* "We learn from private letters that, the last American left in Rome, she [Fuller] was doing her duty in the hospitals as a nurse . . . Women have been sainted at Rome for less." Quoted in Chevigny, *Woman and the Myth*, 403.

31. *W* 126. A tragedy dedicated to Beatrice Cenci was written by Juljusz Slowacki (1809–49) in 1839. But, of course, especially P. B. Shelley's tragedy, *The Cenci* (1819), was very well known by these cultivated Americans, who were simultaneously attracted to and repulsed by such a story and such a heroine. It is not by chance, therefore, that Fuller is mentioned in connection with Cenci. The attribution of the portrait has since changed, but at that time Reni was credited as its author. Felice Romani (1788–1865) wrote the libretto for Bellini's opera (1833). Beatrice di Tenda's tragic story had also been set for the stage by Carlo Tedaldi Flores (1793–1829) in 1825. Beatrice di Tenda lived from 1370 to 1418; left a rich widow by Captain Facino Cane, she married Filippo Maria Visconti. Accused of adultery and of plotting against her husband, she was sentenced to death with her alleged lover.

32. The name is culturally misleading since the most famous Beatrice is Dante's "angel woman"; therefore these women would disguise their true (allegedly evil) nature under this emblematically charged name.

33. Emerson suggests that Fuller was a "sybil" in *Memoirs of Fuller*, 1:228. Adelaide Ristori (1822–1906) is the only Italian actress who attained an international reputation before Eleonora Duse. Ristori privileged roles of strong, dignified, awe-inspiring women, preferably queens. In her repertoire one finds Lady Macbeth, Mary Stuart, Elizabeth, Marie Antoinette. She did not shy away, however, from also representing gruesome heroines such as Legouvé's Medea. See Cristina Giorcelli, "Adelaide Ristori sullè scene britanniche e irlandesi," *Teatro Archivio* 5 (September 1981): 81–155; and Giorcelli, "Ristori on the American Scene," *Voices in Italian Americana* 3, no. 1 (Spring 1992): 29–40.

34. It is not clear what play by Scribe he is referring to, since the only drama by Scribe *and* Legouvé that Ristori performed in was *Adriana Lecouvreur*, which, however, was introduced into her repertoire around 1852 (and not in

1848 as James speculates in *W* 116). Teresa Viziano, *Il palcoscenico di Adelaide Ristori* (Rome: Bulzoni, 2000), 279.

35. *H* 78. James had similarly criticized George Sand for the "force, and mass, and energy" of her "masculine" genius in *French Writers*, 716.

36. *W* 162–63. Interestingly, in *The Scarlet Letter* a character depicts Pearl, the incarnation of Hester's letter *A*, as a "little bird of scarlet plumage" and as a "wild, tropical bird, of rich plumage" (80, 81).

37. Douglas, "Fuller and the Search for History," 66, 69.

38. "Gloria a lei, vera amica d'Italia nostra! Gloria, o fortissima." Barbiera, *Principessa Belgiojoso*, 312 (my translation).

39. Cristina Giorcelli, *Henry James e l'Italia* (Rome: Edizioni di Storia e Letteratura, 1968), 119–46; Henry James, "Madame Ristori," in *The Scenic Art: Notes on Acting and the Drama, 1872–1901*, ed. Allan Wade (New Brunswick, N.J.: Rutgers Univ. Press, 1948), 29. This review was written in 1875, when Ristori was making her third tour of the United States with her company.

40. Being Italian, Eugenio too disguises his real nature under a misleading name: Eu-genio etymologically means well (nobly) born. He succeeds in becoming Daisy's and Milly's guardian and master of ceremony. Amerigo too "almost resembled an actor who, between his moments on the stage, revisits his dressing-room, and, before the glass, pressed by his need of effect, retouches his make-up." Henry James, *The Golden Bowl*, 2 vols. (New York: Scribner's, 1909), 1:248.

41. Belgioioso's biographers insist that her death was little commented upon in the papers. Notwithstanding her active participation in the Risorgimento and her devotion to the House of Savoy, because of her free and adventurous life she had become an embarrassment to the sanctimonious Italian establishment. See Gattey, *Cristina di Belgiojoso*, 257.

42. It is her mother who defines her as such in *Roderick Hudson* (New York: Scribner's, 1907), 247 (hereafter cited in text and notes as *R*).

43. By calling Christina Light a "ghost," Roderick seems also to echo the well-known comment on Belgioioso's paleness, mentioned in Archer Brombert, *Cristina* (see note 8).

44. Given her surname (composed of "grand" + "oni": the latter, a suffix to indicate bigness), one is not surprised that Madame Grandoni is so exaggerated and emphatic in her judgments. For James's quote from Barbiera, see note 13.

45. *Memoirs of Fuller*, 1:238. Belgioioso was portrayed several times and by such artists as Francesco Hayez and Henri Lehmann.

46. *R* 196 and 410. Roland Mallet too calls her "an actress" (*R* 297). In the first version of the novel Christina's characterization as an actress is more insisted upon than in the New York edition.

47. Henry James, *The Princess Casamassima*, 2 vols. (New York: Scribner's, 1908) (hereafter cited in text and notes as *P*). Interestingly, Christina's maiden

surname never appears in *The Princess Casamassima*. Is it because those who have read the previous novel already know that she is luminous and flippant or is it because it is so evident in *this* novel that she is luminous and flippant that she no longer needs a tag? Moreover, it is as if the grandiloquent characteristics of Madame "Grandoni" were taken over by Christina, who, in this novel, has become "Casa-massima": a very big (important) house. "Bel-gioioso" means beautiful (and) merry.

48. *P* 1:305, 2:261. Elsewhere James defines the princess as "an original, and an original with force." *P* 1:252.

49. *P* 2:19. Let us not forget that this novel was written when James had already started thinking of his next one, *The Tragic Muse* (1889), which focuses on the rise of a great actress. In the same years James worked intensely, if unsuccessfully, for the stage.

50. Mark Seltzer, "*The Princess Casamassima*: Realism and the Fantasy of Surveillance," *Nineteenth Century Fiction* 35, no. 4 (March 1981): 519. Brodhead too has emphasized Zenobia's and Christina's "natural theatricality." *School of Hawthorne*, 160.

51. Trilling, *The Liberal Imagination: Essays on Literature and Society* (New York: Viking, 1951) (hereafter cited in text and notes as *LI*); Rowe, *The Theoretical Dimensions of Henry James* (Madison: Univ. of Wisconsin Press, 1984), 167–68. As has been argued, "Acting is . . . the art of the coquette" because the coquette is "a woman who gains power over others by manipulative verbal and body language." Natasha Sajé, "'Artful Artlessness': Reading the Coquette in *Roderick Hudson*," *Henry James Review* 18, no. 2 (1997): 162, 161.

52. Rowe, *Theoretical Dimensions*, 166–67.

53. Seltzer, "*Princess Casamassima*," 524; also Rowe, *Theoretical Dimensions*, 181. On theatricality as the model that organizes James's point of view, see Fredric Jameson, *The Political Unconscious: Narrative as a Socially Symbolic Act* (Ithaca, N.Y.: Cornell Univ. Press, 1981).

54. *P* 2:99. As Rowe maintains, the purpose of this dilettantism "is to constitute the 'other' of th[e] stable social order," because such "other" represents "nothing so much as the power of control, ideological repression, that not only permits [marginal figures or tolerable dissenters] to exist but has in a very real sense 'invented' them as characters." *Theoretical Dimensions*, 175.

55. According to Warren Johnson, "[I]t is usually impossible to distinguish Hyacinth's thoughts from Christina's." In addition, from a narratological point of view, "*The Princess Casamassima* demands that we divide our attentions between two characters and two plots." "Hyacinth Robinson or The Princess Casamassima?" *Texas Studies in Literature and Language* 28, no. 3 (Fall 1986): 306, 298. Hyacinth is even said to have a "double identity" (*P* 1:325), since he does not know whether he is English or French, an aristocrat or a working-class man. There are several other doubles in the novel, such as "day and night, conscious

and unconscious, manifest and latent psychic contents, master and servant."
Rowe, *Theoretical Dimensions*, 185. "Hyacinth's suicide has as much to do with his
inability to identify his proper gender role and sexual identity as it does with his
revolutionary politics." John Carlos Rowe, *The Other Henry James* (Durham,
S.C.: Duke Univ. Press, 1998), 105. Hyacinth's sexual liminality as well as the
other male characters' ambivalent sexuality is discussed in Wendy Graham,
"Henry James's Subterranean Blues: A Rereading of *The Princess Casamassima*,"
Modern Fiction Studies 40, no.1 (Spring 1994). Sara Blair too notes, "In the best tradition of romantic feminine passivity, Hyacinth finds himself everywhere 'em-
barassed, overturned, bewildered.'" *Henry James and the Writing of Race and Nation*
(New York: Cambridge Univ. Press, 1996), 104.

56. Rowe, *Theoretical Dimensions of James*, 179.

57. Christine DeVine, "Revolution and Democracy in the London *Times*
and *The Princess Casamassima*," *Henry James Review* 23, no. 1 (Winter 2002): 69.
While Hyacinth does not want people to know that he is the son of an aristocrat, he does not know that Christina comes from a middle-class background.
Greg W. Zacharias claims that "Hyacinth and the Princess use each other self-
ishly in desperate attempts to stabilize their lives: he to access upper class culture; she lower." *Henry James and the Morality of Fiction* (New York: Peter Lang,
1993), 88.

58. As Trilling pointed out, "[A]t that time anarchism did not attract fac-
tory workers so much as the members of the skilled and relatively sedentary
trades: tailors, shoemakers, weavers, cabinetmakers, and ornamental-metal
workers . . . bookbinding was . . . at once a fine and a mechanic art." *LI* 71.
Deborah Esch notes that "a bookbinder [is] a practitioner of the mechanical
art that operates on the threshold of form and content." "Promissory Notes:
The Prescription of the Future in *The Princess Casamassima*," *American Literary
History* 1, no. 2 (Summer 1989): 321.

59. *Vivier* means "fishpond" in French. Rowe, *Theoretical Dimensions*, 170.

60. The characteristics of the relationships entertained by *The Princess
Casamassima*'s protagonists are thus summarized by Posnock: "The sterility
of the[se] attachments—their minimum of reciprocity and maximum of
exploitation—dramatizes the loss of affect that pervades both the bourgeois
world and the plottings of its allegedly revolutionary redeemers." Ross Posnock, *The Trial of Curiosity: Henry James, William James, and the Challenge of Modernity* (New York: Oxford Univ. Press, 1991), 271.

10

Margaret Fuller on the Stage

MARIA ANITA STEFANELLI

What woman needs is not as a woman to act or rule, but as a nature to grow, as an intellect to discern, as a soul to live freely, and unimpeded to unfold such powers as were given her when we left our common home.

Margaret Fuller, *Woman in the Nineteenth Century*

One, none, and a hundred thousand [women] *is* the protagonist of Susan Sontag's play *Alice in Bed*, written in 1990, published in 1993, and widely performed at academically related theatrical institutions both across the United States—Cambridge, Chicago, Seattle, and New York City, among other places—and Europe.[1] The singular in my previous sentence is as ambiguous as it is intentional in that *Alice in Bed* features but one woman, who disguises as one, another, or yet another woman, thus exhibiting several identities—those of every single female character in the play. Each character, in turn, displays diversity, thus multiplying the possibilities for each different self to be "other" than one's own self. The "house of difference" (to speak in contemporary feminist terms) emerges, therefore, from a plurality of women's identities.[2]

The play—which is "about the grief and anger of women; and . . . about the imagination" (*AB* 117), as Sontag explains in a note following the text—had been "dreamed" by the author ten years earlier while she rehearsed, as director, a production of Luigi Pirandello's *Come tu mi vuoi (As You Desire Me)* in Rome (1980). In the playbill, she had criticized oppression with a feminist statement: "Being created by somebody else's desire is a feature of the human condition, but it is emphatically so for women. The cultural construct of women's oppression can be understood given the assumption that women, differently from men, are created by their being desired."[3]

Both Pirandello's play and her own are centered on the problem of identity; both plays expose man's power over women; both plays present the feminine condition in theatrical terms, according to which the characters are created or dismantled. Alice and "her friends," however, unlike the female protagonist of *Come tu mi vuoi*, L'Ignota (The Unknown One), resist being exploited by the playwright or director, thus exposing, and reducing to zero, the pretense of theater of constructing and defining. By playing with the nonsensical and the theatrical, Sontag defies both Pirandello as author and herself as conniving director, and lets the fictional character Margaret Fuller come alive to oppose the construction of herself by man's, or indeed anybody's, desire.

Alice in Bed

Through eight scenes Alice James, the lifetime invalid, brilliant sister-writer of the famous American novelist, interacts with several personae on stage, entertains a mental social gathering, and utters a long monologue occupying a whole scene. Alice—her own character a combination of bitterness, wit, indifference, resignation, curiosity, and longing—articulates, whether tentatively or provocatively, her own place in her family and in society, her vocation as a woman, her inner strife with herself, and her own desires. In the play, she goes through a series of encounters: with her nurse, who presents her patient's inner conflict as a crisis of the will; with her demanding father, who rationally submits his daughter's wish for death to her friends' distress; and with her brother Harry, who suffers for her condition yet simultaneously appropriates her pains to shape those of his fictional heroines. After her (mental) party with several Victorian female figures including her mother, Alice travels again (mentally) to Rome to recover, in her imagination at least, her lost mobility. She finally meets, in her own home, a young burglar man, who unaware as well as unexpectedly raises her spirit and awakens her will to move; but "Out there it's so big" (*AB* 106), she thinks, so she soon retreats to the isolation of her real and imagined illness.

In scene 5 Alice James's mind is the stage for three historical characters and two fictional ones to participate in the tea party set up for herself by a number of women: the poet Emily Dickinson; Kundry, the mysterious woman from Wagner's *Parsifal;* Myrtha, Queen of the Wilis; and Margaret Fuller, "the first important American woman of letters" (*AB* 115). Another historical character, also dead, makes her appearance at the party: it is Alice's mother, in real life an "unimaginative" woman, "inclined to be gubernatorial" in Leon Edel's words, as much as her husband, Henry James Sr., was maternal, and, according to the later recollection of a young family friend, "genial and delightful . . . out of place in that stiff stupid house in Cambridge."[4]

The time of the play is 1890—two years before Alice's death from breast cancer at forty-three.[5] Both Fuller and Dickinson are ghosts, having died in 1850 and 1886, respectively, while Myrtha and Kundry are fantasy creatures from two musical works of 1840 and 1882, respectively.[6] The year 1882 is also the date of Mrs. James's death.

The setting of the play is mainly London (only one in eight scenes "is a flashback or memory, and takes place two decades earlier in Cambridge, Massachusetts," as the stage direction reads) (*AB* 3). The tea party (which includes opium smoking) takes place on the veranda or sunroom at Alice's lodgings at South Kensington.[7] The atmosphere is Victorian and, as Sontag herself suggests, the name of the protagonist "inevitably echoes the nineteenth century's most famous Alice, the heroine of Lewis Carroll's *Alice's Adventures in Wonderland*" (1865) (*AB* 115). The afternoon reception at Alice's home is quite naturally associated, Sontag confirms, with the nonsensical Mad Tea-party created by the Reverend Charles Lutwidge Dodgson (1832–98).

During the party, Alice is confronted with the opposite roles taken up by Margaret and Emily, who emerge, respectively, as active and contemplative, determined and elusive, in love with life and in love with death.[8] Such historical figures have their counterparts in their two opposite characters: visionary Myrtha and sleeping Kundry. Together the women offer their hostess fragments of their own mental and practical experience, and when Alice's mother—an icon of matriarchal power just as destructive as (if not more destructive than) the patriarchal one— turns up uninvited, she is rebuked by Alice's friends. As the gathering goes on, the women step in and out of Victorian conventions to offer Alice fragments from their biography, fictional world, or writings, and help her voice her own refusal of familial and societal codes. In control of their identities, Margaret and Emily, whether open to sexual engagement or not, show through their performance how to resist the power of the Other's desire. Together—tough Fuller against accommodating Dickinson, active Myrtha against passive Kundry—they act as models for Alice, who tries to learn from them how to partake of their expressed female being and female desire while simultaneously avoiding a crisis of the self. Participating in the collective ritual of the traditional all-women tea party, Alice learns how to resist—at least in her imagination—being patronized by men, women, or life itself.

Complex and richly intertextual, Sontag's play raises questions about the cultural constraints that can limit gifted women's scope of achievement and can turn them into dramatic victims of male power. Moreover, it provides a contextualized comparative analysis of the category "woman," thus revealing the multiplicity of feminine genders in society, their fluidity, and their historical instability.[9]

Margaret Fuller

A person's name, according to Sontag, is potent as it is arbitrary. If it is quite plausible, then, that one scene—scene 5—should have been conceived as an extemporized ceremony at once absurd and logical (nothing less than pure nonsense), one cannot help remarking, as well, that the author of the "notorious proto-feminist book," *Woman in the Nineteenth Century*, does indeed *fill* the scene in ways that fit the character of the woman whom Henry James (also a character—Harry—in the play) called "the talker, the moral *improvisatrice*."[10] Sontag herself, by the way, blends nonsense with good sense when, in her discussion on the aesthetics of silence, she cites an extract from *Through the Looking-Glass* ("Silence" is, incidentally, one theme in *Alice in Bed* that Sontag links with Virginia Woolf's mental creation of Judith Shakespeare, the playwright's imaginary sister).[11] The quotation concerns Lewis Carroll's heroine coming upon a shop "that seemed to be *full* of all manner of curious things—but the oddest part of it all was that whenever she looked hard at any shelf, to make out exactly what it had on it, that particular shelf was quite empty, though the others round it were crowded *full* as they could hold."[12] If, by an arbitrary act of linguistic violence—very common among nonsense addicts—one were to remove from Carroll's "shelf" the *h* (just as one would remove an object from it), one would find that identity exists in its sameness only by reference to otherness. So, as much as "fullness" is perceived as a lack of emptiness and "silence" as a lack of sound, so would "being" be perceived as a lack of nonbeing and "existence" as a lack of representing. In the theater one is trapped between seeming and performing, never in being.

One role Fuller would fulfill most willingly was that of respondent: often with wit and insight, sometimes with impatience and in haste, always with articulation she would interact with her intellectual friends— be it in writing or in conversation—never letting them down. On the other hand, in the forum of intellectual exchange, she would set out to "fill in" the first half of the dialogue, by submitting issues, whether amiably or begrudgingly, for the other participants' critical comments. "I have lost in her my audience," proclaimed Ralph Waldo Emerson regretfully after the Atlantic Ocean prematurely ripped Margaret Fuller Ossoli from this world.[13] To the Transcendentalist poet-philosopher she appeared a "brave, eloquent, subtle, accomplished, devoted, constant soul," while she emerges as "brilliant, witty, imperious, demanding, abrasive, and charming" to the judgment of Robert Hudspeth, who has retrieved from her rich correspondence a much more complex personality than a number of scholars had suggested.[14]

In her literary writings Fuller devoted her efforts to self-definition: whether she portrayed the woman in the nineteenth century or inquired into the universal genius of Goethe, in her letters as in her notes, articles, essays, and dispatches she would claim a role as a multivalent, gendered personality. A promoter of equal opportunities, she trod the stage of the world as a performer who challenged the inadequate categories of gender, power, and sexuality.

Fuller as Actress

Sontag captures Fuller's passion for self-dramatization and summons her ghost to participate in the "free fantasy" situation that takes place in the protagonist's (Alice James's) mind. Throughout her critical prose and the six volumes that contain Fuller's correspondence from infancy to the time she boarded the ship that would take her, her husband, and her child to their deaths, we encounter many of her selves as fictions of her mind. The preoccupation with her identity, the ability to conceal thoughts with words, the disappointment at the impossibility of exercising power, the uneasiness with her sex, and the realization, often, to appear what she was not: all these are motives that are best discussed in relation to role playing and gender construction. To George T. Davis she wrote: "You are the only person who can appreciate my true self" (*L* 1:174); to James F. Clarke she explained the effect on her of reading Goethe: "He comprehends every feeling I have ever had so perfectly, expresses it so beautifully; but when I shut the book, it seems as if I had lost my personal identity" (*L* 1:177). To Davis (presumably, since the document does not reveal the addressee), she vented her bitterness at the lack of compensation for her generosity: "As in a glass darkly, I have seen what I might feel as child, wife, mother, but I have never really approached the close relations of life. A sister I have truly been to many,—a brother to more,—a fostering nurse to, oh how many! The bridal hour of my spirit, when first it was wed, I have shared, but said adieu before the wine was poured at the banquet" (*L* 6:134–35).

In the same letter she wrote that from a very early age she had felt she "was not born to the common womanly lot" and "did not look on any of the persons, brought into relation with [her], with commonly womanly eyes"; her character was, however, "still more feminine than masculine" (*L* 6:134–35). When her father died, she expressed her regret at "being of the softer sex" (*L* 1:237), and in an exchange of letters with William Henry Channing, she utterly rejected all possible charges of frailty: "Certainly I am nowise yet an angel; but neither am I an utterly weak woman, and far less a cold intellect" (*L* 6:99). During her last year in Rome, when events became encumbering, she would dismiss people's negative reaction to her homecoming, which, she was sure, was "not directed against the real Margaret, but a phantom"; she added, "I have acted not inconsistently with myself" (*L* 6:88). Led by a deep admiration for her capacity of impersonation and mimicry, the *Tribune* editor Horace Greeley (1811–72) ventured to hypothesize that "had she condescended to appear before the foot-lights, [she] would soon have been recognized as the first actress of the Nineteenth Century."[15] And Emerson, besides stressing that she made a "disagreeable impression on people" and, indeed, on himself when they first met, also emphasized that she made him laugh, he wrote, "more than I liked," and that she entertained him with "amusing gossip" and an "incredible variety of anecdotes"; he also stated that "her talk was a comedy in which dramatic justice was done to everybody's foibles."[16] "From her childhood on," writes Hudspeth, "Fuller was fond of dramatizing her life, and it is not much to say that she lived with an eye to heightening the drama." Further on he adds, "An actress who wrote her own scripts, she knew how to be commanding and interesting" and then dramatically sums up: "Thus life became a stage" (*L* 1:32, 51, 54).

Nonsense and Intertextuality

Fuller's ability to wear as many hats as she wished to multiply her identities derives from a crossover of gender and sexuality, enacted by the very discourses that have made her into a myth. Definitions of Fuller have been recalled in the various studies devoted to her: from the unwomanly woman emerging from *Memoirs* to the kaleidoscopic portraits supplied by the Higginsons, the Hawthornes, the Poes, the Jameses, and the succeeding generations of scholars. The sparks of her emotions, feelings, and dreams have been captured both within and at the margins of the texts. Sontag's decision to have Alice re-create conversation with the dead spirits of two writers and two imaginary "angry women," more or less her contemporaries, leads to where logic meets absurdity and lets nonsense arise (*AB* 116). This choice of Sontag is in keeping with the idea that a critique of representation is best carried out from within, where theatricality is most evident and there is no limit to possibility, manipulation, or even the ordering of the universe.

What happens at the tea party happens in the form of a dream, on the frontier between language and thinking. In the nonsense world there is no space for more people than are already sitting at a half-empty table, someone who has had no tea can take more, riddles are asked that cannot be answered, and time, though lost, can be prolonged indefinitely. In the nonsense world of Alice's Wonderland many characters are mad: the March Hare, the Mad Hatter, and everybody else too—as the Cheshire cat says—including Alice, who tries to resist. Scene 5 in *Alice in Bed,* in which a dreamlike event takes place, is not a stable locus of meaning, but contains traces (verbal, aural, and visual) that derive from the biographies of the historical characters, the fictional lives of the two imaginary exemplary creatures, and also from Lewis Carroll's nonsensical world as well as the playwright's body of writings, her feminist politics, and her theatrical beliefs.

With the different intertextual elements crossing over, being torn apart, reassembled, and set against one another, meanings are continually renegotiated to provoke amusement, reflection, anxiety, excitement, and desire in a wonderlike atmosphere allowing "woman" to be represented or acted by other women who—though dead or imaginary—"live" on the stage. As the living impersonation of the gendered woman, Fuller deconstructs her own character and the image she represents, and makes the quotation marks around *woman* visible. In this way, she reconstructs "woman" and, likewise, herself. After all, is she not the author-creator of *Woman in the Nineteenth Century?*

Sontag opposes the male-centered discourse in which the subject is male and woman is the object constructed by his desire. While Pirandello's L'Ignota lacks any identity and is defined only by the male subjects around her to which condition she reacts relying on masking, Sontag's Margaret, also aware of the precariousness of such constructions of which she was a victim, sets out to debunk them. Being back in the world as a ghost she recaptures the past by mocking her own self, by creating, as it were, a parody of herself. If one bears in mind one of Sontag's last observations in her "Note on the Play," Margaret is also the counterversion of L'Ignota, who is herself—much like Pirandello's ambiguous idea of Truth—a woman affirmed by belief, although threatened by doubt, namely, a mask, a lifeless creature, one who can only come alive thanks to someone's desire. In contrast, by acting through the transgressive party situation (one need only think of the hookah session), Margaret evades her authoritative contemporary male authors' constructions of herself, and builds herself through her own performance. She then tries to have Alice reject—like L'Ignota—an identity bestowed upon her by a family for whom she is, *passively,* a woman (as well as her brothers' sister, her parents' daughter, a collection of symptoms, etc.), yet *does not live through* her own making of herself.[17] In *Alice's Adventures in Wonderland,* instead, it is the authoritative Caterpillar who gives "advice" to Alice on how to recover her own "self" after her several changes.[18]

By staging aspects of herself that are rhetorical and theatrical, besides, Margaret plays the role of an actress who does not depend on male desire—or, for that matter, anyone's desire. The model is undoubtedly Sarah Bernhardt, who is evoked by Sontag's heroine in scene 2 as proprietor of a mirror Alice now owns and who, as an unconventional and androgynous actress, magnified her own "difference" and

Jewish marginality by "strutting her outrageousness on and off stage across Western Europe and America."[19]

To a certain extent and "embarrassingly" for the people around her, as Sontag puts it, Margaret creates her own self not *as you desire me* (as L'Ignota does) but *as she herself desires*. In Pirandello's conception the price to pay is that of being exposed in one's—supposed—"nudity" that may be repellent and/or unsympathetic, but is one's own.

In acting, though, there are all sorts of risks. Acting is bound up with femininity, but problematic relationships with other women may develop for the woman who "acts," as the introductory polemical exchange over time between Margaret and Emily suggests, after which Margaret addresses Alice thus: "Do you think I offended her? I'm truly sorry. Sometimes I have *acted* on a strong impulse and could not analyze what passed in my mind. I *acted* what was in my character" (*AB* 46; my italics). Action, instead, belongs, by definition, to the controlling male power. Yet assuming a masculine attitude may lead to self-negation if one's identity is not stable: "Margaret: I was very *active*. . . . But now I'm not myself" (*AB* 52; my italics).

In the uncertain world where one may keep drinking tea although there isn't any, where the smoke released by the hookah provokes a trancelike mood, and where Alice's long-dead mother turns up uninvited, the body (which is, on the stage, the physical body of the actress) can express assurance or anxiety: Margaret's "robust" figure is in keeping with her oral aggressiveness and determination while "frail" Emily leaves the party to retire into absence. Margaret—who, when the scene opens, inappropriately reads a book on the table laid out for the tea ceremony—wears a hat that vaguely suggests a sympathetic attitude toward the suffragette movement of Victorian times while Alice—"long hair, childlike" (*AB* 7)—wears an infantilized white gown in the guise of the several "madwomen in the attic" belonging to the history of feminine renunciation.[20] Again, while Margaret's feet are always "on the ground"—"When they are not in the water," she adds with a tragicomic reference to her shipwreck (*AB* 55)—Alice needs the protection of a stack of mattresses to make up for the absence of the body of a man in her life (and in her bed); such presence would turn her into a prisoner and make her a prey to the male power: "Alice: I wanted a man's weight on my body. But then I couldn't move" (*AB* 67).

On the level of self-representation Margaret's courage to defy dominant male prejudices contrasts with, and parallels, Alice's neurotic illness as a form of self-negation.[21] The two women represent themselves differently, of course:

> MARGARET: I was an embarrassment to others. And then to the
> relief of many I died.
> ALICE: I'm an embarrassment to myself. *(Laughs)* (*AB* 47)

The notion of counseling as a specifically male privilege is ironically challenged yet not utterly rebuked:

> ALICE: I wanted advice. From a woman I could respect. I've always
> sought advice from men.
> MARGARET: People were always giving me advice, for my own good.
> Truth was, they did not want me to embarrass them. (*AB* 53)

One extreme act of self-construction involves the romantic sublimation of suffering as a gendered act:

> MARGARET: Women despair differently. I've observed that. We
> can be very stoical. (*AB* 54)

Finally, as a counterpart of the passivity that characterized Pirandello's play—as summed up in L'Ignota's exclamation in act 3, "I am here, I am yours; nothing exists in me, nothing more of mine: make me, make me, as you desire me!"—Margaret weaves erotic excitement within her identity as a residue of the desire experienced in real life.[22] Her depiction of her husband as an innocent, feminized boy—"unlike me, an exceedingly delicate person" (*AB* 73)—unable to speculate about anything at all has a counterpart in the other women's recollections. Alice remembers a young man who was a friend of her brother: "But he liked me," she adds, "I used to imagine that we could go swimming together. I used to imagine his body" (*AB* 67). Emily evokes her goateed brother who cultivated forbidden pleasures ("I stayed at home and wrote. My brother fornicated") (*AB* 73). Kundry is reminded of her attempt to corrupt the young man in *Parsifal*, "To make him desire me. He did desire me, but more as a mother than as a lover. And, still, he resisted me" (*AB* 73). Here men's exploitation of women, exposed by Pirandello as author and Sontag as director on the stage of *Come tu mi vuoi*, is reversed, in *Alice in Bed*, into the staging of female desire.

Uncertainty is doubled up with reversals that in Wonderland the March Hare and the Hatter had warned Alice from confusing: "I mean what I say" is not exactly the same as "I say what I mean" as much as "I see what I eat" is not the same as "I eat what I see," or "I like what I get" is not the same as "I get what I like," or indeed "I breathe when I sleep" is different from "I sleep when I breathe." In *Alice in Bed* Carrollian reversals are duplicated as "I sleep because I am suffering" and "I am suffering because I am asleep," in the pronouncement of Kundry, the Dormouse, who "speaks as if still sleeping" (*AB* 48); or else, they are duplicated as a difference between characters, such as Margaret and Emily, for instance, who at the end of the party leave together because "opposites attract" (*AB* 79), as Margaret puts it; or else, they are duplicated within the same character, as is clear from Alice's realization, "I am betraying myself" (*AB* 50), that she is, indeed, two persons.

In scene 2 Alice, unable to exercise her will power to get up from the bed and presided over by her striped uniform-clad jailor (the nurse), is handed the mirror "which by the way," Alice comments, "once belonged to Sarah Bernhardt" (*AB* 10), as recalled above. After the stack of thin mattresses that cover Alice are removed by two sailors, she is propped up in bed with the help of three cushions and "continues to look at herself in the mirror," as the stage direction goes.[23] While she seems to acquire some confidence in her looks, the nurse who invites her, patronizingly, not to be too vain, promptly rebukes her. Alice makes it quite clear that she has a wider notion of "look" than what is normally associated with makeup—"Perhaps if you put on some powder, a little rouge. You are a woman, you know" (*AB* 9), the nurse had advised—just by adding a comment on the actress who possessed her mirror: "Do you know what I once said about Sarah Bernhardt, do you know . . . She is a moral abscess, festering with vanity. I did say that" (*AB* 12). Soon after she's haunted by visions of herself as man-killer. The mirror— *"a wooden oval on a stick, Italian, ornate, gilt"* (*AB* 10)—Bernhardt hardly needs since she has succeeded in reinvesting the mirror image to gain more and more signifiers at the cost—like Sontag—of her own outward projection.[24] The instrument to create a double of herself Bernhardt can pass on to Alice who, by nonsense, like Alice in Wonderland, can make sense of, and revise, her own attitude. The looking-glass world is reenacted in the mind, while the roles of Mad Hatters and March Hares are played by looking glass, topsy-turvy, or upside-down women.

Reversals signal the inability to find a definite direction in one's sexuality—as psychoanalytic research has maintained; so in this context, one is not surprised at the presentation of Fuller, in her eccentricity, exaggeration, and subtle intelligence, as the Mad Hatter—who, after all, matches, in the degree of artifice and stylization, Sontag's definition of camp.[25] Although she does not embarrass or puzzle Alice with "personal remarks" or "riddles that have no answer" and finds, instead, ready-made logical solutions to the riddles of life (like the question of suicide, for instance: "Alice: I suppose you are against suicide. Margaret: Never seen the point. We die too soon anyway" [*AB* 53]), she lets the language on the stage be indifferently disrupted or taken at face value—as much as in Wonderland—yet manages, by her own example, to have Alice talk herself into a constructive monologue on Rome, filtered through Harry's—Henry James's—and her own lens. There freedom is earned in terms of survival. This is as much as can be done, while the presence of a child with a maimed hand represents "the distressing claims of the world beyond the privileged one in which she lives" (*AB* 116).

Alice in Bed problematizes gender while at the same time problematizing theater. Sontag has written Fuller's life, as well as her afterlife, into the history of American theater. Dramatic texts possess a life that comes through both by being embodied in a real-life character and across the play of discourse. Margaret as product, let us not forget, of Alice's mind is, herself, an idea; she is not a human subject of interest in herself, but in terms of the functions that she fulfills in the nonsensical and paradoxical structure of the tea party, a conversation situation in which the real Margaret Fuller used to play such a prominent role.[26] While the human is displaced, ideas checkmate each other, and meanings are generated "not by the human presences somehow 'stamped' upon [the human element], but by the discourse, the particular language of which it consists operating a kind of free play of signifying practices."[27]

A multiple, decentered, ideologically shaped Margaret Fuller is the theatrical counterpart of a historical, human, psychologically available subject. Both continue playing a role in the impasse of the speculative mind, ever allowing paradoxical, unstable, nonlogical, absurd situations. Dead "to the relief of many," Margaret ceases to be an *embarrassment* to others; yet she defies the others' constructions of her by becoming an idea and coming alive again by means of theater where, however, she can never completely, like Humpty-Dumpty, put her own fragmented self together again.

As Roland Barthes comments: "Such is discourse; if it creates characters, it is not to make them play among themselves before us but to play with them, to obtain from them a complicity which assures the uninterrupted exchange of the codes; the characters are types of discourse and, conversely, the discourse is a character like the others." Sontag's discourse creates in the character of Margaret Fuller her own accomplice and her own mad double. They are both Dark Ladies.[28] They are both, somehow, "angry" in that they enact their own raging desire to escape—as Gilbert and Gubar put it—male houses and male texts. As a matter of fact they both let out the "silent, savage rage" that Alice James, instead, suppresses, thus destroying her own potential.[29] Anger, however, is something both male and female actors (though with different implications) must experience if they want to escape the constraints of life and the body. Sontag's latest novel, *In America* (2000), is about Marina Zalenska, a Polish actress who has made her fortune on the American stage. The last chapter consists of a long monologue, pronounced by the American actor Edwin Booth, whom the protagonist befriends. He says to her: "There is something bland, appeasing, in you, Marina. Perhaps there is in all actresses, with the possible exception of Bernhardt, don't wince, woman, except that her efforts not to be bland seem trivially theatrical . . . Not that I believe what she does. But she says she does it. No, a great actor is turbulent, rarely affable, profoundly . . . angry. Where is your vein of rage, Marina? . . . There's nothing dangerous about you, Marina. You have not accepted your catastrophe."[30]

Sontag's novel reopens the discussion on how stage behavior applies to real life as well as on the importance of duplicity, rage, and dis-ease.

Notes

1. Sontag, *Alice in Bed* (1993) (London: Vintage, 1994) (includes Sontag's "Note on the Play," 111–17; hereafter cited in text and notes as *AB*). The American premiere was presented in the 1996–97 season at the Hasty Pudding by A.R.T. New Stages (director Robert Brustein), Harvard University, under the direction of Bob McGrath. A performance art production of the play, directed by Ivo van Hove, opened at New York Theatre Workshop in May 2000. *Alice in Bed* was also staged in the 1999–2000 season by the Performing Arts Department of Washington University, directed by Andrea Urice, and in the 1998–99 season by the Theatre School of DePaul University (Chicago), directed by J. Kingsford Good; a new Chicago production, directed by Dado, took place at Trap Door Theatre in the 2007 season, after Sontag's death. In the early eighties two plays on Fuller were written and performed: *Zenobia: A*

Life of Margaret Fuller by Agnes Butcher and Sayre Sheldon, and *The Margaret Ghost* by Carole Braverman. (Produced in 1982 by the Charlestown Working Theater, a Boston non-equity theater, *The Margaret Ghost* received its professional premiere in 1984 at the Berkeley Repertory Theater; the last amateur production was by Theatre@First in Somerville, Mass., in 2006.) Bell Gale Chevigny informed me of a study group on Esther Broner's play *The Body Parts of Margaret Fuller*, which met in 1975–76 and in which she played an active role. I wish to thank Bell Gale Chevigny, Rosella Mamoli Zorzi, and Charles Capper for providing information on the 1975–76 events, the 1982 performances, and the New York production, respectively. I am grateful to Ms. Braverman for supplying the details concerning her play. A novel by Cathleen Schine bears the same title as Sontag's play (New York: Knopf, 1983).

2. Mary F. Brewer, *Race, Sex, and Gender in Contemporary Women's Theatre: The Construction of "Woman"* (Brighton, UK: Sussex Academic Press, 1999), 163–64.

3. My translation. (Pirandello's *Come tu mi vuoi* premiered in Milan in 1930.) The original text reads: "Essere creati dal desiderio degli altri è una caratteristica della situazione umana, ma è particolarmente tipica della situazione delle donne. L'edificio culturale dell'oppressione delle donne può essere riassunto dai modi in cui è sotteso che le donne, a differenza degli uomini, sono create dal fatto che sono desiderate." Teatro Stabile di Torino, *Come tu mi vuoi, di Luigi Pirandello, diretto da Susan Sontag. Programma* (Stagione, 1980–81), 4. Adriana Asti took the role of L'Ignota. Sontag's interest in the performance of identity is also evident in her novel *The Volcano Lover*, where Emma is involved in a sequence of poses, a living slide of the iconic moments of ancient myth and literature. *Volcano Lover* (London: Vintage, 1993), 146.

4. Edel, "Portrait of Alice James," in *The Diary of Alice James* (London: Rupert Hart-Davis, 1964), 3–8.

5. For Alice James's life see: Jean Strouse, *Alice James: A Biography* (Cambridge, Mass.: Harvard Univ. Press, 1980). James's journal was originally published under the title *Alice James, Her Brothers—Her Journal*, ed. Anna Robeson (New York: Burr, Dodd, Mead, 1934); it was then republished as *The Diary of Alice James*. Strouse's account of James's therapist Charles Fayette Taylor's ideas of excessive thinking and emotions as causing mental strain and breakdown especially in women (because they are more naturally excitable than men!) may have contributed to Sontag's choice of Fuller as one of the characters acting in Alice's mind: "Reading books gave them ideas—about what else they might be doing, about the disjunction between the interesting panorama of history and their own dull lives, about people who managed to become Joan of Arc, Jane Austen, Queen Elizabeth, or, closer to home, Margaret Fuller, Harriet Beecher Stowe, Louisa May Alcott." *Alice James*, 109.

6. Myrtha, Queen of the Wilis, is a character in the ballet *Giselle ou les Wilis* (book by Vernoy de Saint-Georges and Théophile Gautier, music by Adolphe

Adam). Cyril W. Beaumont explains: "Myrtha is the opponent of Giselle. Jilted by the man to whom she was betrothed, Myrtha died of grief in the flower of her youth. Presumably in her twenties, she would retain the age at which she became an immortal. But she is an unhappy phantom, a female vampire filled with an insatiable lust for revenge which causes her nightly to frequent the mystic glade, to lure any male wayfarer into the web of her fellow vampires, who force the unhappy man to dance until, reduced to exhaustion, he can be toppled to death in the marshy pool close by." *The Ballet Called Giselle* (London: Beaumont, 1944), 82. Kundry is a character in Richard Wagner's *Parsifal:* she is a witch, ambiguously described as an evil agent and a redeeming creature. After bringing a beneficent balm to the king she falls asleep, dead tired. She becomes a prey to a magic sleep, which she tries to resist. She is a sexual temptress, but then falls in love with Parsifal; at the end she falls dead at his feet to expiate some guilt from a previous existence. For further details see Jacques Chailley, *Parsifal de Richard Wagner: Opera initiatique* (Paris: Editions Buchet/Chastel, 1979).

7. This was before she moved to 41 Argyll Road on Kensington's Campden Hill. Strouse, *Alice James*, 297.

8. On Emily Dickinson's role in the play see Maria Anita Stefanelli, "Dickinson on the Stage," *Women's Studies* 31, no. 6 (2002): 785–93.

9. Brewer, *Race, Sex, and Gender in Contemporary Women's Theatre*, 165–66.

10. James, *William Wetmore Story and His Friends*, 2 vols. (Boston: Houghton, Mifflin, 1903), 1:128.

11. Sontag, "The Aesthetics of Silence," in her *Styles of Radical Will* (London: Vintage, 1994), 181–204.

12. Ibid., 187.

13. *The Journals and Miscellaneous Notebooks of Ralph Waldo Emerson*, vol. 11, *1848–1851*, ed. A. W. Plumstead and William H. Gilman (Cambridge, Mass.: Belknap Press, 1975), 258.

14. Ibid., 256; *The Letters of Margaret Fuller*, ed. Robert N. Hudspeth, 6 vols. (Ithaca, N.Y.: Cornell Univ. Press, 1983–94), 1:7 (hereafter cited in text and notes as *L*).

15. Greeley, *Recollections of a Busy Life* (New York: J. B. Ford, 1869), 179. The passage is also cited in Joan von Mehren, *Minerva and the Muse: A Life of Margaret Fuller* (Amherst: Univ. of Massachusetts Press, 1994), 288.

16. *Memoirs of Margaret Fuller Ossoli*, ed. R. W. Emerson, J. F. Clarke, and W. H. Channing, 2 vols. (London: Richard Bentley, 1852), 1:202–3.

17. See Pirandello, *As You Desire Me* (London: Oberon Books, 2007), act 3.

18. The Caterpillar smokes a long hookah, then takes it out of its mouth and says to Alice: "Who are *YOU*?" She replies, embarrassed about her own identity: "I—I hardly know, Sir, just at present . . ." (chaps. 4 and 5).

19. Alisa Solomon, *Re-dressing the Canon: Essays on Theatre and Gender* (London: Routledge, 1997), 98; Bernhardt performed, among many others, the role

of Hamlet, the most effeminate of Western tragic heroes, with a harsh, virile, and disruptive air scarcely put on by any male actor (95–129). For details of Bernhardt's life see Arthur Gold and Robert Fizdale, *The Divine Sarah: The Life of Sarah Bernhardt* (New York: Vintage Books, 1991).

20. The reference is to Sandra M. Gilbert and Susan Gubar, *The Madwoman in the Attic: The Woman Writer and the Nineteenth-Century Literary Imagination* (New Haven, Conn.: Yale Univ. Press, 1979).

21. Sontag elaborates on the mythology of disease in nineteenth-century society in *Illness as Metaphor* (New York: Farrar, Straus and Giroux, 1978).

22. One could detect sexual overtones in the title of Sontag's play, "bed" being ambiguously a reference to both invalidism and sex.

23. *AB* 11. The sailors are probably the same stewards that had helped Alice—in the historical reality—to be moved, after the ocean crossing in 1884, from the *Pavonia* at Liverpool to the rooms booked by her brother Henry at the Adelphi Hotel. Strouse, *Alice James*, 234.

24. A Jew, like Sontag herself, now aged and without one leg, she would bravely dismiss her own invalidity to look after wounded soldiers in World War I, a choice similar to that of Fuller, who did not hesitate to leave her baby in the care of a nurse in Rieti to become Regolatrice of Fatebenefratelli Hospital in Rome during the war.

25. Paul Schilder, "Psychoanalytic Remarks on *Alice in Wonderland* and Lewis Carroll (1938)," in *Aspects of Alice*, ed. Robert Phillips (Harmondsworth, UK: Penguin Books, 1971), 333–43; Sontag, "Notes on 'Camp' (1964)," *A Susan Sontag Reader*, intro. Elizabeth Hardwick (New York: Farrar, Straus, and Giroux, 1982), 105–21.

26. This aspect of Sontag's theory is in keeping with the poststructuralist approach to character and subject, as discussed in Edward Burns, *Character: Acting and Being on the Pre-Modern Stage* (London: Macmillan, 1990), 226.

27. Ibid., 227.

28. Barthes, *S/Z*, tr. Richard Miller (New York: Hill and Wang, 1974), 178. In reviewing Sontag's *Against Interpretation*, Burton Feldman wrote: "Miss Sontag is the latest heir and perhaps leading example today of that strenuously intellectual woman starting with Margaret Fuller and coming forward to Mary McCarthy. She shares with these a quick mind, a good education, a high-handed manner, and an inability to stop nagging." "Evangelist of the New," *Denver Quarterly* (Spring 1966): 152. Elaine Showalter, who has called Fuller the Dark Lady of the American Renaissance, suggests that Dark Ladies are punished for accepting the eminence thrust upon them, as has been the case with the harsh criticism of Sontag's previously highly influential work (as reported by Donna Dickenson in her introduction to Fuller's *Woman in the Nineteenth Century and Other Writings*, ed. Dickenson [New York: Oxford Univ. Press, 1994], vii). Norman Podhoretz has identified Sontag as the Dark Lady of her generation,

adding that she has replaced Mary McCarthy as "clever, learned, good-looking, capable of writing family-type criticism as well as fiction with strong trace of naughtiness." *Making It* (New York: Random House, 1967), 154–55.

29. Gilbert and Gubar, *Madwoman in the Attic*, 85, 483.

30. Sontag, *In America* (London: Jonathan Cape, 2000), 383.

Appendix

Biographies

Chronology

Contributors

Index

Appendix

*Documents in the State Archive of Rome: Margaret Fuller's
Hospital Service during the Roman Republic*

Contrary to what one might think, the State Archive of Rome contains few documents relating to Margaret Fuller. In particular, despite considerable research, I found no papers written in her own hand. Fuller was a friend of Giuseppe Mazzini and of other leaders of the Roman Republic, and her letters to them were not official and bureaucratic, but confidential and informal. They were not directed to government figures in their official capacity, but to friends who happened to be leading the republic. Consequently, her letters did not find their way into the state archive.

If Fuller's presence in the papers of the Roman Republic of 1848–49 seems today no more than a tantalizing shadow, it is also owing to the incomplete nature of the archives for this period. They have been handed down in great disorder, mixed with those of the papal administration. Furthermore, after the fall of the Papal State in 1870, many state archive documents were extracted from their original bureaucratic context and grouped into miscellanies by subject and for research purposes, as was typical of the period.

Yet, in reexamining the records related to the Roman Republic in the hope of finding documents, letters, or acts mentioning Margaret Fuller, I felt her presence continually. In these records, which allow us to reconstruct some of the notable events of the Italian Risorgimento, the history she lived emerges from letters, petitions, directives, and dispatches in which her individual story is fused into a larger historical drama. These documents vividly convey the hectic intensity of life in Rome, and particularly in the medical services for the wounded, as French forces besieged the city and threatened the newly proclaimed republic. They also reveal the hostility that, even in this moment of crisis, a male-dominated medical bureaucracy directed against a cadre of dedicated female volunteers, including Margaret Fuller.

A recent publication of the State Archive of Rome, following an exhibit commemorating the 150th anniversary of the Roman Republic, demonstrates the documentary richness of this institution.[1] In this publication, however, Fuller is cited only briefly (page 174) for her activities as a volunteer in the hospital wards, together with the Swiss Giulia Calame, wife of the actor Gustavo Modena, and in connection with the Comitato per i soccorsi ai feriti (Committee for Aid to the Wounded), directed by Fuller's good friend Cristina Trivulzio di Belgioioso. Actually, we know that Fuller played a larger role, having expressly received the charge of directing the Fatebenefratelli Hospital from Belgioioso, whose personal letter, written in English, was published in Italian translation by Emma Detti in 1942:[2]

April 30, 1849

Dear Miss Fuller,

You are named *Regolatrice* of the hospital of *Fate Bene Fratelli.* Go there at twelve if the alarm bell does not ring before. When you arrive there you will receive all the women coming for the wounded and give them your directions so that you are sure to have a certain number of them, night and day.

May God help us.

Fuller's name does not immediately appear in the daily chronological series of documents constituting the second part of the Miscellanea della Repubblica romana (Miscellany of the Roman Republic) record group. This record group, however, does include an original manuscript decree of April 29 issued by the Triumvirate, the three-man governing body named by the Constituent Assembly of the Roman Republic in February 1849. This document instituted the Comitato per l'Amministrazione delle Ambulanze (Committee for the Administration of Field Hospitals), composed of Cristina Trivulzio di Belgioioso and thirteen other citizens:[3]

The Roman Republic, in the name of God and the People
The Administration of the Field Hospitals is hereby entrusted to

a committee composed as follows: citizens Enrichetta Pisacane, Cristina Trivulzio Belgioioso, Giulia Paolucci. Citizens P. Gavazzi, Pasquali, Panunzi, Feliciani, Sani, Mengherini, Vivardi, Savorelli, Dr. Carlucci, Vannuzzi, Cleter. The committee sits in the Municipal Residence in the Campidoglio and communicates with the administration of Military Health, with the town council, and with the Ministers of War and the Interior. The Triumvirate.

A later document in the May 1 file names the individuals responsible for the city's hospitals and related field hospitals, including "Margherita Fuller" as director of Fatebenefratelli, and gives them practical instructions:

Trinità dei Pellegrini—Central Field Hospital
Controlling members of the Central Committee—Cristina Trivulzio di Belgioioso, Giulia Bovio Paolucci, Director Galletti.

Santo Spirito—Modena, Giulia
S. Giacomo—Constabili, Malvina
S. Gallicano—Baroffio, Adele
S. Giovanni—Lupi, Paolina
S. Pietro in Montorio—Pisacane, Enrichetta
Fatebene Fratelli—Fuller, Margherita
Santa Teresa di Porta Pia—Filopanti, Enrichetta
S. Urbano—Nazzani, Olimpia

Everyone above mentioned who has bedding and linen dressing ready should bring the donation to the Hospital where she is assigned this morning; the other citizens and in general all the compassionate individuals who have considered giving such items to the wounded Brothers should send these objects to the Committee Managers at the *Trinità dei Pellegrini*. The mattresses subject to restitution should be visibly marked, and will be declared as such in the receipt. Courage Romans! The moment nears in which we shall show the world how we honor the love for our Country. Rome, April 30, 1849.
The Central Committee: Pisacane, Enrichetta, Cristina Trivulzio di Belgioioso, Giulia Bovio Paolucci.

From a comparative examination of sources we know that Fuller also worked with Belgioioso in the Central Field Hospital at Trinità dei Pellegrini, assisting the wounded. They also succeeded in setting up a hospital on the grounds of the Palazzo Quirinale, the former papal residence, on a hill northeast of the city center. Fuller speaks about the latter in her dispatches to the *New-York Daily Tribune* and in

her letters. In one letter dated June 10 she writes to Ralph Waldo
Emerson:

The palace of the Pope, on the Quirinal[e], is now used for
convalescents. In those beautiful gardens, I walk with them—
one with his sling, another with his crutch. The gardener plays
off all his waterworks for the defenders of the country, and gathers
flowers for me, their friend.[4]

On June 28 Fuller was issued a pass by the "Roman Republic-
Triumvirate" that reads: "Miss Margaret Fuller is permitted to circulate
freely in the gardens of the Quirinale and to bring acquaintances with
her. Giuseppe Mazzini. *Triumviro.*"
    This formal pass was accompanied by a much more familiar letter
from Mazzini, a member of the Triumvirate:

I send the permit to enter the Gardens. My having forgotten
it these two days will show you, dear friend, how my poor
head is.
    On your showing the other pass to the "Direzione di Pubblica
Sicurezza" you will have the pass for the gates. As for the rest, I
don't know whether I am witnessing the agony of a Great Town,
or a successful resistance. But one thing I know, that resist we must,
that we *shall* resist to the last and that my name will *never* be appended
to a capitulation.

Yours in haste,
Jos. Mazzini.[5]

Fuller was personally and emotionally committed to providing medical assistance to the wounded not only because of her support for the
Roman Republic and her friendship with Mazzini and other republican
leaders, but also and especially because of her relationship to Giovanni
Angelo Ossoli, who as a captain of the Civic Republican Guard com-
manded a battery at Pincio, a park overlooking the city above the
Piazza del Popolo. Fuller therefore lived in constant trepidation, afraid
of seeing Ossoli among the wounded or even of receiving news of his
death in combat. In order to serve the patriotic cause, she had left their
newborn son in Rieti, some forty miles north of Rome. And to avoid the
disinheritance of her revolutionary husband by his noble family, who

also could contest his tie to a Protestant, the presumptive marriage was probably kept secret as the couple awaited better times.

With all this on her mind, Fuller plunged into her volunteer hospital work, joining the group of female volunteers to whom the Triumvirate had assigned certain tasks related to the care of the wounded. On June 8 the minister of the interior, Aurelio Saffi, wrote to "Citizen Bovio Paolucci" to announce the Triumvirate's decision to nominate a directorial and administrative Commission of Field Hospitals. After listing the commission members (Giulia Bovio Paolucci, Cristina di Belgioioso, Malvina Constabili, Giuseppe Lunati, Carlo Grillenzoni, Gaetano Pulini, Dr. Pastori, Gen. Luigi Salvati, Dr. Giuseppe Pastorelli, Domenico Bolasco), he went on:

As the number of the wounded increases and so does the care of these gentle souls who laboriously and with extraordinary zeal work to succor them, it is deemed necessary to form a Commission to tend to the direction and administration of all the field hospitals. Therefore, the Triumvirate of the Roman Republic, desiring, for the benefit of the Government, to take advantage of your intelligence and virtue, has chosen you as a member of the said Commission together with others noted in the margin. Your well known zeal and precision will reflect on the Republic and on the defenders of the Fatherland to the advantage of the Government. In announcing this deliberation I fraternally salute you.

The Minister.

Documents relating to the hospitals' day-to-day operations give us an idea of the situation Fuller confronted, including the extreme difficulty of obtaining the minimum resources necessary for the functioning of a military-hospital system organized in just a few days' time. Furthermore, the presence of volunteers, and especially women volunteers, was not always looked upon favorably by the medical officials, traditional nursing staff, and medical students. Indeed, formal complaints were lodged against the "inopportune" presence of women in the hospitals, especially "aristocratic" and "foreign" women. These criticisms were muted owing to the tragic nature of the situation and also to the indefatigable work done by these extraordinary and patriotic women, among whom Fuller was doubtless one of the most active. Nevertheless, the efforts of Fuller and the other volunteers were unquestionably complicated by the hostility of male doctors and attendants. For example, in June 1849 the medical community of Santo Spirito protested as follows:

To the citizen Dr. Andrea Pasquali,
director of the Hospital of *Santo Spirito in Sassia*
    Citizen director, Our Community is rather indignant about the superiority and tyranny displayed by the women who are said to preside over the field hospital; of course today it would not restrain from violent demonstration, if it did not place its faith in your justice and wisdom. By tradition as old as the founding of the hospital, the lance corporals are entitled to two desks. Today one of these was to be removed. Certain rights, however, are inalienable, despite the will of he who is temporarily invested with them. The only pretext produced for this usurpation is that the noise of youths gathered here can harm, indeed actually harms the wounded. Who could deny that it is so? But renew the prohibition to the corporal to allow the gathering of youths and other people at his desk and, what's more, the raising of voices; let the responsibility be his, let him be punished if the order is not maintained: thus the goal will be reached. But in the meantime may our community not see, to the detriment of its dignity, a woman seated at a desk (exercising almost the greatest power in the hospital) whose intelligence is neither enough nor can ever be enough. Citizen director, the love you have for the Community and, even more, your sense of justice assures us that we will not see our complaints lodged uselessly; nor will we be forced to come to acts which are not fitting and which we loath. Long live the Republic! *S. Spirito,* June 12, 1849
                                    Signed: Dr. Giovanni Negri, Vice Director;
                                                P.E. Apolloni, Vice Director;
                                                Grilli Giulio, M. Assistente
                                            [twenty-six other signatures follow]

Dr. Pasquali forwarded the protest to the higher authorities with these words:

To the Citizen Minister of the Interior.
    Most of the *S. Spirito* Community, as per the complaint, is opposed to the female invasion that every day occurs in the hospital of the same name. Without wanting to participate entirely in the indignation

of the students, I beg you to take their complaint into consideration and, using your well known wisdom, to give me orders suitable for satisfying the already very lively youths, who today are persuaded to avail themselves of reasonable and legal means.

Superintendent general Dr. A. Pasquali.

A letter of June 12 to Aurelio Saffi, a member of the Triumvirate, evokes the tragic situation in which the wounded found themselves and in which the women of the Auxiliary Corps had to operate:

Citizens Anna Galletti and Anna Mandolesi inform the *Triumviro* Saffi that the many remaining wounded at *Trinità dei Pellegrini* lack many things that it is necessary to provide if the said house is to stay open. Not having seen any measure adopted by which to remove both the wounded and the Female assistants from imminent danger of bombs (one of which fell a few rods away) they warn the *Triumviro* that the Husbands of the undersigned do not want them exposed any longer when there are central locations where to place them in safety. June 12, 1849, half-past three in the afternoon.

Furthermore, the institutional decree (general regulations) of the General Superior Council of Management and Administration for the Temporary Hospitals for the care of the wounded includes the following statement restricting the women's work: "To the Committee of the Ladies voluntarily dedicated to the assistance of the wounded is especially entrusted the direction of the linens."[6] Clearly this remained only a paper command, however, and the female volunteers' activities extended far beyond caring for linens.

As if all this weren't enough, one of the superintendents responsible for administering the field hospitals, a certain Gaetano Vannozzi, addressed a long petition to the acting minister of the interior, the attorney G. De Angelis, on May 28, 1849, contesting the very legitimacy of a "Center for Field Hospitals in the area of *Trinità dei Pellegrini* in which certain people take part, though extraneous and with absolute presumption of command and absolute indifference to the nominated individuals." Vannozzi's petition clearly referred to those nominated in the governmental dispatches of April 29.

Without mentioning the Princess Belgioioso (or her close friend, Margaret Fuller) or Belgioioso's membership in the Committee of

Ladies, Vannozzi took aim precisely at the volunteer organization established by the women. With pretentious and flimsy justifications concerning economic and judicial factors related to the traditional uses of the hospital locations, he advanced his complaint and even mentioned having sought a meeting with the minister of the interior to persuade him to "lend his authority to defeat every arbitrary arrangement in the matter, so the administration might operate only with the work of the individuals nominated ad hoc by the government; and especially in so far as those officially announced in the Minister's Gazette were and are the only ones truly responsible, even in the eyes of the public."

With an accountant's petty mentality, and without any sensitivity to the extraordinary situation, the petition goes on to insist that a precise accounting be given of the "voluntary oblations," that is, the contributions to the field hospitals by Roman citizens and foreign residents. It further alleges administrative irregularities, condemns the lack of written financial accounts, and demands that "such a report be presented to the town council bearing the sum of many thousands *scudi*." What should have been laudable is stigmatized as if it were a crime.

As this petition proceeds, the source of Vannozzi's venom becomes clear:

> It is even a wonder that the above-mentioned Field hospital Center, without regard for the meaning of the word, should be set up, in the same location, as a permanent, no, perpetual field hospital, to the exclusion of pre-established acts of charity . . . and consequently, as well as for other reasons omitted here, this member believes it to be his duty to warn that the idea of converting the *Trinità de' Pellegrini* field hospital into a central field hospital and therefore a permanent field hospital, in addition to having been a whim, since it was not executed with everyone's knowledge, is, what is more, a true paradox equal to that of walking and standing still.

In conclusion, Vannozzi asked the acting minister of the interior "to put an end as soon as possible to the field hospital in question and to every other branch," threatening resignation if his request was denied.

Conflicts, if not actual obstructionism, erupted in other hospitals as well. For example, the Comitato di Soccorso pei Feriti (Committee for Aid to the Wounded) itself asked the minister of the interior to replace the director of S. Gallicano:

Citizen Minister, the serious mishaps occurring in the Hospital of S. Gallicano, the insults with which both our wounded and those who assist them are assailed daily, and the evident ill will of the Director of this Hospital, voluntary author of all these mishaps, force us to ask directly for the immediate substitution of the current Director with a new one. Without such a measure we will not be able to answer for the health of our wounded. *Salute e fratellanza.*

For the central committee,
Cristina Trivulzio di Belgioioso,
Giulia Bovio Paolucci,
don Alessandro Gavazzi.

A June 20 message from the minister of the interior to the field-hospital supervisors, including Fuller, conveyed how desperate the supply situation had become:

The Motherland owes you much because you have done much for her. However, it is not enough. The circumstances worsen every day and your extraordinary energy cannot flag. Beds are needed for the establishment of a general field hospital. With your usual courtesy, collect them whether whole or in pieces; together we will be able to supply what is necessary. In executing this collection try to obtain as well a quantity of bandages. Zealous as you are for the public good you will offer new proof of your prodigious activity in this endeavor.

On June 22 the military field hospital of the Quirinale, where Fuller gave assistance while also directing the Fatebenefratelli Hospital, made its pressing necessities known to the government, and the minister wrote immediately to the commissioner of the Colonna district:

The military field hospital of the Quirinale urgently requests one hundred chairs, two large tables, and a dozen small tables. Please, therefore, procure the above-mentioned objects and send them as soon as possible to that field hospital. *Salute e fratellanza.*

This hasty document is the last that has been found in the State Archive of Rome relating to the administration of field hospitals during the French attack—an effort that absorbed Margaret Fuller's energies in the spring and early summer of 1849. Other documents relating to Fuller are located in the Ossoli archive, left to the State Archive of Rome in 1991 after the death of Maria Ossoli, Giovanni Angelo Ossoli's great-grandniece. The Ossoli archive contains documents pertaining to the Ossoli family's hostility to Giovanni's relationship with Margaret and the couple's tragic end with their young son in 1850. It also contains subsequent legal documents and correspondence between the Ossoli and Fuller families regarding financial matters and the disposition of the estate. These additional documents, while not directly relevant to the theme of this book, are of considerable interest to scholars and others interested in the life of this remarkable woman.[7]

In the records reproduced here, Margaret Fuller's intense and passionate life in Italy becomes part of the collective history of a group of women of high democratic ideals who, while confronting male prejudice and hostility toward their activities, participated with great energy and notable civic virtue in the political and military struggle for Italian independence.

DONATO TAMBLÉ

Notes

1. State Archive of Rome, *"Roma, Repubblica, venite!" Percorsi attraverso la documentazione della Repubblica Romana del 1849,* ed. Monica Calzolari, Elvira Grantaliano, Marina Pieretti, Angela Lanconelli, *Rivista Storica del Lazio,* 7 (1999), 10, notebook no. 2.

2. Emma Detti, *Margaret Fuller Ossoli e i suoi corrispondenti, con lettere inedite di Giuseppe Mazzini, Costanza Arconati, Adam Mickiewicz* [et al.] (Florence: Felice Le Monnier, 1942), 209, 352 (in English).

3. The translations of this document and other archival documents that follow are mine.

4. *The Letters of Margaret Fuller,* ed. Robert N. Hudspeth, 6 vols. (Ithaca, N.Y.: Cornell Univ. Press, 1983–94), 5:239.

5. Detti, *Margaret Fuller Ossoli,* 279.

6. Two manuscript copies of the decree are in the State Archive of Rome, Miscellanea della Repubblica romana, bundle 15.

7. Documents from the Ossoli archives may be consulted in the State Archive of Rome. The records referring to Margaret Fuller appear in Donato Tamblè, "Le carte di Margaret Fuller nell'Archivio di Stato di Roma," in Cristina Giorcelli and Giuseppe Monsagrati, eds., "Margaret Fuller: tra Europa e Stati Uniti d'America," *Dimensioni e problemi della ricerca storica,* vol. 1 (Rome: Carocci, 2001), 165–87.

Biographies

Major Italian and Foreign Political Figures at the Time of the Roman Republic

Camillo Benso, Count of Cavour (Turin 1810–Turin 1861), statesman. He opposed both King Charles Albert's bigotry and Mazzini's revolutionary program. A profoundly lay and rational man (he always believed in the separation between State and Church), before entering the parliament of the Kingdom of Piedmont-Sardinia (comprised of Piedmont, Liguria, Savoy, and Sardinia), he had traveled to Switzerland, France, England, and Belgium to study the effects of the industrial revolution; he visited hospitals, prisons, and schools and inspected railway systems. He was in favor of fiscal reforms to update Piedmont (and the rest of the kingdom) and turn it into a modern state. In 1850 he became minister of agriculture and finance. A conservative liberal, he joined Urbano Rattazzi's central left party in 1852 and became prime minister. He was capable of matching a realistic sense of limits with audacious initiatives. In 1855, to overcome Piedmont's international isolation, he entered the Crimean War. At the Congress of Paris (1856) following the war, he succeeded in bringing the Italian situation to the immediate attention of the major European powers, above all, to that of Napoleon III, who in 1858 signed a military alliance with the Kingdom of Piedmont-Sardinia against Austria, its historical enemy and the major obstacle to the unification of Italy. After Naploeon III signed with Austria the armistice at Villafranca (1859), however, only Lombardy (and not also Veneto) was annexed. Cavour resigned in protest. He resumed power at the beginning of 1860, when, by surrendering Savoy and Nice to France, he annexed Tuscany. Meanwhile Emilia, Romagna, Umbria, and the Marches also freed themselves from papal authority with the help of Piedmontese troops. In the same year, thanks to Garibaldi's campaign with his thousand men, the Kingdom of the Two Sicilies became part of the Kingdom of Piedmont-Sardinia. On March 14, 1861, in Turin the first Italian parliament proclaimed the Kingdom of Italy; only Veneto, Trentino, Latium, and Rome were still missing to complete the mosaic. At his death Cavour saw almost the whole of his program of a united Italy under the Savoy crown realized.

Carlo Cattaneo (Milan 1801–Lugano 1869), a historian and political figure. He sponsored democratic ideals and federalism for Italy. He believed that such a state system had to be achieved through pacific means. He extolled science and technology as a means to secure development, progress, and social renewal. He believed in the social importance of the middle class. As a republican, he opposed monarchy and the House of Savoy to the point that, elected to the parliament of the Kingdom of Italy, he rarely participated in its sessions.

Ferdinand II of Bourbon (Palermo 1810–Caserta 1859), king of the Two Sicilies. In 1830 he granted some extension of liberties but retracted a few months later. In January 1848 he granted a constitution and autonomy to Sicily and allowed some of his troops to fight against Austria. In May, however, he carried out a coup with the help of Swiss mercenaries, dissolved the parliament, bombed Messina, recalled his troops from Northern Italy, and reestablished absolute monarchy. He prided himself on his kingdom's strong steel industry, mercantile fleet, and the first railway system in the country. He was succeeded by his son, Francis II, called Franceschiello, because he was young and insecure (1836–94). In 1860, when Garibaldi and his men entered his kingdom, Francis II withdrew to Gaeta, then to Rome, and finally to Paris (1870).

Giuseppe Garibaldi (Nice 1807–Caprera 1882), military leader and political figure. In his youth he joined "Giovine Italia," Mazzini's revolutionary and republican movement. In 1835 he went into exile in Latin America, where he fought for the liberty of Brazil and Uruguay and against the Argentine dictatorship. He returned to Italy in 1848 and fought against the Austrian troops. In 1849 he was elected deputy of the Roman Republic parliament. He defended the city strenuously but, after its fall and the ensuing collapse of the Roman Republic, he went to Morocco, the United States, and Peru. In 1854 he returned to Italy and established himself on the island of Caprera, off the coast of Sardinia. Having abandoned Mazzini's republican program, he adhered to the monarchy of Victor Emmanuel II. In 1860 he protested in vain for the cession of Nice (his birthplace) to France. The same year, with a thousand volunteers, he sailed from Liguria to Sicily to free the Kingdom of the Two Sicilies from the Bourbons. In four months he turned the whole of Sicily and the southern mainland over to the Piedmontese king. In 1862 and in 1867 he tried to free Rome, but was stopped by the Italian and the French troops in Aspromonte and Mentana, respectively. In 1874 he was elected deputy to the Italian parliament. Admired by the common man, internationally famous, intensely patriotic, he had complete confidence in and always enjoyed the confidence of his troops. He was alien to both Mazzini's dogmatism and Cavour's brand of diplomacy. Fundamentally a democrat, he believed in a united Europe, women's emancipation, education for all, equality among races and classes, and workers' rights, and he opposed capital punishment.

Vincenzo Gioberti (Turin 1801–Paris 1852), a priest and political figure. He wrote *Del primato morale e civile degli Italiani* (1843). Since he believed that the Church safeguards the moral and social values essential to the progress of humanity, he thought that in Italy the pope should assume leadership and head a federation of states. He was thus opposed to Mazzini's unitarian and republican program. A moderate, he also opposed revolutionary movements. He was often involved in polemics with the Jesuits. Elected deputy to the Piedmontese parliament in 1848, he supported universal suffrage and education.

Leopold II (Florence 1797–Rome 1870), Grand Duke of Tuscany. Meek and tolerant, he planned many important public works (railway construction, enlargement of the port of Leghorn, the draining of the swamps in Maremma). In 1847 he eased press censorship and promulgated a statute similar to the one passed by Charles Albert in Piedmont. In February 1849, after having been compelled to hand over power to the radicals (F. D. Guerrazzi, G. Mazzoni, and G. Montanelli), Leopold II left Tuscany and repaired to Gaeta, in the Kingdom of the Two Sicilies. He returned to Florence in July 1849, aided by the Austrian troops. He then annulled the statute, persecuted Protestants, and reinstituted the death penalty. During the Second War of Independence (1859) he did not fight with Piedmont against Austria. A pacific revolution sent him into exile the same year. He first took refuge in Austria, but eventually went to Rome, where he died.

Ferdinand Marie de Lesseps (1805–1894), diplomat. Sent to Rome in 1849 to act as mediator between France and the triumvirs of the Roman Republic, he conducted, apparently in good faith, peace negotiations. He was then called back by Louis Napoleon, who had given General Oudinot different instructions.

Giuseppe Mazzini (Genoa 1805–Pisa 1872), political theorist, revolutionary, and propagandist. Born of a Jansenist mother, he was a democrat, a secular republican, and a believer in the people and in the ideal of national unity, in Italy and elsewhere. As a member of the Genoese Carboneria (the secret society that conspired for the liberation of the country from reactionary and foreign governments), he was arrested in 1830 and went into exile the following year. In Marseilles, influenced by Charles Fourier and Chartism, he founded "Giovine Italia," a movement that promulgated his ideals throughout Italy. He had an ethical-spiritualistic conception of revolution. Expelled from France, he went to Switzerland and then to London. In 1834 he founded "Giovine Europa," convinced as he was that the whole of Europe deserved to be free, independent, democratic, and republican. He believed that it was the duty of intellectuals to mediate between God and the people, absorbing and clarifying their aspirations. Although he upheld universal education and the need to reduce working hours and to raise wages, he opposed both communism and socialism. After the fall of the Roman Republic, of which he was one of the triumvirs, he fled back to London. He often returned to Italy in disguise and inspired revolutionary uprisings, which mostly failed. He died in Pisa in the house of his friends the Nathan Rosselli family. His republican ideal became a reality after World War II.

Napoleon III (Paris 1808–Kent 1873). As a young man, Louis Napoleon Bonaparte—son of Louis Bonaparte, king of Holland, Napoleon I's brother—lived in Italy, Switzerland, Bavaria, England, and the United States. After a revolutionary youth, during which he expressed ideas in favor of workers, peasants, and the lower bourgeois, in December 1848, as a consequence of the fall of Louis Philippe of Orleans, he became president of the French Republic with the support of

Catholics and conservatives. Three years later (December 2, 1851), he staged a coup: he banished the republican party and promulgated a new constitution, which gave him presidential powers for ten years. A year later he turned the republic into the Second Empire. During the Second War of Independence (1859) he fought successfully with the Kingdom of Piedmont-Sardinia against Austria, thus proving his capacities as a strategist and a general. Because of his aid to the Kingdom of Piedmont-Sardinia he obtained Nice and Savoy in 1860. A tenacious and clever political figure, he was gifted with a formidable sense of timing. He gave a great impulse to French industrial investments: railway construction, streets, canals (the Suez Canal was built between 1859 and 1869). In 1870, in the Franco-Prussian War, his army was defeated at Sedan by Bismarck. For a short time he was taken prisoner; when freed, he repaired to England. On September 4, 1870, the Third Republic was proclaimed in France.

Nicolas Charles Victor Oudinot (Bar le Duc 1791–Paris 1863), French general. As a young man he fought in the army of Napoleon I in Russia. After a military campaign in Algeria (1835), he was appointed general. In 1849 he was sent to Rome to suppress the Roman Republic. When he returned to Paris, he opposed Louis Napoleon's coup and was arrested. Released, he retired to private life.

Pius IX (Giovanni Maria Mastai-Ferretti; Senigallia 1792–Rome 1878). Elected to the papacy in 1846, he quickly granted amnesty to some political prisoners and some press freedom; he also created a State Council, instituted the Civic Guard, and formed a Council of Ministers. First hailed as a liberal pope, after the revolutionary uprisings that took place in March 1848 and the beginning of the First War of Independence (1848) he only reluctantly conceded a constitution. A month later he sent troops to take part in the war between Piedmont and Austria, but, afraid to alienate Catholic Austria from the Church, he soon recalled them. On April 29, 1848, he delivered an allocution in which he separated the interests of the Church from those of Italian independence. From that moment the so-called Roman question began—it would last until 1929. Caught between the fear of compromising the holy character of papal authority and the desire to please his subjects, he came to the conclusion that a constitutional government was impossible in his states. When his minister Pellegrino Rossi and his secretary were killed in November 1848, he fled Rome and went to Gaeta. In 1850 he returned to Rome and reestablished a conservative and reactionary government. In 1854 he proclaimed the Dogma of the Immaculate Conception. During the Second War of Independence, Emilia, in 1859, and Romagna, Umbria, and the Marches, in 1860, freed themselves from the Papal States and were annexed to the Kingdom of Piedmont-Sardinia. With the fall of the Kingdom of the Two Sicilies in 1860 he became entirely isolated. In 1870 the Italian troops entered and occupied Rome. King Victor Emmanuel II took up residence at the Quirinale and Pius IX retreated to the Vatican, considering himself a prisoner of the Kingdom of Italy. He refused to consider papal authority as merely spiritual, and condemned liberalism as well as communism and socialism, thus enforcing Catholic integralism. At Ecumenical Vatican Council I (1869–70) he proclaimed the Dogma of Papal Infallibility.

Johann Joseph Franz Karl Radetzky (Bohemia 1766–Milan 1858), Austrian general. From 1831 to 1857 he was the military governor of Lombardy and Veneto, which were under Franz Joseph of Habsburg, Emperor of Austria and Hungary. He was defeated during the Milan insurrection called the "five days" (March 1848), but fought successfully against Charles Albert during the First War of Independence (1848 and 1849). A capable strategist, he was convinced that to maintain control over Lombardy and Veneto Austria should deepen the divide between the local peasantry and gentry. Lombardy was annexed to the Kingdom of Piedmont-Sardinia in 1859 (after the Second War of Independence) and Veneto was annexed in 1866 (after the Third War of Independence).

Pellegrino Rossi (Carrara 1787–Rome 1848). Professor of constitutional law at the University of Bologna, he taught also in Geneva and in Paris. Ambassador of France to Rome, he endorsed Pius IX's constitutional reforms. On September 16, 1848, Pius IX appointed him home minister. He was assassinated on November 15, 1848.

Victor Emmanuel II of the House of Savoy (Turin 1820–Rome 1878), first king of Italy. The son of Charles Albert, he fought with him during the First War of Independence and was defeated at Custoza (1848) and at Novara (1849). He succeeded to the throne of the Kingdom of Piedmont-Sardinia in 1849 when his father went into exile. His first prime minister was Massimo d'Azeglio; his second, Camillo Benso,

Count of Cavour. Although a conservative, Victor Emmanuel maintained the constitution in his kingdom, the only sovereign to do so in the Italian panorama after 1848. He endorsed the Crimean War (1855) and the Second War of Independence (1859), seeing in both the possibility for his state to be taken into consideration at an international level. He cultivated the habit of carrying on unofficial political dealings beside the official ones. Thus, he often reached private agreements with political figures like Garibaldi, somewhat in disaccord with his prime minister. During the Third War of Independence (1866) he insisted upon leading the troops and suffered defeat at Custoza. He also tried to drag Italy into the war between France and Prussia (1870). A none-too-subtle politician and a not-too-great military commander, he was nonetheless able to establish his line as the one that united Italy (he was hailed as "the father of the country"), thanks to the talent of Cavour, who believed in monarchy as the best form of government for the Italians of the time, and to the military abilities of Garibaldi.

CRISTINA GIORCELLI

Chronology

1846

June 16	Giovanni Maria Mastai-Ferretti is elected pope and begins a thirty-two-year reign as Pius IX. The pontiff grants political amnesty.
August 12	Margaret Fuller arrives at Liverpool.
October 1	Fuller arrives in London.
October 7	Fuller visits Thomas and Jane Carlyle for the first time.
October 24	Fuller meets Giuseppe Mazzini in London.
November 13	Fuller arrives in Paris.

1847

February 8	Fuller visits George Sand for the first time.
February 15	Fuller meets Adam Mickiewicz in Paris.
March 3	Fuller arrives in Genoa.
March 15	Piux IX grants some press freedom.
March 27	Fuller arrives in Rome.
April 1	Fuller first meets Giovanni Angelo Ossoli (Holy Thursday).
May 27	Fuller leaves Rome for a four-and-a-half-month journey through northern Italy.

August 10	Fuller meets Alessandro Manzoni in Milan.
September 8	Fuller witnesses violent clashes between Milanese demonstrators and the Austrian police after the Great Feast of the Madonna.
October 10	Fuller arrives back in Rome.
October 14	Pius IX introduces the State Council.

1848

January 1	Milanese antismoking campaign begins.
January 12	Insurrection occurs in Palermo.
January 29	Ferdinand II, King of the Two Sicilies, grants constitution.
February 2	End of the Mexican-American War.
February 17	Leopold II, Grand Duke of Tuscany, grants constitution.
February 28	France is proclaimed a republic.
March 13	Prince Metternich resigns following a revolution in Vienna.
March 14	Pius IX grants constitution for Papal States.
March 24	Kingdom of Piedmont-Sardinia declares war on Austria.
April 29	Pius IX delivers an allocution denouncing the war against Austria and pleading for peace.
May 15	In a "coup" Ferdinand II storms the National Guard's barricades, disavows the constitution, and withdraws from the war against Austria.
May 28	Fuller travels with Ossoli to Tivoli and arrives in L'Aquila ca. May 30.
July 29	Fuller leaves L'Aquila and arrives in Rieti.
August 9	Salasco treaty is signed ending the Kingdom of Piedmont-Sardinia's war against Austria.
September 5	Angelo Eugene Philip Ossoli is born to Fuller in Rieti.
November 5	Angelo is baptized in Rieti.
November 8	Fuller returns with Ossoli to Rome.
November 15	Pellegrino Rossi, home minister of the Papal States, is stabbed, possibly by Angelo Brunetti (Ciceruacchio)'s son Luigi.

November 16   A popular rally in front of the Quirinale (the pope's residence) demands a democratic government. Monsignor Palma, the pope's secretary, is killed.

November 24   Pius IX flees Rome in the night and takes refuge in Gaeta, a fortified city in the Kingdom of the Two Sicilies, ruled by Ferdinand II.

November 25   Council of Ministers of the Papal States forms a new government.

December 5   Pius IX writes to foreign kings pleading for protection and for the safeguard of the Holy See's territories. Giuseppe Mazzini writes to the Romans, advocating a republic as the best form of government.

December 10   Louis Napoleon Bonaparte is proclaimed president of the French Republic.

December 12   Giuseppe Garibaldi enters Rome with his "volunteers."

December 17   Ciceruacchio organizes a popular rally in favor of the proclamation of an Italian constitution.

December 29   After eight days in Reiti Fuller arrives back in Rome and moves into an apartment at number 60 in the Piazza Barberini. In Rome the Council of Ministers and the State Executive Committee summon the Constituent Assembly.

1849

January 1   Pius IX releases an encyclical against the decree that summons the Constituent Assembly.

January 7   Ciceruacchio organizes a popular rally against the encyclical.

January 21   Elections with male universal suffrage are held in the Papal States to form the Constituent Assembly.

January 23   Charles Albert, King of Piedmont-Sardinia, declares he will recall his delegation from Rome and recognize only the pope as the legitimate temporal and spiritual head of the Papal States.

January 27   *La Battaglia di Legnano,* Giuseppe Verdi's historical opera with patriotic overtones, enjoys great success at the Teatro Argentina in Rome.

February 5	Constituent Assembly convenes. Garibaldi proposes the proclamation of the republic and a deputy seconds it. Some of the ministers are against the proposal.
February 6	Mazzini arrives in Leghorn in Tuscany from Marseilles.
February 8	Granduke Leopold II flees Tuscany.
February 9	Constituent Assembly proclaims the Roman Republic. (The vote is 120 in favor and 10 against, while 12 abstain.)
February 11	Servants in livery of the Roman nobility are insulted in the streets of Rome.
February 12	The Executive Committee of the Roman Republic Constituent Assembly orders that all laws be released "In the name of God and the People" and that the flag be the tricolor (red, white, and green).
February 14	Pius IX protests against the proclamation of the Roman Republic.
February 21	All ecclesiastic property is declared to belong to the republic.
February 23	The republican police enter the headquarters of the Santo Uffizio and set its archives on fire.
February 24	Church bells are requisitioned to make coins.
March 2	Constituent Assembly decrees the coinage of the Roman Republic currency.
March 5	Mazzini arrives in Rome as a deputy of the Constituent Assembly.
March 8	Mazzini visits Fuller at her apartment.
March 23	After the Kingdom of Piedmont-Sardinia reopens its war against Austria (March 20), its army is defeated by Austria's at Novara. Charles Albert abdicates in favor of his son, Victor Emmanuel II.
March 26	Fuller arrives in Rieti.
March 28	The pope's "Guardia Nobile" (a guard of honor composed of Roman noblemen) is dissolved.
March 29	Executive Committee is dissolved and the Triumvirate (Mazzini, Aurelio Saffi, and Carlo Armellini) is proclaimed.
April 16	Fuller returns to Rome.
April 24	A first contingent of French troops (5,200 men), sent by Louis Napoleon to restore Pius IX to power, lands in

	Civitavecchia under the command of General Nicolas Charles Victor Oudinot.
April 26	The Assembly resolves to resist the French and Giuseppe Avezzana is appointed war minister and head of the Roman Republic army.
April 27	Garibaldi and his legion (3,000 men) arrive in Rome.
April 28	A state of siege is declared in Rome. All foreigners in the city are set under the protection of the Roman Republic. The French troops move toward Rome.
April 30	French troops are beaten back at Porta Cavalleggeri, one of the gates of Rome. They wave the white flag and retreat to Castel di Guido (20 kilometers west of Rome). Neapolitan troops enter the territory of the Roman Republic. Fuller is appointed director of the Fatebenefratelli Hospital.
May 1	Roman hospitals accept wounded French soldiers.
May 3	Fuller moves to the Casa Dies in the Via Gregoriana.
May 4	Fresh French troops (4,000 men) join the former ones.
May 9	Ferdinand de Lesseps leaves Paris for Rome to start negotiations with the Triumvirate. Garibaldi, who defends the Roman Republic along its southern borders, successfully fights against the Neapolitan troops in Palestrina.
May 13	Garibaldi and Pietro Roselli are appointed lieutenant generals for their courage and military merits. Roselli is appointed commander in chief. In the French elections the "Party of Order," a coalition of three monarchist factions, wins a majority of seats in the Assembly.
May 15	Lesseps arrives in Rome and starts talks with the Triumvirate.
May 28	The Neapolitan troops are joined by 4,000 Spaniards. General Oudinot is impatient to enter Rome and secure a French victory before the troops from other foreign countries join in.
May 31	Lesseps sends a note to the assembly in which he declares that the French troops will enter Rome to defend the Roman people from foreign invasion.
June 1	Lesseps returns to France. Oudinot declares war on the Roman Republic.

June 3	French troops launch an attack at Villa Pamphili, Porta San Pancrazio (on the Gianicolo), and Ponte Molle. At the end of the day the French count 14 dead and 229 wounded; the Italians 551 dead or wounded. At this point the French forces consist of 35,000 men and 75 cannons. The Roman Republic has 19,000 soldiers, only 12,000 of whom are regular ones.
June 12	Oudinot enjoins the Italian troops to surrender.
June 13	French troops shell the city.
June 23	French bombs fall on Trastevere, Sant'Andrea della Valle, Piazza Argentina, and the Church of the Gesù.
June 30	The republican assembly declares the end of the defense of Rome. Roselli surrenders the city to Oudinot.
July 2	Garibaldi and his troops leave Rome.
July 3	French troops enter Rome.
July 12	Mazzini leaves Rome and goes to Civitavecchia and Marseille and then to London. Fuller leaves Rome for Rieti.
August 10	Ciceruacchio, who had fled Rome with Garibaldi, and two of his sons (Luigi and thirteen-year-old Lorenzo) are shot by Austrian troops near Comacchio.
August 31	Fuller writes to her mother about her husband and child. She leaves Rieti for Perugia for a month before going to Florence.

1850

April 12	Pius IX returns to Rome.
May 17	Fuller sails with her husband, the Marquis Giovanni Angelo Ossoli, and their son, Angelo, from Leghorn on the *Elizabeth*.
July 19	The *Elizabeth* runs aground off Fire Island in the early morning and breaks up eleven hours later.

CHARLES CAPPER and CRISTINA GIORCELLI

Contributors

CHARLES CAPPER is professor of history at Boston University. He is the author of *Margaret Fuller: An American Romantic Life,* volume 1, *The Private Years* (1992), which won the Bancroft Prize in 1993; and volume 2, *The Public Years* (2007). He is also the coeditor (with David A. Hollinger) of the two-volume *American Intellectual Tradition,* fifth edition (2006), and (with Conrad E. Wright) of *Transient and Permanent: The Transcendentalist Movement and Its Contexts* (1999). He is the coeditor of the journal *Modern Intellectual History.*

BELL GALE CHEVIGNY is professor emerita of literature at State University of New York, College at Purchase. Her books include *The Woman and the Myth: Margaret Fuller's Life and Writings* (revised, expanded edition, 1994); *Chloe and Olivia,* a novel (1990); coeditor (with Gari Laguardia) of *Reinventing the Americas: Comparative Studies of Literature of the United States and Spanish America* (1986); and *Doing Time: 25 Years of Prison Writing,* a PEN American Center Prize Anthology (1999), which she edited as a Soros Senior Justice Fellow.

CRISTINA GIORCELLI is professor of American literature at the University of Rome Three, where she directs the Department of American Studies and coordinates its Ph.D. program. She has published extensively on nineteenth-century fiction and modernist poetry. She cofounded and codirects the quarterly journal *Letterature d'America* (Literatures of the Americas) and is the editor of the series *Abito e Identità* (Clothing and Identity) of which seven volumes have been published. Former vice president (1994–2002) of the European Association of American Studies, she is "foreign delegate" to the MLA Assemblies (2006–8).

FRANCESCO GUIDA is professor of history of Eastern Europe at the Faculty of Political Sciences of the University of Rome Three. He has published numerous essays on the history of Bulgaria, Greece, Poland, Romania, Russia, and Hungary and on their relationships with Italy in the nineteenth and twentieth centuries. His books include *Italy and the Balkan Risorgimento* (1984), which received the Howard R. Marraro Prize; *Michelangelo Pinto, a Literate and Roman Patriot between Italy and Russia* (1998); and *Romania* (2005).

ROBERT N. HUDSPETH is research professor of English at the Claremont Graduate University in California. He has edited *The Letters of Margaret Fuller* (1983–94) and a volume of selected letters, *My Heart Is a Large Kingdom* (2001). He is currently editing *The Correspondence of Henry D. Thoreau* for the Princeton edition of Thoreau's works.

LESTER K. LITTLE is Dwight W. Morrow Professor Emeritus of History at Smith College, and former director of the American Academy in Rome. He served for five years on the Italian Fulbright Commission and was president of the International Union of Institutes of Archaeology, Art History, and History in Rome and of the Medieval Academy of America. His works include *Liberty, Charity, Fraternity: Lay Religious Confraternities at Bergamo in the Age of the Commune* (1988) and *Benedictine Maledictions: Liturgical Cursing in Romanesque France* (1993).

LARRY J. REYNOLDS is Thomas Franklin Mayo Professor of Liberal Arts at Texas A&M University and founding executive officer of the Margaret Fuller Society. He is author of *European Revolutions and the American Literary Renaissance* (1988), editor of *Woman in the Nineteenth Century* (1998), and *Historical Guide to Nathaniel Hawthorne* (2001), as well as coeditor of *"These Sad But Glorious Days"* (1991), *New Historical Literary Study* (1993), and *National Imaginaries, American Identities* (2000). His current projects include the book-in-progress *"'So Like Murder': Political Violence and the American Renaissance."*

JOHN PAUL RUSSO is professor of English and interim chair of the Department of Classics at the University of Miami, Florida. He is the author of *I. A. Richards: His Life and Work* (1989) and *The Future without a Past: The Humanities in a Technological Society* (2005). He is coeditor and book review editor of *Italian Americana* and has published essays in cultural and ethnic studies, poetics, and the history of criticism.

ANNA SCACCHI is assistant professor of American literature at the University of Padua. She is the author of *A una voce sola. Il racconto della storia in Benito Cereno di Herman Melville* (2000) and has published essays on nineteenth-century American women writers. She has coauthored a volume on multilingualism and language policies in the United States (*Babele americana*, 2005) and is the editor of a collection of essays on the mother-daughter relationship (*Lo specchio materno*, 2005).

JOSEPH C. SCHÖPP is professor of American literature at the University of Hamburg. He is the author of *Allen Tate: Tradition als Bauprinzip dualistischen Dichtens* (1975), *Ausbruch aus der Mimesis: Der amerikanische Roman im Zeichen der Postmoderne* (1989), and *Deciphering the Darkness of the Past: Essays zur amerikanischen Literatur*, ed. Bettina Friedl. He coedited *Postmoderne: Ende der Avantgarde oder Neubeginn?* (1989) and *Transatlantic Modernism* (2001). His current research interest focuses on the American Transcendentalists as travelers.

MARIA ANITA STEFANELLI is associate professor of American literature and North American theatre in the Department of American Studies at the University of Rome Three. She is the author of *Figure ambigue. Disgiunzione e congiunzione nella poesia di William Carlos Williams* (1993). Her scholarly interests are mainly in modernist and postmodernist American poetry and twentieth-century American drama. She has recently edited a collection of essays, *City Lights: Pocket Poets and Pocket Books* (Rome 2004), focusing on works published by the famous San Francisco publisher.

DONATO TAMBLÉ is director of the state archives in Potenza and archival superintendent for the Basilicata Region. He is also professor of archival science and of history of archives at the School of Archival Science, Latin Palaeography, and Diplomatics in Rome. He is the author of numerous books and essays on archives, history, cultural property, and humanities, and is president of the Society for the Specialists in Archival Science ("ACTUM") and vice president of the International Center for the History of Towns.

Index